DETACHMENT FROM PLACE

DETACHMENT FROM PLACE

Beyond an Archaeology of Settlement Abandonment

EDITED BY
Maxime Lamoureux-St-Hilaire AND **Scott Macrae**

UNIVERSITY PRESS OF COLORADO
Louisville

© 2020 by University Press of Colorado

Published by University Press of Colorado
245 Century Circle, Suite 202
Louisville, Colorado 80027

 The University Press of Colorado is a proud member of
the Association of University Presses.

The University Press of Colorado is a cooperative publishing enterprise supported, in part, by Adams State University, Colorado State University, Fort Lewis College, Metropolitan State University of Denver, Regis University, University of Colorado, University of Northern Colorado, University of Wyoming, Utah State University, and Western Colorado University.

∞ This paper meets the requirements of the ANSI/NISO Z39.48–1992 (Permanence of Paper)

ISBN: 978-1-60732-814-8 (hardcover)
ISBN: 978-1-64642-008-7 (ebook)
https://doi.org/10.5876/9781646420087

Library of Congress Cataloging-in-Publication Data

Names: Lamoureux-St-Hilaire, Maxime, editor. | Macrae, Scott, 1984– editor.
Title: Detachment from place : beyond an archaeology of settlement abandonment / edited by Maxime Lamoureux-St-Hilaire and Scott Macrae.
Description: Louisville : University Press of Colorado, [2020] | Includes bibliographical references and index.
Identifiers: LCCN 2019039436 (print) | LCCN 2019039437 (ebook) | ISBN 9781607328148 (cloth) | ISBN 9781646420087 (ebook)
Subjects: LCSH: Land settlement patterns, Prehistoric. | Human settlements. | Human ecology. | Landscape archaeology. | Place attachment.
Classification: LCC GN799.S43 .D48 2020 (print) | LCC GN799.S43 (ebook) | DDC 307.1/4—dc23
LC record available at https://lccn.loc.gov/2019039436
LC ebook record available at https://lccn.loc.gov/2019039437

Cover art by Aaron Alfano

To our wives, Mary Kate Kelly and Eniko Macrae, who, beyond supporting us throughout the challenges of academia, embody the importance of attachment to place.

Contents

DETACHMENT FROM PLACE

1

Introduction

Maxime Lamoureux-
St-Hilaire and
Scott Macrae

A place's enduring human occupation creates bonds between people and their inhabited landscape. This people-place relationship attaches groups to their homeland in a way that largely defines their economic, ideological, and cultural identity. Yet, no human occupation is everlasting. As individuals, households, or whole communities inevitably end their occupation of a landscape, the ties binding them are either altered or severed. This process—*detachment from place*—transforms both the landscape and how it is conceived by its former inhabitants.

This universal process has many distinct and contrasting modern manifestations. Endemic warfare forces populations into exile toward more peaceful, but often more densely populated, areas. Rising sea levels across the world gradually displace cultural groups. Young academics become nomads, migrating between cities on a yearly basis. These distinct cases of detachment from place differentially alter, erase, or disrupt social ties and human-place entanglements (following Hodder 2016a). Each detachment leaves distinct material signatures on abandoned landscapes; in some cases, they are invisible or very subtle and in others dramatic.

THEORETICAL FRAMEWORK OF THE VOLUME

This volume takes a comparative approach to detachment from places located across the Americas, Africa,

DOI: 10.5876/9781646420087.c001

and Eurasia. Its chapters study physical manifestations of detachment that vary in relation to geopolitical and environmental contexts and to degrees of attachment to place. Since all its authors study relatively sedentary people, they emphasize anthropogenic landscapes and geography, while relying upon cultural-historical backgrounds. Questions of land modifications, the socioeconomic values associated with these, and the valuable knowledge of inhabited landscapes (Balée and Erickson 2006; Brookfield 1984; Feld and Basso 1996; Knapp and Ashmore 1999) all play a role in defining human-place entanglement (Hodder 2011a, 2016a).

Yet, this volume emphasizes how settled landscapes were detached from, thus highlighting the conundrum of sedentism which, ultimately, is a historical illusion. By focusing on archaeological proxies of detachment—artifacts, features, burials, architecture, and landscape modifications—most chapters have methodological and theoretical overtones, bringing forth the theme of settlement abandonment. Concepts of settlement abandonment and formation processes—including the contrast between archaeological and systemic contexts—are rooted in processual archaeology, specifically in the writings of Robert Ascher (1968) and Michael B. Schiffer (1972, 1976, 1985, 1987), who first theorized how archaeologists can study abandonment behaviors. Beyond owing to these foundational theories, this volume is aligned with comparable efforts geared toward a cultural and environmental understanding of how places were left in the archaeological past (Cameron and Tomka 1993; Inomata and Webb 2003a; McAnany and Yoffee 2010; Middleton 2012; Mock 1998; Nelson and Strawhacker 2011).

We began a recent article as follows: "What makes a settlement an archaeological site? It could be said that once a settlement is abandoned, it enters the archaeological record" (Lamoureux-St-Hilaire et al. 2015:550). Until recently, we felt confident about this "Schifferian" assertion, which remains true for some archaeological sites—especially within areas having suffered civilizational collapse and regional depopulation. However, it does not apply to many sites that are considered foundational for the identity of cultural groups—as living places for sacralized ancestors (e.g., see Birch and Lesage, chapter 4 in this volume; Birch and Williamson 2013; Colwell-Chanthaphonh and Ferguson 2006; de Barros, chapter 8 in this volume; Glowacki 2015, chapter 3 in this volume), or as modern ceremonial centers (e.g., see Iannone, chapter 10 in this volume; Palka 2014).

As people go, places remain. Yet, most archaeological sites may never be truly abandoned and may simply be awaiting to be reinvested—be it by migrants, pilgrims, or researchers. We are not suggesting to discard advances from settlement abandonment studies, which have made strong middle-range contributions to help us interpret the archaeological record, since "whether one sees abandonment processes as transforming the material record (e.g. Schiffer 1983, 1985), or as integral components of site formation (e.g. Binford 1981), all archaeologically recovered remains have been conditioned by abandonment processes" (Tomka and Stevenson 1993:191). Yet, recent advances highlight the limitations of the behavioral concept of "settlement abandonment" and call for a more nuanced approach to people-place disentanglement; hence our proposal of *detachment from place*.

As towns and regions are today abandoned by segments of their populations, these same people, or distinct groups, will inevitably return and idiosyncratically attach themselves to these transformed landscapes. Alternatively, vacant and even never-revisited places may retain essential cultural value for former, out-migrated inhabitants (see Stanton and Magnoni 2008). As an analytical framework, detachment from place goes beyond archaeological proxies of abandonment; it involves migration and resettlement, and inquires into the dynamic relationship between people and their landscapes before, during, and after abandonment. By studying detachment from place as such a decisive social process, this volume also emphasizes the formative powers of leaving—in other words, migration (see Anthony 1990). This perspective is rooted in ethnography, ethnographically minded archaeology, and heritage or engaged archaeology (see Cameron 2013; Colwell-Chanthaphonh and Ferguson 2006; Glowacki 2015; McAnany and Rowe 2015) and contributes important nuances to settlement abandonment studies by reminding us that (1) ancient people may not be heuristically reduced to the landscapes we study; and (2) our scientific, archaeological approach is but one perspective on these landscapes, which value and significance may be entirely different for related cultural groups. Consequently, the authors of this volume rely on more than archaeology to study detachment from place, providing interdisciplinary and/or multivocal perspectives through the lenses of history, epigraphy, ethnoarchaeology, ethnography, oral history, and fictional accounts.

Besides its theoretical influences, the scope of this volume has been defined by internal academic dynamics. The life of this volume began with the 78th Annual Meeting of the Society for American Archaeology (Honolulu, 2013), for which this first author coorganized a session with Patricia McAnany, entitled "Living Abandonment: The Social Process of Detachment from Place." This productive session featured thirteen papers by scholars working in the Americas, the Near East, and East Asia and discussions by Catherine Cameron and Ian Hodder. After a hiatus, this concerted project was revived by inquiries from the University Press of Colorado, giving momentum to the editors of this volume. A new (double) session was organized for the 116th Annual Meeting of the American Anthropological Association (Washington, DC, 2017), entitled "Detaching from Place: A World Archaeology Perspective to Settlement Abandonment." This session was effectively a rehearsal for this volume and grouped twelve presenters, several of whom were part of the "Living Abandonment" session. This volume was thus six years in the making, granting its authors a certain perspective on its themes and composition. As will become apparent, the following chapters represent distinct theoretical and methodological perspectives unified by the objective of exploring the multifaceted complexities of detachment from place.

VOLUME OVERVIEW

This volume covers a wide geographic distribution of case studies, which are sometimes separated by millennia: the Huron-Wendat region of Northeast America, the Mesa Verde region, the Archaic Southeast United States, the Classic Maya of Mesoamerica, the historical Bassar region of Togo, the Bronze Age Near East, and the Southeast Asian medieval capital of Bagan, Myanmar. These case studies are tied together by a desire to explore the complexities involved in processes of detachment from place; complexities that may be summarized by a set of interrelated questions:

1. What do we mean by detachment from place?
2. What were the *stressors* and *enablers* that prompted detachment from place?
3. How were cultural groups transformed during this process?
4. How were places transformed during this process?
5. How did "abandoners" continue to interact with groups that remained home?
6. How were "abandoned landscapes" reused by newly attached groups?
7. How can we study these questions with archaeological data?
8. How can archaeological studies and cultural studies of migration inform each other?
9. How do anthropologists and indigenous groups differently understand abandonment?

The chapters tackle these questions in distinct fashion through case studies spanning a variety of spatial and temporal scales, as well as theoretical perspectives. The following chapter 2, an initial foray into the topic of detachment from place by Patricia A. McAnany and Maxime Lamoureux-St-Hilaire, breaks down the complexities of place-making and unmaking. The authors use several archaeological cases, along with contemporary and popular culture analogies, to challenge traditional archaeological approaches to periodization and settlement abandonment by exploring questions of migration, memory, and reattachment to place. The ensuing, relativistic approach broadens the archaeological scope to study abandonment-framing *stressors* and *enablers* in relation to processes of community formation and their (dis)entanglement with landscapes.

In chapter 3, Donna M. Glowacki focuses on the thirteenth-century ancestral Pueblo people of the Mesa Verde region in the American Southwest. By placing a contextual understanding of Pueblo migrations within an ethnographically informed perspective, the author describes the social dislocation, reorganization, and continuity that occurred within Mesa Verde landscapes. Glowacki also critically reviews settlement abandonment literature to provide a strong theoretical framework—exploring "the when and how of leaving that inform on the why of it"—which ties together the interrelated concepts of leaving and migration. In addition, Glowacki addresses cultural issues that may derive from the blanket application of the archaeological concept of abandonment.

In chapter 4, Jennifer Birch and Louis Lesage address detachment from place at both the local and regional scales amongst the Northern Iroquoian peoples of the northeastern woodlands. Combining archaeological and historical data, oral histories, and contemporary indigenous perspectives, the authors investigate processes of detachment from place among ancestral Huron-Wendat communities. This case study, with its fine-grained chronology, challenges conceptions of both sedentism and abandonment by exploring practices of planned abandonment and short-distance migration by extended kin groups within a regional framework. The authors also expose the inadequacy of the concept of abandonment from the perspective of indigenous groups tied to ancestral landscapes.

In chapter 5, Kenneth E. Sassaman and Asa Randall explore macroregional abandonment within the Archaic Southeast United States. Their chapter focuses on several archaeological sites from this region (especially coastal Florida) that coalesced within the *cosmunity* of the early monumental site of Poverty Point, Louisiana. The authors draw connections between cosmology, the natural landscape, and environmental change—specifically sea-level rise. This ambitious, high-level theoretical exercise, anchored in a rich empirical framework, addresses the predictability of the detachment from and repositioning of archaeological sites among the Archaic indigenous groups of the northeast coast of the Gulf of Mexico.

In chapter 6, Scott Macrae, Gyles Iannone, and Pete Demarte shift the focus of this volume to Mesoamerica and the ancient Maya of the North Vaca Plateau of western Belize. The authors emphasize the strong ties established between ancient Maya people and their landscape, while contrasting two closely related agrarian communities in terms of settlement history, climate change, and sociopolitical context. By exposing these *longue-durée* processes, the authors adopt and develop the concepts of *landesque capital* and *sense of place* to explain the differential abandonment scenarios for their two case studies.

In chapter 7, Maxime Lamoureux-St-Hilaire, Marcello A. Canuto, Tomás Q. Barrientos, and José Eduardo Bustamante provide a second case-study from the ancient Maya world centered on the Classic Maya center of La Corona, Guatemala. Drawing on the historical record and rich archaeological datasets from the site's regal palace, the authors discuss the process of detachment from power experienced by the La Corona government. By studying a program of ritual termination, preabandonment middens, and on-floor assemblages, the authors explore how the La Corona regime adapted to a changing geopolitical context by gradually reducing the size of its political institution. This chapter takes a focused approach to processes of detachment from place related to the Classic Maya political collapse.

In chapter 8, Phillip L. de Barros turns our attention to the Later Iron Age in the Bassar region of Northern Togo, West Africa. Drawing on incredibly rich datasets derived from history, ethnography, archaeological excavations, and survey, de Barros studies warfare-induced detachment from place at the regional scale. The author evaluates questions related to site abandonment, relocation and reattachment to place, and connections and disconnections with abandoned landscapes. This case study convincingly ties together matters of settlement abandonment and migrations within a well-documented geopolitical context—slave raiding by organized military forces on smaller-scale societies.

In chapter 9, Michael D. Danti brings us to northern Mesopotamia to address the detachment from urban communities and increasing transhumant pastoralism of the later third and early second millennia BC. Questioning the relevance of the "megadrought hypothesis" for explaining regional abandonment, Danti provides a nuanced discussion of shifting regional subsistence economies. This rich empirical archaeological case study, strengthened by ethnographic data, addresses abandonment and continuity in the settlement patterns of northern Syria. Along with Macrae et al.'s chapter 6, Danti's chapter provides sound environmental and ecological perspectives to the volume.

In chapter 10, Gyles Iannone shifts the volume's focus to Southeast Asia and to sociopolitical entanglement and disentanglement at the Medieval Burmese capital of Bagan. In this final case study, Iannone provides a comprehensive discussion of Bagan's rich historical and settlement records by addressing the relationship between its ruling elites, the Crown and Sangha (the Buddhist Church). This discussion, centered on the site's prominent architectural landscape, highlights the merit-building and patron-client relationships that made, unmade, and remade Bagan. The author's longue-durée approach provides a dynamic sociopolitical model for studying the recursive process of detachment from place at Bagan—which today remains an important ceremonial center.

The volume concludes with two discussion chapters, chapters 11 and 12. First, in chapter 11, Catherine Cameron provides a detailed discussion of each chapter's theoretical and methodological contributions. Cameron takes advantage of her decades of engagement with the field of settlement abandonment to provide insightful comments about all case studies, which she organizes along scales of detachment and sociopolitical organization. This discussion astutely summarizes the volume's contribution to archaeological approaches to landscape and population movement. Finally, in chapter 12, Jeffrey H. Cohen provides a nonarchaeologist's perspective to the study of how migration transforms the social and economic landscapes that are left behind. This methodologically minded commentary discursively engages discrepancies between the analytical frameworks of ethnography and archaeology.

CONCLUSION

This volume represents a first attempt to study archaeological processes of leaving places from a world archaeology, comparative perspective. This collection of case studies centers on relatively sedentary communities that all detached from their home at very different times, under distinct circumstances, and following idiosyncratic practices tied to their attachment to landscapes. Assembling these diverse perspectives on detachment from place brings forth many anthropological themes, especially those related to identity, memory, subsistence, and sociopolitical and economic organization. As geopolitical and environmental contexts dramatically shift in the modern world, studying archaeological cases of detachment from place may become increasingly relevant. We hope that this effort is of interest for all students of population displacements, both ancient and modern.

ACKNOWLEDGMENTS

All the contributors have conducted significant archaeological research to document detachment from place around the globe. We would thus like to thank all our host countries and their dedicated Departments of Archaeology and staff who, over the years, have encouraged and supported our research. We also thank the funding agencies that have seen fit to support these many studies. The editors are grateful for the timely contributions and hard work of the authors for both the American Anthropological Association (AAA) symposium and for the compilation of this volume. We are also very appreciative of the comments provided by the two anonymous reviewers, as well as those provided by Catherine Cameron and Jeffery Cohen. Gratitude is also extended to Patricia A. McAnany for guidance through this process and to the UPC acquisition editor Charlotte Steinhardt and her predecessor, Jessica d'Arbonne, whose work was instrumental to the completion of this volume. We also thank Bryce Sledge from Davidson College for his help with the volume's index. The final stages of this volume were completed while Lamoureux-St-Hilaire was a George Stuart Residential Scholar at the Boundary End Center, which is acknowledged for its peaceful environment and great resources.

2

The telescopic lens of archaeological research brings definition to distant action. Yet the palimpsestic character of this long-focus-with-low-resolution view leaves many unanswered questions and arguably can produce spurious narratives of how a place was founded, left, and possibly refounded. The difficulties of understanding the processes of arriving, leaving, and returning are considered here in light of larger theoretical issues, such as collapse discourse. Historical and archaeological examples from the Maya region provide specific contexts. By engaging with human intentionality—how movement through space and in relation to place structures archaeological deposits—we hope to expand the epistemic limits of founding/abandonment/refounding discourse within archaeology. Related issues—such as the scalar complexities of understanding total or partial abandonment, the way in which leaving attenuates the relationship between people and place, and the difficulties of recognizing (archaeologically) recursive place-making—are tangentially addressed.

By emphasizing the recursiveness of human action and a specific kind of agency that involved interacting with built environments that were animated as well as neutralized through human action, a perspective is employed that works to hybridize theories of materiality (Brown 2001; Gell 1998; Hodder 2016a; Miller 2005) with those of migration/mobility (Cohen and Sirkeci 2011; Dorigo and Tobler 1983, among others). These two approaches seemingly are at odds since materiality

An Archaeological Perspective on Recursive Place-Making and Unmaking

Patricia A. McAnany and Maxime Lamoureux-St-Hilaire

DOI: 10.5876/9781646420087.c002

11

stresses human entanglement with things (and all of its associated complexity), while migration/mobility attempts to understand the conditions under which humans relinquish claims on things and places. Throughout this chapter, we suggest that this tension is central to the human experience—at least since sedentary lifeways began to recraft the way in which humans relate to places and things. The centrality of this tension is matched by its recursive quality. Farming communities, for instance, often seem utterly rooted in place with intimate knowledge of their landscape and a suite of associated ritual practices. Yet, on the scale of a century (more or less, the resolution of the archaeological record), mobility—rather than rootedness—is often the prevailing leitmotif. Such an example from Yucatán, Mexico is presented below. Entanglement with place—as part and parcel of sedentism—often is perceived as occupying one end of a continuum of movement that ranges from highly mobile on a seasonal or annual basis to highly sedentary or fixed in place. Often, the fixed-in-place end of the continuum is valued by researchers over the highly mobile end. For instance, a foundational study of migration (Dorigo and Tobler 1983) models population movement as the result of *stressors* and *enablers*, suggesting that a sedentary posture is disrupted by specific kinds of stress or opportunity (see Kohler, Varlen, and Wright 2010 for an archaeological application). Another example of the valorization of sedentism comes from the literature on climate change in which human movement/migration is predicted to be a deleterious result of sea-level rise and drought intensification.

Such differential valorization leads us to ask why we—as humans of the Anthropocene—so value rootedness and disdain uprootedness when the history of our species is primarily a story of movement and migration. We value stasis when, in light of the longue durée, it might be more accurate to think of periods of stasis as highly unstable (and unsustainable) moments that punctuate more prevalent periods of movement. It is rootedness in place that creates the (often painful) experience of uprooting from place. In the Maya region, archaeologists have correlated uprooting with political chaos and/or drought cycles that are thought to have interrupted a period of stability and spurred detachment from Late Classic royal courts and hinterland settlements (for good examples, see Iannone 2014; Inomata and Webb 2003a). Thinking about mobility in terms of human emotions and decision making is important since—despite the prevalence of movement/migration—real pain and anguish may accompany the process of uprooting. However, when movement is framed purely in abstract demographic terms, human suffering is easily overlooked.

In this chapter and several others in this volume, there is an attempt to reevaluate the archaeological discourse of abandonment, which arguably has been framed around concepts of property and property rights derived from the influential Enlightenment thinker John Locke. Locke ([1689] 1993) proposed a labor theory of property from which abandonment of property rights could be deduced from the withholding or cessation of labor in relation to a place. As we shall see as this chapter proceeds, Locke's concept of property rights is not a very good fit with non-Western ontologies of place. Without an engagement with other ontologies of being-in-place, it will be very difficult for archaeologists to understand detachment from a non-Western perspective.

This chapter begins with a review of archaeological approaches to detachment from place and then moves to an agent-oriented discussion of *stressors* and *enablers*, which have been so influential in framing discussion of human mobility/migration. Examples from US popular culture, specifically television and literature, illustrate both the stressing and enabling factors that spur mobility. Then, place-making, unmaking, and remaking are discussed from an archaeological/historical perspective. Finally, we return to the question of rootedness—how and why it is valued—and why mobility has been so villainized.

ARCHAEOLOGICAL APPROACHES TO
DETACHING FROM THE STASIS OF PLACE

Persons, households, and sedentary communities are entangled with the materiality of their landscape in a contextually distinctive fashion. Multigenerational occupation of a dwelling and investment in a built landscape only serve to intensify this attachment. Consequently, disentanglement of a sedentary group from their landscape is a particularly complex process (Hodder 2016a:142).

Although human agency is situated within a large array of impinging forces, decisions regarding residential mobility and migration generally take place on the scale of a family or household unit (Cameron 2003:209). Within this context, however, a sense of place tends not to be atomized to household but rather is inclusive of the entire community (Basso 1996). Members of agricultural communities who move through the process of detachment from place leave behind, by necessity, many meaningful constituents of their inhabited landscape (Lamoureux-St-Hilaire et al. 2015). These components include immovable elements of their constructed and natural landscapes, houses and related structures, agricultural lands, and surrounding environmental features such as forests and hills. The built environment is associated with artifactual assemblages and cultural features such as ancestral burials, which altogether constitute a rich ideational landscape (Knapp and Ashmore 1999). Agricultural lands often represent investment in intensive production techniques that modify landscapes (such as terracing or canals) and create valuable landesque capital (Brookfield 1984; Håkansson and Widgren 2016; see Macrae et al., chapter 6 in this volume). Local ecological knowledge associated with an environment is extremely valuable and creates conceptualized landscapes with a sense of place—even for groups inhabiting less domesticated worlds (Basso 1996; Jojola 2006; Knapp and Ashmore 1999). Detachment from constructed, ideational, conceptualized, and natural landscapes involves complex sets of behaviors and practices that have differential material impacts and, significantly, are loaded with a range of emotions that may include loss or nostalgia. Arguably, the emotional state of those who are leaving will have a strong impact on how a left-place is encoded in social memory. As archaeologists have noted, the materiality of detachment can result in distinctive archaeological signatures (Cameron and Tomka 1993; Inomata 2003; Inomata and Webb 2003b; Lamoureux-St-Hilaire et al. 2015; Schiffer 1987).

Archaeological explanations of detachment typically employ large-scale political or economic trauma, meteorological hazards, or environmental abuse to drive the abandonment of place. In an effort to go beyond the push-pull modeling of human migration pioneered by Guido Dorigo and Waldo Tobler (1983), this chapter emphasizes how the process of abandonment and relocation takes place at the interface of humans, landscapes, and relevant stressors/enablers.

STRESSORS AND ENABLERS OF MOBILITY/MIGRATION

Consider two fictional accounts that portray, in a romanticized fashion, how detachment from place may be undertaken by households: the Clampett family of television fame and the Joad family from the 1939 John Steinbeck novel, *Grapes of Wrath*. The Clampetts were the subjects of the farcical TV comedy *The Beverly Hillbillies*, which aired from 1962 to 1971. In a nutshell, the Clampetts abandoned their rustic cabin due to an unexpected windfall of cash from the discovery of oil on the family farm. Their new wealth *enabled* a residential move to a home in Beverly Hills, California, which was considerably more upscale than their rural farmstead. Oddly, the social matrix of their rural extended family was alluded to, but not visible, and none of the Clampetts, except Granny, harbored longings to return to the social matrix of which the rustic cabin was but one node.

In contrast, the Joad family's journey, featured in the *Grapes of Wrath* (released as a film in 1940), did not conclude with a happy Hollywood ending.

The family left the windswept Oklahoma "dustbowl" during the 1930s and moved, under trying and dehumanizing circumstances, to labor in the agricultural fields of the Sacramento Valley. For the Joad family, *stressors* prevailed: their livelihood had been compromised by environmental hazards and the economic devastation of the Great Depression. They had few options other than to buy a truck and move the household west. Their arrival in California amidst thousands of migrant workers only served to exacerbate their misery and hardship. Housing in migrant camps was worse than the modest frame home they left behind and to which there apparently was no possibility of returning. Steinbeck alludes to the notion that the migrants' only salvation would be through unionization—the forging of new attachments to a community based not on kin but on shared economic circumstances.

These vignettes from popular culture highlight contrasting examples of migration at the scale of the household. For the Clampetts, enabling factors allowed migration; but for the Joads, stressing factors prevailed. Both narratives emphasize motorized transport of people and valued possessions, which is of doubtful relevance to the deep past, except in long-distance migration via water-borne craft such as occurred with the peopling of Polynesia. In both examples, connections with the sending community were severed—a rare event in contemporary migration. In fact, persistence of social linkages with those left behind (dead or alive) is a structuring characteristic of detachment from place in the archaeological past. In addition, if we train an archaeological eye on the modest dwellings from which the Clampetts and the Joads detached, these fictional examples give insight to the fact that two very different acts of leaving may look archaeologically similar, thus presenting a problem of equifinality and adding another layer of complexity to archaeological understanding of detachment from place.

DETECTING PLACE-MAKING ARCHAEOLOGICALLY

Although human intentionality is materially displayed and archaeologically detectable in different ways, deliberate place-making by way of diacritical archaeological deposits that announce the onset of a relationship between people and place is a prevalent feature of the architectural record. These deposits—particularly in those parts of Mesoamerica where they are classified as dedicatory or foundational caches (Mock 1998)—often are compared to dedication plaques placed on large buildings in the Western world. But in the former archaeological or ethnographic context, the deposit does not so much celebrate construction completion but rather initiates a new relational realm between humans and a newly built or rebuilt construction that will need to be nourished recursively. In other words, a dedicatory deposit codifies the work to be done in relation to a place and often includes something of great value, possibly as a demonstration of good faith and a commitment to a relationship that some call covenantal (Monaghan 1995, 1998).

Initiation of Preclassic place-making at K'axob in Belize could include reverential interment of human remains that sometimes were intrusive and other times incorporated into the basal construction unit (McAnany, Storey, and Lockard 1999; Storey 2004). This residence-based ancestralizing activity (Adams and King 2011; Hill and Hageman 2016; McAnany 2013) also signaled a continuing relationship with a deceased family member and a commitment to safeguard/nurture both the corpse and the soul of the deceased (McAnany 2019).

If place-making can initiate relational actions with material consequences, then place-leaving likely involved termination or transformation of relational arrangements between people and place (Stanton and Magnoni 2008). But termination can be more subtle and blurred than dedication. The material signatures of this phase often are difficult for archaeologists to read; intentional deposits may be intermingled with material from postoccupational reuse/visitation, all of which may be close to the surface and not sealed beneath later constructions as often occurred with place-making deposits. Yet, evidence for dedication and termination, since they are ideationally related, can be expected to be contextually related; they can, for example, be located in the same building, or be stratigraphically superposed (see Lamoureux-St-Hilaire 2011:21–25, 33–42). The process of leaving—detaching—from place, thus, presents unique challenges for archaeologists. These challenges are exacerbated by the emotionally freighted quality of leaving, such as that which occurred at the end of the Maya Classic period throughout much of the Maya Lowlands, a topic to which we now turn.

LEAVING ON THE SEAM OF AN ARCHAEOLOGICAL PERIODIZATION CHART

In 2012, Guy Middleton weighed in on an overheated collapse discourse, entitling his contribution "Nothing Lasts Forever" (see also Middleton 2017). Few would dispute the wisdom of this age-old adage, yet archaeologists tend to interpret detachment from place as an aberrant deviation from a slavish attachment to home and a red flag for societal failure and/or environmental abuse (McAnany and Yoffee 2010; Nelson 1999:186; Wilcox 2010). The drawdown of population residing in the lowland Maya cities at the end of the

Classic period provides a salient case in point. Situated at the seam between what are characterized as the Classic and Postclassic periods, this century-long process of political and demographic reorganization has been evaluated repeatedly as a tragic and unexpected failure.

Yet, there is a significant body of archaeological evidence indicating that Classic Maya cities were "abandoned" in an intentional and oftentimes recursive fashion. Shallowly buried "termination" deposits—often rich in broken pottery and artifacts—indicate the intentional severing of relations between people and place (e.g., Harrison-Buck, McAnany, and Storey 2007). Close examination of termination deposits indicates that reverential as well as desecrational intentions could underlie ritual practices involved in unmaking a place (Canuto and Andrews 2008).

In reference to the US Southwest, Chip Colwell-Chanthaphonh and T. J. Ferguson (2006) as well as Michael Wilcox (2010) note the uncanny convenience of applying the term *abandonment* to landscapes subject to European colonization. Honing in on the Mogollon area of the Southwest, Nelson (1999:193) attributes overuse of this term by archaeologists to a fascination with the mystery of leaving, and a neglect of evidence indicating continued connection with a landscape of former inhabitation. Nelson, as well as Ferguson and Colwell-Chanthaphonh, allude to the challenges of sustainability that are intensified by sedentism. In other words, farming communities—although anchored in place as discussed earlier—may choose to detach periodically from a place and relocate in order to maintain a sustainable livelihood. Market forces of capitalism and concepts of private property have all but erased this option for most farming communities, but precolonial patterns of settlement movement within the Americas allude to the efficacy of residential relocation, particularly in the northeastern part of North America (see Birch and Levage, chapter 4 in this volume).

When archaeological periodization schemes (in reality, models of punctuated stasis) are fused with environmental and settlement pattern research, abandonment studies can take on apocalyptic dimensions. Exempting cases of abandonment, such as those following volcanic eruptions or military invasions and contrary to the finality of the fictionalized abandonments in *The Beverly Hillbillies* and *Grapes of Wrath*, detachment from place is a gradual process. It begins with anticipation, as "abandoners" both mourn and contemplate their home community while planning the enterprise of migration. Following movement to a new place, abandoners differentially recall, commemorate, and revisit older place(s) of inhabitation. Then, abandonment may be reversed by a return to a community after months, years, or even decades have passed.

Thus, detachment from place is not unilinear, but rather a dialectical process during which faraway landscapes remain active in the social memory of those who left, sometimes even acquiring the mythic proportions of an Aztlan for subsequent generations.

THINKING BEYOND HOUSEHOLDS: WHEN COMMUNITIES COME APART

The fictionalized accounts discussed earlier focus on interaction among members of a coresidential household who relocate from their natal place and attempt to find new community. The focus on household resonates with contemporary migration patterns, which may hold insights to the past if we analyze detachment from place employing the "meso"-level that Jeffrey Cohen and Ibrahim Sirkeci (2011:35) suggest. Yet, no matter how gradual the process of leaving, households do not exist within a vacuum but rather are part of the relational web of an interdependent community. A decision to leave is crossthreaded with social and environmental entanglements within a community. When Chinua Achebe (1958) wrote *Things Fall Apart*, he was referring to that elusive sinew that holds communities together and facilitates maintenance and reproduction of daily practice. For example, documenting the lowland Maya royal court of Waká, Olivia Navarro-Farr and Ana Lucía Arroyave-Prera (2014) find a late Classic attempt to maintain relationality with deities after abandonment of the royal court by its courtiers.

Referring to contemporary migration, Cohen and Sirkeci (2011:109) emphasize "environments of human insecurity" (from the scale of households to nation-states) that prompt migration. Human perception of insecurity can stem from a large array of stress-inducing variables—social, economic, environmental, political, or military. The refugee crisis prompted by the Syrian "civil war" of the mid-2010s provides a painful reminder of how regional warfare, as a stressor, may force groups to detach from landscapes with which there may be temporally deep attachments. In this case, enablers in the form of prospects for economic well-being attracted refugee households to resettle in other nation-states as close as Jordan and as far away as Canada. Warfare plays the role of a catastrophic stressor not dissimilar from volcanism (see Cooper and Sheets 2012 for extended discussions of environmental hazards). Both result in the mass depopulation of a region that is left as a desolate, underpopulated landscape. In a world carved into territorially bounded nation-states, the scale of mobility has greatly amplified. Often refugees must relocate outside the borders of a nation-state in order to improve (in the parlance of Cohen and Sirkeci 2011) their environment of human security.

In reference to the Maya Lowlands, we have explored through agent-based modeling how smaller-scale political entities could differentially attract migrant population during periods of political turmoil (McAnany et al. 2016). While the dissolution of Classic Maya divine rulership is not comparable to the militarized political turmoil of the contemporary Near East, both cases illustrate how vulnerable households and larger communities may be pushed into detaching from place by forces beyond their control.

The large-scale migration resulting from the Syrian crisis is not so dissimilar from what happened in West Africa during the sixteenth and seventeenth centuries. At that time, the impact of a devastating transatlantic slave trade disrupted large swaths of settlement and intercultural relations among communities. De Barros (chapter 8 in this volume) documents how warfare in the form of raids by organized Dagomba armies and other centralized polities forced less tightly organized groups such as the Bassar of Togo to abandon their constructed landscapes in fertile valleys and relocate to less accessible hilltops. Bassar households and those of other ethnic groups resettled in a much denser fashion on a landscape in which they could establish an environment of human security and economic stability. Significantly, the landscape of seventeenth-century Togo afforded nearby, less densely settled areas available for resettlement. The Togo example reminds us that the presence of proximate, less-settled areas can act as a magnet for populations under stress and that this option diminishes in more densely populated contexts of nation-state sovereignties such as exist in the twenty-first century.

Entangled human-nature relationships characterize agricultural communities and strongly affect the expression of stressors and enablers, and possible migration. Such relationships impact the timing, sequence, and degree of landscape abandonment. For instance, by leaving agricultural lands located in the rich alluvial plains of the Togo River (as well as iron-smelting facilities) and relocating in defensible hilltops, the Bassar communities reinvented their economy and developed new ways to secure a livelihood. This case exemplifies how detachment from place due to the threat of captive taking, in reality, was an emotionally and economically complex process.

MYTHIC MEMORIES AND THE DEAD

Colwell-Chanthaphonh and Ferguson (2006) stress that many indigenous peoples of the US Southwest do not regard detachment from place as deactivation of a landscape and its contextual meaning; it is not equivalent to a Quitclaim Deed in Western legal terms. Instead, places where ancestors once lived, died, and were buried are seen as a vital part of an ongoing metaphysical cycle (Colwell-Chanthaphonh and Ferguson 2006:39). Returning to a place—especially one where precursors were interred—often is marked materially by subtle signs that are difficult to detect much less interpret archaeologically.

In a study of household groups from the Contreras Valley, which were attached politically to the Classic Maya center of Minanha, Belize, Lamoureux-St-Hilaire et al. (2015) found that detachment from place spanned centuries and was intimately related to household contingencies, both economic and ceremonial. These factors were not necessarily dependent on the fate of the ruling body of their polity. Yet, excavations within the royal precinct of Minanha indicate that agents—either abandoners returning on pilgrimage or unrelated groups still living in the vicinity—revisited the ideologically rich, royal architecture to inter their dead long after the precinct was deactivated as a political center and royal residence (Lamoureux-St-Hilaire, Iannone, and Snetsinger 2013). Thus, just as households were disentangling from their landscape in the nearby Contreras Valley, agents opted to further entangle with Minanha's monumental landscape—two contrasting behaviors that highlight the complex dialectical processes involved in "settlement abandonment."

RECURSIVE PLACE-MAKING

Sometimes, the process of detachment is reversed and after a period of time a place is reactivated. This kind of place remaking may or may not be visible to an archaeologist but is an important part of unmaking and remaking, even if a place is remade by a group that is unrelated to earlier inhabitants. Today, if one drives through the eastern part of Yucatán, Mexico, the landscape seems like one of timeless occupation—immense, early colonial missions sit astride pre-Columbian pyramidal temples. Yet, as recently as the nineteenth century, this landscape was nearly depopulated—torn apart by a social war that pit Indigenous peoples against Mexican nationalists. A particularly crisp example of this traumatic period is provided by current archaeological and archival research at Tahcabo, Yucatán (Batun Alpuche et al. 2017).

Mexican independence from Spain in 1821 ushered in a restlessness in Yucatán that soon turned to open revolt. As the landscape in and around Tahcabo became militarized, townsfolk fled to the South with some relocating as far as Belize. Tahcabo census data indicate that in 1841 the town held about

2,500 people, but during the latter half of the nineteenth century residents fled the violence, upheaval, and grinding poverty that plagued eastern Yucatán.

As the violence subsided, many towns were slowly repeopled during the first half of the twentieth century. This was the case at Tahcabo where only 195 *habitantes* were counted in a 1930 census. Remaking the community and refounding the church, however, appear to have happened decades earlier. Late in the nineteenth century, the statue of San Bartolomé was equipped with a new metal halo and knife fabricated by Maya metalsmith Juan B. Chan, who incised the halo with his signature and the year 1892 (McAnany and Brown 2016:fig. 9). Remarkably, despite the upheaval and population dislocation of the nineteenth century, memory was retained of a patron saint who had been designated 300 years earlier. Recursive place-making can draw upon social memory to reactivate the relationality of founding events and effectively erase or obscure earlier detachment from place.

CONCLUDING THOUGHTS

Rootedness seems like a neutral or slightly positive term. It denotes stability and yet is a term embedded in Western notions of progress in which sedentism is perceived as a pinnacle of success and prosperity—the achievement of freedom from moving. But is such an achievement sustainable? The foregoing discussion suggests that periods of stasis may be highly unstable, in the long run, and that dynamic processes of making, unmaking, and remaking tend to typify the human experience more so than rootedness. Place-making arguably is a celebrated activity with material consequences that can be found nearly everywhere, even if the meaning of *place-making*—whether it signals completion, a new relationality, or conquest of nature—differs widely by place and time. Unmaking places, in contrast, may or may not be materially encoded through intentionally structured deposits. Humans are more ambivalent about the unmaking of places that hold social memory, and remaking places can completely mask abandonment periods with a simple sleight of hand. Recursively practiced at the scale of household and community, these dynamic processes may or may not synchronize with larger climatic and political cycles. Regardless, these processes typify what is distinctly human about engagement with place.

In this chapter, we have worked to effect a rapprochement between theories of materiality and migration. Seemingly at odds because materiality stresses human proclivity toward entanglement with things, while migration attempts to comprehend the conditions under which humans relinquish or loosen such entanglements, we suggest that the polarity of this contrast does not square with empirical reality, except in cases of popular fiction. Moreover, the many ways in which humans tend to "stay connected" to places of prior residence indicate that archaeology should move beyond the Enlightenment discourse of labor-based property rights and abandonment as argued by John Locke.

Historically, innovation within the field of "settlement abandonment studies" has been primarily methodological and less frequently engaged with the how and why of landscape inhabitation and detachment. An inductive fueling of abandonment and collapse discourse has constrained interpretive space and privileged inferences that rely too heavily on presentist concerns about environmental damage, middle-class materialist values, and crises of late capitalism. The topic of detachment would be well served by increased attention to field methods and careful, contextual analysis of stratigraphy, structures, and artifacts. In the Maya region, more precise excavation of surficial deposits has yielded extraordinarily detailed information about place-making and unmaking. By refining both the theoretical framing of place-making/unmaking/remaking and the investigation of its materiality, we better position archaeology as the preeminent science of human response to challenges and opportunities over the long term.

3

The Leaving's the Thing

The Contexts of Mesa Verde Emigration

DONNA M. GLOWACKI

The social and physical processes involved in leaving a place are of course intrinsic to migration; they initiate all that comes after. By setting the stage, if you will, these processes have a wide range of ramifications for how quickly people leave and where and how far they go, for how easily they reestablish themselves and how completely they disassociate from their homelands, and for what happens to those who stay behind. Thus, to understand much of migration, the leaving's the thing.

A key issue is that leaving is highly individualized and circumstantial, yet enmeshed in broader social, political, and economic relationships that create situations and events with differential effects. Even if deeply rooted in factors such as security (e.g., food access), climatic conditions, socioeconomic status, or ideological differences, most reasons for leaving are realized through interpersonal dynamics. Social circumstances such as feuds and familial strife, unrequited love, and the marginalization of people who do not "fit in," for example, can all lead to leaving or being forced out of a home. Archaeologists cannot "see" these types of interactions readily in the archaeological record, which is most revealing about settlement organization, subsistence practices, exchange networks, and ecological settings. Consequently, archaeological studies of regional depopulation and migration often result in explanations for leaving that are overly reliant on Malthusian narratives. The "classic" story is things were fine until there was a severe, prolonged drought or some other

DOI: 10.5876/9781646420087.c003

disaster reducing food availability and other necessities such that the resulting insecurity and increasing conflict led to a societal breakdown, and people left. The thread of this narrative may explain what happened on one level and to some people, yet we know the circumstances were much more complex and shaped as much by social relationships as anything else (e.g., Butzer 2012). The challenge, then, is reconciling the disparity between what can be measured and how it actually happened for regional depopulations really are the culminations of many "leavings."

Archaeologists contend with this challenge by focusing on what specific aspects of society are discontinued versus those that change or continue, and by developing methods and frameworks that engage with multiscalar causalities. An important step in this regard was the recognition that leaving (abandonment) is not solely an event, but also a process (Cameron and Tomka 1993). This needed paradigm shift opened intellectual space to consider more fully the intersection of multiple factors at multiple scales that affect the circumstances of leaving. Another important conceptual shift is being explicit about what it is that is collapsing, and the cultural continuities maintained through the transformation (McAnany and Yoffee 2010; Middleton 2012; Yoffee 1988). Subsequently, research has focused on developing deeper understandings of the contexts from which people leave that stress the role of historical contingencies and variation in the lived experience (Butzer 2012; Glowacki 2015), the intersection of stressors and enablers (McAnany and Lamoureux-St-Hilaire, chapter 2 in this volume), and the use of ethnography to develop interpretive models (Cameron 2013).

Holistic understandings of migrations involving regional depopulation also require specific knowledge of the timing and pace of emigration (e.g., S. Ortman and Cameron 2011). This information is an essential component for assessing the nature and pattern of migration streams and understanding how migrants moved into new areas and the context for migrant-local interactions at destinations (Anthony 1990). For example, those leaving during the initial stages of regional depopulation establish connections to other areas that are then relied upon by later emigrants from the region. Although key information, timing and pace are often difficult to determine as many archaeological cases of regional depopulation do not have adequate chronological resolution.

In one of the more dramatic cases of regional abandonment in the world,[1] the Mesa Verde (Northern San Juan / Four Corners) region went from being the most densely Pueblo-occupied area in the Southwest United States (SWUS) to completely vacated by Pueblo people within just two generations. Yet, what may appear to be a complete collapse from the perspective of the

Mesa Verde region actually involves dislocation, reorganization, and continuity when viewed from the broader Pueblo World. It is a powerful case study for developing rich contextual understandings of the when and how of leaving that inform on the why of it. The region also has the archaeological advantage of high-resolution chronological data (i.e., decadal level) for environmental and occupational reconstructions that builds on more than a century of archaeological research. More important, the outcomes of the processes of dislocation from the Mesa Verde region are known from contemporary Pueblo people and their oral histories (e.g., Naranjo 2008), the archaeological record of the fourteenth- and fifteenth-century Pueblo World, and the ethnographic records of historic pueblos (e.g., Adams and Duff 2004; Cushing 1896; Parsons 1939; Ware 2014).

After more than a century of inquiry into this compelling topic, the "classic" Malthusian narrative continues to dominate scholarly accounts of the Mesa Verde regional depopulation (e.g., Bocinsky and Kohler 2014). The prime movers implicated in causing the depopulation are the negative impacts of droughts and cooler-than-average temperatures on agricultural production, population pressure, resource depletion, and increased violence (Kuckelman, Lightfoot, and Martin 2000; Lipe 1995; Schwindt et al. 2016; Varien Van West, and Patterson 2000; Wright 2010). These factors certainly impacted circumstances during the 1200s and are keys to understanding what happened, but really at issue is how they were handled socially, which is much more difficult to discern. Substantial inroads into addressing the social dimensions of the departure from Mesa Verde have been made in recent years (Varien 2010). Studies focused on the role of religious and cultural change, the influence of historical contingencies, and the religiopolitical collapse of the ceremonial centers of Chaco and Aztec (Arakawa 2012; Glowacki 2011, 2015; Lekson 2008; Lipe 2010; S. Ortman 2012) make it clear that leaving Mesa Verde was more than an expected response to increasing population and climate change. In fact, K. W. Kintigh and S. E. Ingram (2018) recently found little to no correspondence between the timing of extreme climate events and dramatic cultural transitions in the SWUS; a finding that is supported in the Mesa Verde (MV) region as we now know that substantial numbers of people had begun leaving decades before the late thirteenth-century drought (Glowacki 2015). Thus, the social dimensions are the key.

My recent synthesis of the thirteenth-century regional dynamics in the Northern San Juan (Glowacki 2015) lays important groundwork in this regard by showing how regional balkanization occurred as the ceremonial and economic centers of Chaco and Aztec disassembled; the study addresses how

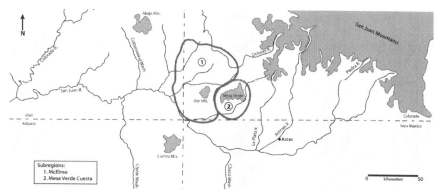

FIGURE 3.1. *Regional map showing the MV Core with the McElmo and MV Cuestas subregions.*

circumstances varied across the region and how deeply the processes were rooted in historical contingencies (in the broad sense of Hegmon 2017). Using this framework as the foundation, this chapter continues to expand on this in-depth contextual approach by focusing specifically on the MV Core within the broader Northern San Juan (Mesa Verde) region (figure 3.1). Using a more ethnographically informed perspective, I examine how the contexts of leaving the MV Core changed over time and affected the processes involved in widespread emigration and depopulation. In doing so, the variation in when and where emigration occurred is elucidated and suggests that migrants leaving in the late 1200s were moving into landscapes with connections and knowledge gained from those who had migrated in the late 1100s and early 1200s.

BUILDING CONTEXTUAL UNDERSTANDINGS OF LEAVING: DYNAMISM, HISTORY, AND SCALE

People are always leaving (and arriving). Populations flow in a variety of ways including: short-distance moves within familiar territory, longer-distance moves to new frontiers, moves to get away from something, moves to join people, and moves to return home. What changes are the numbers of people leaving and the nature of the reasons for doing so, even if the underlying motivator is always to improve their circumstances somehow. When the frequency and quantity of leaving lead not only to widespread departure from a region, but also from specific ways of living, then it is not just relocation, but transformation. Such is the case for the Pueblo people who once lived in the Mesa Verde region.

At any given time and place, multiple factors and historical processes converge that induce people to leave their homes. Some decisions to leave are an immediate response, while others are the culmination of building circumstances. In all cases, departures result from a combination of factors that galvanize and facilitate leaving and change personal connections to place-making people willing to relocate or forcing them to leave. Stressors, whether perceived or actual, are those factors that heighten insecurities, whereas enablers are advantages that individuals have and/or gains found at potential destinations. Stressors and enablers are also not necessarily mutually exclusive, as some factors can be at once stressing and enabling. Using these terms, rather than push-pull factors (Dorigo and Tobler 1983), places more emphasis on what the people are experiencing and doing rather than on the external forces themselves. However, simply identifying stressors and enablers is not enough and can also lead to static narratives.

Constantly evolving, stressors and enablers are socially mediated (Butzer 2012; McAnany and Lamoureux-St-Hilaire, chapter 2 in this volume). Thus, their intensity and combination vary for each person, household, and village, producing numerous narratives of leaving, even during periods of widespread emigration. This dynamism also has scalar and historical dimensions that further complicate the entanglements. Macrolevel stressors, for example, tend to be broadly shared and external, including factors such as climate change and political upheaval, which are then experienced and mitigated at the local and individual levels. Consequently, reactions to even shared circumstances vary and would therefore variably affect when and how people move away and where they decide to go. Emergent local stressors, which also vary between people and among groups, arise from interpersonal situations and inequalities, especially those involving food insecurities. It is the intersectionality of the varied stressors and enablers at multiple scales and how they change over time that create the dynamics of leaving.

Leaving is a historical process affected by contingencies that can also create path dependencies (e.g., Hegmon 2017). Elsewhere I used the concept of historical landscapes—long-lived traditions and social configurations tied to place that creates some degree of social order (Robb and Pauketat 2013:25)— to show how the history of Pueblo occupation in the MV region was integral to understanding how people reacted to circumstances during the 1200s (Glowacki 2015). Because the intensity and combination of stressors and enablers change over time and space, the emigration process is itself also historicized. This perspective is particularly important for understanding emigrations that lead to regional depopulation. In these cases, delimiting the timing and intensities of emigration streams and their associated contexts can help characterize the vectors for change that are the most influential for prompting emigration. This analysis is critical because the reasons for which people begin leaving an area are likely not the same for those who leave later in the process. Additionally, there can be cumulative effects to consider. For example, the number and intensity of stressors can compound rather than subside, particularly if new factors, such as the onset of a severe drought or a war, are introduced. This progression would also cause an increasing proportion of the population to experience shared and prolonged stress.

ETHNOGRAPHY AND LEAVING IN THE PUEBLO WORLD

In the Pueblo Southwest, it is increasingly apparent that contexts for leaving cannot be fully understood without ethnographic perspectives, the disruption brought about by Spanish and US colonialism notwithstanding (Bernardini 2005; Cameron 2013; Colwell-Chanthaphonh and Ferguson 2006; Fowles 2005; Schachner 2012; Ware 2014). For Pueblo people, movement (and corn) is life (Naranjo 2008). Pueblo oral traditions and ethnographic histories are replete with stories about individuals and families leaving villages because of their social circumstances, and in some cases, about entire villages relocating (e.g., Whiteley 1988; Yava and Courlander 1978). These histories elucidate two key social processes that shaped contexts of leaving with ramifications for archaeological interpretation: serial migrations and social group fission and fusion.

Serial migrations are successive movements of families and clans as they stopped at various points along their migrations, sometimes joining other clans to form villages, before moving on to settle elsewhere. For example, using Hopi oral tradition and archaeological evidence, Wesley Bernardini (2005) shows how social diversity and independence in Hopi identity construction and community formation emerged from the serial migrations unique to each clan's history. His analysis of settlement patterns, rock art, and pottery showed that Anderson Mesa and Homo'lovi villages contained multiple groups with diverse origins and connections. Bernardini (2005) not only contextualizes how individuals and groups move, creating multiple habitation sites, but also stresses how the diverse clan histories enable both village formation and dissolution. Moreover, he shows that spatial proximity does not always equate to a shared identity, an assumption commonly employed when interpreting site data.

Social group fissioning and fusion are social processes that underlie village formation (immigration) and dissolution (emigration), and thus also identity construction. Group fissioning occurs when fracture lines between individuals, families, and groups (factions) develop allowing social conflict, competition, violence, or disenfranchisement to intensify (e.g., Chagnon 1992; Kopytoff 1987). In these cases, stressors have greater influence, even if factors enabling the dynamics are at play. Often, the actual act of fissioning from a group is instigated by an event and happens quickly, even if tensions may have been building gradually (Cameron 2013). Pueblo ethnography and oral traditions (e.g., Levy 1992; Schlegel 1992; Whiteley 1988; Yava and Courlander 1978) commonly describes factional disputes and dissension that causes fissioning, most often along lineages and clan group lines (Schlegel 1992). Although not always the case, when groups fission, short-distance moves are more common (Anthony 1990) and are often to areas that are not yet occupied (e.g., "internal frontiers," Kopytoff 1987).

Group fusion is the process of coming together, which archaeologists study as processes of aggregation and coalescence (e.g., Kohler and Sebastian 1996; Kowalewski 2006). The social dynamics involved in these processes bear on the contexts of leaving because multicultural villages, with diverse groups and histories that intermix populations, such as described by Bernardini (2005), can be stressors, for they have inherent lines of fracture that can lead more readily to fission depending on the degree of social cohesion. Diverse social histories can also act as enablers because social networks beyond the village that could facilitate migration through information or contact points would differ.

Both fissioning and fusion are influenced by the distribution of power and status, which can be both a stressor and enabler. For example, individuals who were ritual specialists or held other powerful traditional knowledge could be actively recruited to join villages (Brandt 1994; Bernardini 2005, 2011). However, those lacking power, such as those who are socially marginalized (e.g., witches; Darling 1998) or are lower-status clans, are among the first to leave or be forced out (Cameron 2013; Schlegel 1992).

The Story of Ojegeh

Pueblo oral histories and stories are deep understandings of how and why Pueblo people move, and contain essential cultural information for addressing the complexity inherent in contexts of leaving a place (Bernardini 2005; Naranjo 2008). Therefore, to conceptualize the importance of serial migrations and social group fission and fusion more fully, I summarize a story. Frustrated by archaeologists' explanation of migration and village formation, and the absence of the human experience in their narratives, Rina Swentzell (2000)—a Santa Clara Pueblo artist, architect, and scholar-activist,—wrote *Younger-Older*

Ones. It is not an oral history, but a Pueblo story created by Rina that incorporates her own experiences and observations. The story is about Ojegeh, a self-sufficient potter shunned from her village when she became a focus of discord and blamed for the energy associated with several deaths that had recently occurred in the village. Over the course of the story, Ojegeh, her husband, and four children (not always together) move from Wo-Ping Owingeh (Medicine Mountain Village) to a small stone house just outside the village, to a more distant house made of juniper, to an even more distant alcove in a canyon located near the Posongeh (River). While near the river, Ojegeh continued to make pottery and traded it with other nearby villages. Meanwhile, the people of Wo-Ping village continued to have problems, even after Ojegeh had moved away. The leaders of Wo-Ping decided it was because they had treated Ojegeh poorly. To remedy this mistreatment and restore balance, they decided to join Ojegeh and established a new village by the river, Posongeh Owingeh, though some people changed their minds and returned to Wo-Ping.

The story of Ojegeh illustrates how migration happens, how people live, and ultimately how their actions produce what becomes the archaeological record. Of importance, in this story, largely the same group of people is responsible for five residential sites of different sizes, construction, and settings including a relocated village (and this count does not include the village one of Ojegeh's sons joined after getting married). By showing how serial migration and social group fusion-fission happened, Ojegeh's journey elucidates the serious challenges we have not only in identifying the specific behaviors and reasons involved in leaving, but also in estimating population and interpreting settlement patterns.

Implications for Mesa Verde

These examples from Pueblo culture and the ethnographic record have direct implications for our archaeological narratives of the Mesa Verde migrations. First, as Catherine Cameron (2013) notes the ethnographic literature indicates that reasons for moving are often not economic and transactional in nature; rather, they tend to be socially driven—another reason the classic Malthusian MV narrative falls short of reality. Second, the influence of serial migration and processes of fusion-fission requires reconsideration of population estimates and settlement pattern interpretation. Third, the early 1200s in the Mesa Verde Core was a period of intensified growth, when many of the largest villages formed quickly as diverse groups with different backgrounds coalesced (Glowacki 2015; S. Ortman 2012). Thus, the social processes—both stressors and enablers—associated with social group fusion and fissioning described above were an intrinsic part of the social landscape that resulted in regional depopulation.

THE MESA VERDE CORE AND HOW MANY PEOPLE LEFT IT

The Mesa Verde core—comprised of the MV Cuesta and McElmo subregions (figure 3.1)—was the most densely occupied part of the region with more than 2,300 habitation sites dating to the 1150–1290 period (Glowacki 2015:table 3). McElmo encompasses the Great Sage Plain including the McElmo drainage and the Hovenweep, Dolores, and Ute Piedmont districts (Schwindt et al. 2016). Best known for its cliff dwellings, the Mesa Verde cuesta (also known as Mesa Verde Proper) is a geologic uplift about 460 meters higher than the rest of the MV Core area and is cut by north-south trending canyons and mesas. The cuesta has the highest annual precipitation and longest growing season in the region, and thus the best conditions for dry-land agriculture (K. Adams and Petersen 1999).

To understand how regional depopulations happen requires knowing how many people were involved. Mesa Verde core population estimates range from 5,000 to 30,000 (Lipe 1995; Schwindt et al. 2016). The most recent estimate is from the Village Ecodynamics Project (VEP), which puts peak population at 26,700 people between 1225–60, with roughly 25 percent of them living on the Mesa Verde cuesta at higher densities than in McElmo (Schwindt et al. 2016:table 2). This estimate is based on Bayesian analyses of pottery, architecture, surveyors' assessment, and tree-ring dates to estimate the number of households, which were momentized using structure use-life per period (Ortman, Varien, and T. L. Gripp 2007). It is our best effort to model population in the Mesa Verde core to date; however, an implicit assumption is that each site represents different people. Nonetheless, if Rina Swentzell's story—inspired by her history—is any illustration of the impact of serial migration and fusion-fission processes, we are double counting to some degree, and even the momentized estimates are inflated, by perhaps as much as 25 percent. If nothing else, the story of Ojegeh and her community should serve as a parable for archaeologists about how inadequately our methods capture population movements, and sizes, not to mention reasons for moving (as Rina intended).

The story should also stress the need for the cautious use of population estimates, which we know are not absolute figures, but tend to reify in our application of them. For the VEP estimate, researchers calculated an informal 80 percent confidence interval (Schwindt et al. 2016:table 4, fig. 3). Using the lower interval, the MV Core estimate is decreased by 30 percent, between

14,000 and 18,500 people, with 3,500–5,000 people on the MV Cuesta, and 10,500–13,000 people in McElmo. And, within this more conservative and perhaps more realistic population estimate, it is also prudent to use the lowest end of this range (~14,000), because the VEP II methods are not as sensitive to the earlier occupations of multicomponent sites, and, thus, the latest occupation estimates are somewhat inflated. This estimate, which is nearly half of the proposed peak population, would significantly alter models for the impact of Mesa Verde migrants at destinations and therefore has important implications for answering the "Where did everybody go" question.

UNPACKING THE CONTEXTS OF LEAVING: TIMING IS EVERYTHING

Thirteenth-century Mesa Verde began in the aftermath of the most severe droughts to hit the SWUS (Cook et al. 2004). The severity of these conditions sent shock waves throughout the Pueblo world, affecting confidence in long-standing Chaco and related, but nascent, Aztec institutions. Ultimately, leaving Mesa Verde was in many ways the result of sociopolitical upheaval stemming from resistance and religious reformation that increased conflict and collapsed the emergent Aztec-Chaco religious and sociopolitical system (Glowacki 2015). These vulnerable circumstances were worsened by difficult agricultural conditions (i.e., cooler-than-normal temperatures), and for those remaining in the region during the mid-to-late 1270s and into the 1280s, severe drought. The intensity and diversity of stress factors, both external and emergent, played out in various ways, even if ultimately most Pueblo people ended up leaving or dying in the region.

To unpack these circumstances further, I next describe the changing contexts of emigration from the MV Core between 1140and 1290 CE, relying most heavily a regional tree-ring database and settlement pattern data (Glowacki 2015; Schwindt et al. 2016). The regional tree-ring database is the one used in VEP analyses and is curated by researchers at Crow Canyon Archaeological Center. This database contains 10,681 dates from sites across the MV Core, and 1,289 of these are cutting dates from between CE 1100 and 1290. Of these, 505 cuttings dates are from thirty-three sites in the McElmo subregion, and 784 cutting dates are from thirty sites on the MV Cuesta. Although the number of sites is relatively equal, the number of samples is higher from the MV Cuesta because of the remarkable preservation that the cliff dwellings afford. However, a greater proportion of the samples from the McElmo subregion are from systematically excavated contexts. As described below, using the percentage of

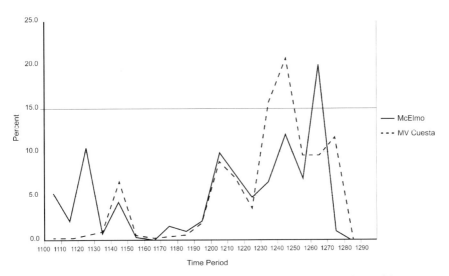

FIGURE 3.2. *Tree-ring dates for the Mesa Verde Core—construction and remodeling episodes for the Mesa Verde cuesta and McElmo subregions. The x-axis is the percent of the sample from each subregion for each decade.*

the total sample within each subregion, the distribution of these dates shows important similarities and differences in the intensity and timing of construction and remodeling between the MV Cuesta and McElmo (figure 3.2).

The VEP II paleodemographic model of population changes across the Mesa Verde core is used only to compare *general trends* in the occupation of the MV Cuesta with that of McElmo (see table 3.1 and figure 3.3, which are based on data presented in Schwindt et al. 2016). Although specific numbers of momentary population are presented in table 3.1, per the discussion above, the emphasis here is on the relative degree and direction of change in population across space and over time, as opposed to the specific estimated numbers of people.

1140–1180 CE—POST-CHACO DROUGHT

This hot and dry period had a severe, prolonged drought from 1130 to 1158 CE, with another shortly on its heels from 1164 to 1178 CE (Wright 2010:89, figs. 4.2 and 4.3). Consequently, agricultural productivity was below average for much of this period, rebounding slightly by the end of it (Varien et al. 2007:figs. 3 and 8). Maize niches—the size and density of areas suitable for growing corn—contracted in the McElmo area during this period, but not on the MV

TABLE 3.1. Momentary population estimates from Schwindt et al. 2016:table 2, and percent change between periods

ce				McElmo				
Begin	*End*	*Centers*	*% change*	*Small Sites*	*% change*	*All Sites*	*% change*	*Ratio*
1100	1140	1536		13361		14897		8.7
1140	1180	1824	16	13894	4	15718	5	7.6
1180	1225	3282	44	10968	-27	14250	-10	3.3
1225	1260	6846	52	14080	22	20926	32	2.1
1260	1280	5886	-16	9767	-44	15653	-34	1.7

ce				MV Cuesta				
Begin	*End*	*Centers*	*% change*	*Small Sites*	*% change*	*All Sites*	*% change*	*Ratio*
1100	1140	528		5318		5846		10.1
1140	1180	486	-9	4793	-11	5279	-11	9.9
1180	1225	576	16	4352	-10	4928	-7	7.6
1225	1260	792	27	4978	13	5770	15	6.3
1260	1280	708	-12	5431	8	6139	6	7.7

ce				Mesa Verde Core Total				
Begin	*End*	*Centers*	*% change*	*Small Sites*	*% change*	*All Sites*	*%c hange*	*Ratio*
1100	1140	2064		18677		20741		9.0
1140	1180	2310	11	18688	0	20998	1	8.1
1180	1225	3858	40	15320	-22	19178	-9	4.0
1225	1260	7638	49	19057	20	26695	28	2.5
1260	1280	6594	-16	15198	-25	21792	-22	2.3

Cuesta (Schwindt et al. 2016). Unsurprisingly, there was attendant conflict with intense and widespread violence that occurred at higher frequencies than would be expected given the number of people living in McElmo during the 1100s (Kohler et al. 2014). This violence included dismemberment and postmortem processing (Billman, Lambert, and Leonard 2000; Kuckelman, Lightfoot, and Martin 2000). These extreme conditions changed attitudes about where and how to live and among other responses prompted shifts in settlement locations, such as increased positioning in canyon rim settings (Glowacki 2015).

Relatively little new construction occurred between 1140 and 1190 (figure 3.2; Lipe and Varien 1999). The low number of cutting dates for this period may result from sampling bias, but, given the extreme conditions of the time, may also reflect drought-related conservation practices, such as reduced

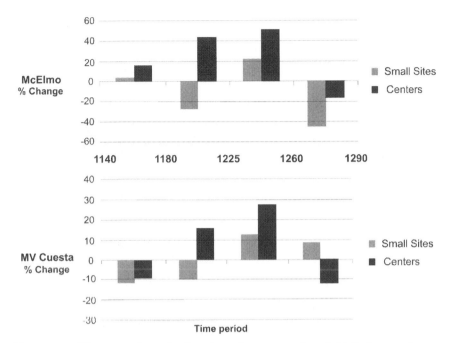

FIGURE 3.3. *The percent change in the estimated momentary households for large centers and small sites. Based on table 3.1.*

wood harvesting or increased recycling (Ryan 2010). Although some archaeologists correlate the paucity of cutting dates with population decline (Berry and Benson 2010), VEP estimates suggest the McElmo population remained relatively stable with possibly some increase in the numbers of people joining large villages, perhaps for security reasons. On the MV Cuesta, however, people were clearly leaving the area regardless of the size of their villages (table 3.1). Here, the drought conditions and conflict compounded an ongoing twelfth-century depopulation and reorganization on the cuesta as connections to Chaco and Aztec attenuated and changed, such that emigration intensified. Regardless of where in the MV Core people lived, the consequences of how they coped with these conditions created new challenges and contingencies that affected Mesa Verde society for generations.

Emigration Contexts. Across the MV Core, everyone contended with the severity of the times. The drought and violence heightened food insecurity and other uncertainties that likely made for fractious interactions and difficult conditions to which mobility and relocation are common responses (e.g.,

Halstead and O'Shea 2004). Thus, leaving and moving were prevalent, but the specific contexts and ways movement was used to cope with personal circumstances and stressors differed among residents of McElmo and the MV Cuesta. For example, in the McElmo subregion, where population levels were somewhat stable, leaving and relocation involved more local movement and fusion-fission processes than long-distance emigration. That the large villages experience some growth suggests that aggregation may have afforded needed stability during an unstable time (Glowacki 2015). In these cases, enablers such as key knowledge or skills would have facilitated joining the established villages.

However, on the MV Cuesta, prior to the drought and violence, many people were already on the move given the widespread settlement relocation and reorganization (Glowacki 2015). The drought and increased violence were thus added stressors that intensified interactions and challenges, such that one of the subsequent outcome of this period was the establishment of the cliff dwellings. In contrast to the situation in the McElmo subregion, not only were people moving around on the cuesta, but also were leaving it altogether. It is possible that some of these people joined some of the large villages in the McElmo area, but they also were moving out of the core entirely.

1180–1225 CE—Recovery and Revitalization

Following the mid-1100s megadrought, there was a cold and wet period with prolonged wet conditions from 1179–97 CE, and generally below-average temperatures that begins in the 1190s and lasts throughout the rest of this period (Wright 2010:89, fig. 4.3). Agricultural productivity in the McElmo area was relatively good until 1200, and then below average through the 1220s (Varien et al. 2007:fig. 8). In general, the MV Cuesta was agriculturally better off than anywhere in the region (Adams and Petersen 1999; Benson 2011; Schwindt et al. 2016), and residents of the cuesta likely fared better than those in McElmo during this period.

Construction and remodeling increase (figure 3.2), and both in McElmo and on the MV Cuesta, large villages increase in number and their populations grow in size (table 3.2, figure 3.3). Yet, population in the smaller settlements decreases as people either joined larger settlements or left the MV Core altogether (table 3.1). These settlement pattern changes suggest heightened aggregation was one of the responses people had to the severity of the prior period (Glowacki 2015). This tendency toward living in larger settlements is especially interesting on the MV Cuesta as it comes after a period when people had been leaving the cuesta altogether.

TABLE 3.2. The number of community centers that were newly constructed, continued to be occupied, and abandoned during each period

McElmo (n=69)

CE	New	% New	Continue	% Continue	End	% End	total
1100–40	6	30.0	13	65.0	1	5.0	20
1140–80	5	21.7	16	69.6	2	8.7	23
1180–1225	13	37.1	19	54.3	3	8.6	35
1225–60	28	46.7	28	46.7	16	26.7	60
1260–80	3	6.3	0	0.0	48	100.0	48

Mesa Verde Cuesta (n=36)

CE	New	% New	Continue	% Continue	End	% End	total
1100–40	2	10.5	14	73.7	4	21.1	19
1140–80	4	22.2	13	72.2	2	11.1	18
1180–1225	5	23.8	13	61.9	3	14.3	21
1225–60	8	30.8	15	57.7	6	23.1	26
1260–80	1	4.8	0	0.0	21	100.0	21

With aggregation into existing villages and the establishment of new ones, new types of village configurations emerged. These villages were more contained and centrally oriented than many of the earlier centers that tended to be dispersed and strongly north-south oriented (Lipe and Ortman 2000). There is also evidence of the instigation of significant religious organizational changes. At the turn of the thirteenth century, the shift from great houses that signaled connections to traditional Chaco, to circular multiwalled structures indicative of an Aztec-Chaco revitalization movement reflects the changing influence of the Aztec-Chaco ideological complex in Mesa Verde society (Glowacki 2015; Lekson 2008). These changes in village organization and associated practices and the initial benefits of heightened aggregation, all promoted stability in the MV Core, at least for a time, which is indicated by low levels of violence during this period (Kohler et al. 2014).

Emigration Contexts. Despite evident aggregation, emigration from the MV Core continued as indicated by the apparent decline in the overall population (table 3.1). Given changes in settlement patterns, it seems two broad modes of emigration characterize this period. One mode entails intraregional, short-distance moves within and beyond communities (e.g., the Goodman Point and Sand Canyon communities [Varien 1999]). Growth in the large villages while population in the smaller settlements declined suggests that fusion and fissioning, among other processes, were occurring. Alternatively, a small proportion of the overall population left the MV Core completely. That people were leaving the MV Core when violence was low and agricultural conditions were relatively good suggests that the stressors and enablers prompting emigration had more to do with social dynamics and interpersonal interactions associated with the reorganization and aggregation that was taking place in the aftermath of the severity of the mid-1100s.

1225–1260 CE—McElmo Intensification

Temperatures were colder than average until the 1250s, and then prolonged wet conditions began (Wright 2010). The 1230s and 1240s were tough years for agriculture, but the 1250s were good ones (Varien et al. 2007). However, analyses suggest the size and density of areas suitable for growing corn contracted across the MV Core during this interval (Schwindt et al. 2016). Thus, as population was increasing and aggregating, it was also becoming more difficult to grow adequate amounts of corn (see also Glowacki and Ortman 2012). Despite this apparent stressor, people experienced low levels of violence (Kohler et al. 2014), but this does not mean there was also little or no social tension or conflict. Architectural features associated with villages during this period suggest an increasingly defensive social landscape as indicated by more people moving into alcove and cliff settings and the proliferation of enclosing walls and towers (Glowacki 2015).

New construction and remodeling continued across the MV Core, with increased activity in the 1230s and 1240s, and a decline in the 1250s (figure 3.2). The peak in construction on the MV Cuesta in the 1230s and 1240s corresponds with settlement reorganization and a shift to living in alcoves (Glowacki 2015). The VEP II estimates indicate population growth occurred during this period (table 3.1). Some of this growth resulted in increased aggregation into large villages as nearly 35 percent of the centers in the MV Core were established during this period (table 3.2; Glowacki 2015; Varien 1999). The coalescence of these large villages involved both local fission and fusion processes, but also low-to-moderate levels of immigration (Schwindt et al. 2016) with some of the migrants likely coming from west-central Mesa Verde (Glowacki 2015). Thus, social dynamics involved the integration of new people who had different histories and ideas.

Within this social landscape, the changes in settlement configuration toward an organization that was more focused on inwardness and village-level, and the adoption of circular, bi- and tri-walled structures initiated by the early 1200s intensified. Additionally, a new form of building analogous to the circular, bi-wall structures—the D-shaped structure (e.g., Sun Temple)—is evidence of new ideas and diverging connections, symbolism, and ritual practices among some of the large centers (Glowacki 2015). Many of these changes transformed social, ritual, and political relationships, which involved social negotiations that may have caused friction between individuals, families, groups, and villages. The defensive architectural positioning and posturing lend some credence to this inference. Ultimately, given that within a generation all Pueblo people were leaving the MV Core, factionalization within and among villages caused Pueblo people to reconceptualize fundamental aspects of where and how they were living. The cultural and organizational changes at this time affected internal village dynamics and intervillage relationships, especially with respect to how, or if, they remained connect to Aztec and the institutions of the Aztec-Chaco ceremonial system (Glowacki 2015). The impacts of these social processes cascaded across the Pueblo World, ultimately transforming it from being culturally predicated on vertically oriented Chaco ideologies to being more horizontally oriented (Glowacki 2015; Pauketat 2011). This seismic shift, more than anything else, was the reason why Pueblo people left Mesa Verde.

Emigration Contexts. Many of the reasons for leaving during this period were shaped by the situatedness of individuals and families in relation to the dramatic changes in settlement organization and the challenges of agricultural production that intensified during this period. Although VEP II estimates suggest population in the MV Core grew between CE 1225 and 1260, other analyses focusing on the large centers show that starting in the 1240s and during the 1250s, the rate of emigration was steadily increasing (Glowacki 2015:table 4). Certainly, construction activity ebbed during the 1250s (figure 3.2). That just over one in four of the largest villages were completely depopulated by the end of this period (i.e., 27 percent, table 3.2) is a strong indicator that social tensions and conflict were becoming more pervasive as everyone negotiated the intense social changes, worsening climate, and agricultural capacity.

1260–1290 CE—Fracture, Refuge, and the Last Decades

The final decades were cooler on average, and the prolonged wet conditions of the 1260s were followed by a devastating fifteen-year drought (1273–88), even if it was less severe than the mid-1100s megadrought (Wright 2010:89, fig. 4.3). During the 1260s, the potential maize yield was modeled below average, followed by a brief period of good years in the early 1270s, before the drought cycle began (Varien et al. 2007:fig. 8). Across the MV Core, variability in maize niches increased (Schwindt et al. 2016). Thus, farming was more unpredictable than the preceding years, further intensifying uncertainty and instability during these last decades.

The social and subsistence stressors were palpable as violence spiked in the MV Core (Kohler et al. 2014). Villages such as Castle Rock and Sand Canyon pueblos, have clear evidence of traumas and extreme postmortem processing commensurate with attacks and raids (Kuckelman, Lightfoot, and Martin, 2002). A particularly gruesome battle ended the occupation of Castle Rock Pueblo.

Construction activity in the McElmo area reached its height in the 1260s (figure 3.2), when population concentration and aggregation were at their most intense (Glowacki and Ortman 2012; Schwindt et al. 2016; Varien et al. 2007), but then it sharply declined. In contrast, on the MV Cuesta construction activities lessened in the 1260s, but increased in the 1270s, specifically in the cliff dwellings. These differences suggest that by the 1270s, widespread and substantial emigration out of the region from McElmo was underway. Although some people were also leaving the MV Cuesta, the active construction and slight population increase that occurred in the last decades (table 3.1; Glowacki 2015) suggest that the cuesta and the cliff dwellings in particular became a last refuge as conditions continued to worsen (Glowacki 2015; Lipe 1995). Not only did the cliff dwellings afford protection, but also the agricultural advantages of the cuesta made it a desirable location during these troubled times and allowed more people to remain for a longer period than elsewhere in the region (Glowacki 2015; Schwindt et al. 2016).

Emigration Contexts. By these last decades, the prolonged stressors had become acute and everyone was struggling and eventually leaving or dying. Not only did the timing and pace of emigration from McElmo and the MV Cuestas differ, but also did the strategies used by those attempting to remain in the region, before they too were forced to leave. For instance, people leaving McElmo vacated the small sites faster than they did the largest ones (table 3.1; figure 3.3), suggesting that large centers may have provided more security, at least for a time. However, on the MV Cuesta, people may have been leaving the large centers faster than the smaller settlements (table 3.1; figure 3.3). This issues requires more analysis, as site documentation in Mesa Verde National Park is biased toward small sites because historically each room block or architectural feature was assigned a separate site number, yet residual populations remained in the cliff dwellings as indicated by tree-ring dates in the late 1270s and early 1280s (e.g., Varien 2010:table 1.3). If true, however, it suggests that people living on the cuesta chose a more dispersed settlement strategy for coping with these difficult times, which points to some interesting differences in strategies and interpersonal relationships between McElmo and the MV Cuesta (see also Glowacki 2015). By the end, of course, migration became a means of survival as people were fleeing drought, violence, and imbalance to find a better place to live.

IMPLICATIONS AND CONCLUSIONS

As shown here, relocation within and emigration from the region were always shaping the Mesa Verde social landscape. Between CE 1140 and 1290, the contexts and frequency of leaving differed in character and intensity. During the severity of the mid-to-late 1100s, there was deliberate emigration and relocation under duress. On the one hand the social contexts of those living in the McElmo area favored more local movement. On the other hand, the severe climatic conditions intensified the circumstances for those living on the MV Cuesta that were already involved in social and settlement reorganization, and prompted more emigration from the cuesta. At the turn of the thirteenth century, as people recovered from the harsh conditions of the late 1100s, there was coalescence into larger villages that depopulated small settlements (fusion and fissioning), as well as emigration from the MV Core. Coalescence and organizational change intensified into the mid-1200s, but tensions resulting from integrating new groups and migrants from beyond the MV Core, as well as sociopolitical strains as the Aztec-Chaco system balkanized, exacerbated regional emigration. In the end, these conditions became insufferable and were made worse by drought and widespread violence, such that short-term refuge and flight were the only options.

Much of our archaeological inquiry has focused on the migrations at end of the 1200s (e.g., Ortman 2012). However, to understand where and how Pueblo people left the region during these decades also requires consideration of the timing and contexts of regional emigration preceding the final exodus. Often when people move, they rely on established connections and prior knowledge of places obtained through resource procurement, exchange networks, or familial ties, which can create migration streams between destinations and homelands (e.g., Anthony 1990). Thus, emigration contexts and their temporality are a necessary foundation for developing models for identifying where and how people migrated, including a determination of how far people might travel, their direction, and their potential visibility en route and at destinations. For example, recent modeling of migration pathways of MV migrants through the Gallina area correlates with sites that have evidence of violence and date to the post-1250s (Borck 2012). Given the contexts of emigration at this time, these migrants would have been leaving the MV Core, especially the cuesta, as conflict and social tensions were rising in the context of coalescence and reorganization (see also Glowacki 2015).

The dominant MV migration narrative is that the Northern Rio Grande (NRG) was the primary destination for migrants because population synchronically increases on the Pajarito Plateau at the end of the 1200s (Bocinsky and Kohler 2014; Ortman 2012). Tewa oral traditions, linguistic patterns, and bioarchaeology also suggest MV migrants played a role in NRG developments (e.g., Ortman 2012). However, the extent to which this is the case is highly debated, for despite evident population increase, the MV migrants themselves are not readily visible in the NRG archaeological record (Boyer et al. 2010; Schillaci and Lakatos 2016). This contradiction leads to questioning the degree to which the population increase was the result of MV migrants who moved more or less directly to the NRG or the consolidation of local populations that relocated due to pressure from increasing immigration in areas such as the southern San Juan and Galisteo Basins (Cameron 1995; Davis 1964; Habicht-Mauche 1993). Mesa Verde archaeologists often attribute the low visibility of MV migrants in the NRG to a pervasive willingness to disassociate from their past life (Glowacki 2015; Lipe 2010; Ortman 2012), yet, paradoxically, MV material culture is present in other parts of the Southwest.

The nature and timing of emigration from the MV region preceding the final migrations are essential for explicating variation in the visibility of MV migrants en route and at their destinations and the social processes and histories responsible for them. Outside of the region, Mesa Verde connections, if not migrants, are most readily apparent from the Chinle Wash in northeastern Arizona (Dean 2010) and east across northwestern New Mexico (i.e., the southern San Juan Basin). The distribution of MV-style pottery covers this area (Roney 1995:fig. 3), which conforms with potential routes, stopovers, and destinations of those leaving the MV Core using southern routes.

Southerly migrations were facilitated by natural corridors such as the Montezuma Valley that would direct travelers toward the Chuska Mountains. Some sites in the Chuska Valley, dating to the early-to-mid-1200s, contain MV-style pottery, both imported and produced with local resources, a few MV-style ("keyhole") kivas, and a bi-walled structure, called Red Willow, with MV and McElmo black-on-white pottery (Murrell and Vierra 2014; Peckham 1963). Although some MV traits could have been locally adopted, the timing and nature of the evidence suggest that they may relate to MV migrants who, having left their homeland during the unsettled period of recovery and reorganization (ca. 1180–1225 CE, described above), needed to reconstitute their social identity in a new place. The same is true of areas such as the Puerco Valley, where sites such as Prieta Vista have strong affinities with Mesa Verde settlement organization and pottery styles, and appear to have been established in an unoccupied area around 1220 (Roney 1995). Further south, near Magdalena, New Mexico, there are also probable MV migrant enclaves ("site-unit intrusions") that date between CE 1230 and 1275 (i.e., Gallina Springs and Pinnacle Ruin; Clark and Laumbach 2011; Lekson et al. 2002).

Thus, it seems those leaving Mesa Verde because of disruptions caused by the severity of the mid-1100s or the subsequent social upheavals resulting from coalescence and social change in the early 1200s were more likely to retain material expressions associated with their homelands. The retention of material culture would also be strengthened if the migrants pathways and intended destinations were more direct than in later periods. Apparently, these circumstances, both with respect to emigration contexts and pathways, changed with MV migrations later in the 1200s as migrants became less visible in the archaeological record. Notably, these types of differences also likely play a role in why Kayenta migrants were more visible in the late 1200s than the MV migrants (e.g., Clark et al. 2019).

Strong connections to the homeland would have created social networks that included return migration flows and other visits that facilitated migration and relocation. As circumstances continued to worsen in the homeland, these connections likely became important influences when deciding which general direction to travel or potential destinations. Not only do our models need to account for these realities better, but also for the reality that, especially when leaving in the mid-to-late 1200s, many MV migrants likely stopped, sometimes for extended periods, at intermediary places during serial migrations before they potentially arrived in the NRG. These movements would have allowed MV migrants time to change and adapt as they moved to new locations, even if temporary, and encountered new groups of people with differing practices and traditions. This important consideration may help explain why MV migrants were not visible in the NRG and why they may have seemingly rapidly adopted new cultural practices upon arrival. Reconstructing detailed understandings of the contexts and timing of emigration and addressing the potential serial migration histories of MV people as they left their homeland are essential for nuanced models and understandings of Pueblo migration. In this way, and by emphasizing the historical contingencies associated with what happened when they migrants Mesa Verde, we may come closer to the stories of leaving, such as the one illustrated by Ojegeh and her family, which constituted the Mesa Verde migrations.

ACKNOWLEDGMENTS

The data used in this chapter were synthesized as part of the Village Ecodynamics Project (VEP), work with Crow Canyon Archaeological Center, dissertation research, and large site survey fieldwork. Research was funded through the NSF (CNH-0816400; SES-1132226, Tim Kohler, Senior PI) and grants awarded to the author by National Geographic (#9100–12) and Notre Dame (ISLA Research Grant). Thank you to Mesa Verde National Park and its archaeological staff, Mark Varien, Tim Kohler, Kyle Bocinsky, and the VEP research team. Special thanks to Tessie Naranjo for our conversations and friendship, and for introducing me to Rina Swentzell's story about Ojegeh, I have learned much.

NOTE

1. Pueblo people do not view this region as *abandoned* in the sense of "to neglect or to give up completely," for they remain integrally connected to this landscape, both physically and spiritually. I use the term sparingly with this implicit understanding to convey that Pueblo people no longer lived in the region year-round and discontinued some of the cultural practices associated with the region.

4

Archaeologists recognize processes of abandonment and detachment from place as a normal component of the occupational histories of structures, settlements, and regions (Cameron 1993; McAnany and Lamoureux-St-Hilaire, chapter 2 in this volume). Societal collapse or regional depopulation exists at one extreme end of a continuum of responses that may include abandonment. These abandonment processes may result in profound transformations that affect virtually every aspect of a society and its culture (e.g., Clark et al. 2013; Cobb and Butler 2006; Faulseit 2015; Glowacki 2015; S. Ortman 2012). Other processes of detachment from place may unfold as part of normal processes of settlement use—and with less immediate crisis—but are just as thoroughly enmeshed in processes of place-making and unmaking. The archaeological signatures of such processes can provide important data on human behavior in these varying contexts (e.g., Ascher 1968; Cameron 1993; Schiffer 1976). Oral histories and the perspectives of contemporary native peoples also provide important viewpoints on the enduring attachment to place that may run counter to archaeological constructions of abandonment processes (Colwell-Chanthaphonh and Ferguson 2006; Richard 2016; Warrick and Lesage 2016).

For the Northern Iroquoian peoples of the northeastern woodlands, flexibility was the defining characteristic of the settlement landscape (Birch 2015:305–6). Migration, amalgamation, coalescence, dispersal,

When Detachment Is Not Complete

Emplacement and Displacement in Huron-Wendat Ancestral Landscapes

JENNIFER BIRCH AND
LOUIS LESAGE

DOI: 10.5876/9781646420087.c004

resettlement, incorporation, and abandonment occurred at the local and macroregional scales throughout Iroquoian history. As such, processes of site abandonment and population relocation were the norm, rather than the exception.

In this chapter, we consider processes of detachment from place at the local and regional levels in Northern Iroquoia and, more specifically, how these processes apply to members and ancestors of the Huron-Wendat. Together, processes of attachment to place and subsequent movement created landscapes composed of territories that were spiritually, strategically, and politically charged for ancestral and contemporary Huron-Wendat peoples. Concepts of emplacement (in the sense of Cobb 2005; Rodning 2009), social memory (Wilson 2010), and contextual experience (Snead 2008) are employed to frame the processes of population movement that entangled kin-groups in social and physical landscapes, creating associations that persist to the present day.

Variable social, political, economic, and subsistence-related contexts motivated population movements and village relocation at different points in Huron-Wendat history. Archaeologists have often relied on environmental considerations, such as constraints on agricultural productivity and the exhaustion of wood resources as primary motivators for village relocation and the rationale behind relocating settlements every 20–30 years on average in prehistoric times and as frequently as every 8–12 years in the contact era (Trigger 1969; Warrick 1988). At the village scale, community relocation would have been an occurrence that all people would have experienced at least once in their lifetimes. At the local and regional scales, the frequency and predictability of settlement relocation created sequences of abandoned village sites and "communities of the dead" that remained meaningful places for living populations. Less frequently, entire subregions were abandoned and transformed into zones of conflict and resource extraction. Relocation of villages due to sociopolitical issues was also documented during the historic period (Trigger 1976:158, 509, 517).

Processes of settlement relocation, aggregation, and abandonment created ancestral landscapes that later evolved into politicized territories and buffer zones during processes of confederacy formation. Today, these associative landscapes remain meaningful places for the contemporary Huron-Wendat Nation. Although historical circumstances resulted in the Huron-Wendat resettling near Quebec City, away from the principal area they occupied at the beginning of the seventeenth century, they are asserting their rights to defining how their ancestral landscape is perceived and constructed. This reframing includes challenging the notion that they were ever "displaced" from their ancestral lands.

DISPLACEMENT AND EMPLACEMENT

In order to understand processes of detachment from place, we also need to understand how people become attached to places. Wendy Ashmore (2002) has observed that archaeological studies of place tend to fall into two themes: (1) establishment and affirmation and (2) the subsequent afterlife of a locality. Recent conceptualizations of place-making in human societies recognize that social relations and spatial structures are not only linked recursively but that these relations are dynamic, fluid, and always potentially in flux (e.g., McAnany and Lamoureux-St-Hilaire, chapter 2 in this volume; Pauketat 2003, 2007:107). Multiscalar studies of settlement dynamics that consider the temporality of occupations, abandonments, and the practices through which peoples choose, develop, and maintain relationships to place are key to understanding such flexibility. While large-scale abandonment and population movement is a highly visible form of detachment from place, such processes can also include small-scale, repetitive relocations that were highly significant in shaping people's relationships to settings and landscapes (Bernardini 2005; Cobb and Butler 2006).

In this context, the concept of emplacement is a useful construct. Christopher Rodning defines emplacement as "the set of practices by which a community attaches itself to a particular place through formal settlement plans, architecture, burials, and other material additions to the landscape" (2009:629). In some parts of pre-Columbian North America, communities and their leaders used monuments and architecture in order to create and perpetuate connections to places. In the Southwest, masonry pueblos or Great Houses served this function (Van Dyke 2004). In the Woodland and Mississippian Southeast, the construction and expansion of mounds made of earth and shell served to reinforce or legitimize group identity and authority (Cobb 2005; Rodning 2009; Thompson and Pluckhahn 2012). The construction and renewal of the built environment were one way that groups enacted their connection to place (Rodning 2009, 2013; Thompson and Pluckhahn 2012). Such persistent monumental places have accordingly drawn a great deal of archaeological interest. However, processes of emplacement can also take place in wider cultural landscapes. Emplacement has also been conceived of as "how people are drawn to, and into places" (Cobb 2005:564; see also Cobb and Butler 2006). These attachments do not necessarily depend on material correlates of human activity. For many Western scholars, the relationship between community and landscape tends to be framed in oppositional or Cartesian terms (Cobb and Butler 2006:332). The relational turn in archaeology recognizes that any phenomena we seek to understand must be interpreted in the context of its relative positioning within webs of other entities and activities (Hodder 2012; Ingold 2007; Watts 2013). Wider geographic and cultural landscapes can become settings for emplacement via repeated movement through and engagement with various settings, including trails, forests, fields, and a range of "natural landscape features" (e.g., Bourdieu 1977; Joyce and Hendon 2000; Tilley 1994). This sense of attachment may also include formerly inhabited places, such as abandoned villages, former field systems, and other sites of anthropogenic modification and utilization (McAnany and Lamoureux-St-Hilaire, chapter 2 in this volume; Fowles 2009). James Snead (2008:18, 85) argues that culturally constructed perceptions of the landscape combine complex arrays of natural and cultural features into landscapes of "contextual experience," where history and action are tied to cultural concepts of identity, legitimacy, and a sense of place.

Acts of remembering encourage continuity in the landscape through observation and reflection on the recent and distant past. While remembering can be a deeply personal act, social and collective memories can also be harnessed as powerful political tools (Shackel 2001). Gregory Wilson (2010:4) observes that at the Mississippian Moundville site, inhabitants brandished memory as a political resource for negotiating social and economic conditions and through "careful and persistent claims to space." While social memory can also be used to establish claims to place, Tsim Schneider (2015:697) notes that establishing continuity of place may also involve "contestations, strategic forgetting, and the genesis of new memories and place associations."

In the remainder of this chapter, we consider how the archaeological record of Iroquoian settlement dynamics circa AD 1000–1450 served to emplace households and communities in ancestral landscapes. We then examine how these landscapes became politically changed territories during processes of nation- and confederacy-building, population movement, and geopolitical realignment, circa 1450–1650. Finally, contemporary Huron-Wendat perspectives on attachment to and detachment from place are considered with respect to the relationship between St. Lawrence Iroquoians and Huron-Wendat peoples and ancestral territories.

ST. LAWRENCE IROQUOIAN AND HURON-WENDAT HISTORY

The term Iroquoian refers to both a cultural pattern and a linguistic family, of which Northern Iroquoian is one branch. Iroquoian archaeology is generally concerned with the material remains of groups ancestral to several seventeenth-century Iroquoian-speaking peoples, including the Five Nations of the Haudenosaunee (Iroquois), the Wendat (Huron), Tionotaté (Petun),

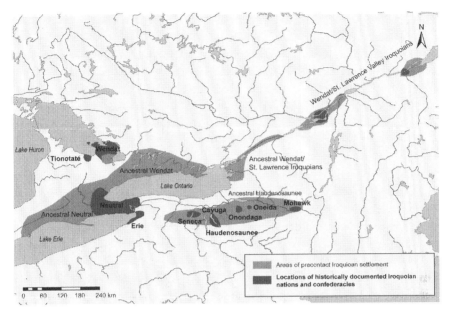

FIGURE 4.1. *Location of historically documented Iroquoian-speaking groups and the ancestral territories formerly occupied and/or claimed by those groups in the Lower Great Lakes and St. Lawrence Valley.*

Attawandaron (Neutral), Erie, and groups inhabiting the St. Lawrence Valley, known collectively to archaeologists as St. Lawrence Iroquoians (figure 4.1). These sedentary societies spoke different dialects but shared similar cultural traits, including spirituality, beliefs, and subsistence based on maize horticulture supplemented by hunting, fishing, and gathering; settlement in longhouse villages that were often enclosed with palisades; and distinctive material culture, including collared ceramic vessels. In this chapter, we focus primarily on the archaeology of the ancestors of the contemporary Huron-Wendat Nation.

The name Wendat has been interpreted as meaning "dwellers on a peninsula" (Hodge [1913] 1971: 24) or people of a "drifting" or "floating" island, represented by the back of a turtle in the Wendat conception of the world. The precise translation remains unknown (Steckley 2007:26–28). The open nature of Wendat society meant that in order to become a member of a Wendat Nation or Wendat society, a person or group need not have necessarily originated in Wendat territory. For example, the Attignawantan and Attigneenongnahac became the "most populous" nations in the Wendat Confederacy, owing to their adoption of many "families" (Thwaites 1896–1901:16:227–28) who had most likely gradually migrated north in the years between AD 1350 and 1600 (Birch and Williamson 2015).

The integration of St. Lawrence Iroquoian populations into Wendat society illustrates how unification, adoption, and incorporation relate to processes of attachment to and detachment from place. From the early fifteenth century to late sixteenth century, there is evidence that populations originating from the St. Lawrence Valley relocated to the Upper Trent Valley, Toronto, and Georgian Bay regions (Ramsden 1990; R. Williamson 2016), integrating with communities who had been inhabiting these regions for generations. Although the unification of populations with St. Lawrence identity markers may not have always proceeded seamlessly (Ramsden 2009), the integration of St. Lawrence and ancestral Huron-Wendat populations also involved the development of shared metaidentities and symbols (Ramsden 2016a, 2016b). From a linguistic perspective, observations by the recollet Gabriel Sagard in the early 1600s suggest the retention of St. Lawrence Iroquoian terms and etymology in the Wendat common language (Steckley 2016). Evidence for strong connections between Wendat and St. Lawrence Iroquoian peoples and territories include primary rights to trade with eastern groups, including early Basque and French trade connections between the St. Lawrence Valley and southern Ontario (Fitzgerald 1995 Williamson, Fox, and Grant 2016). The current consensus is that by the early seventeenth century, certain St. Lawrence Iroquoian peoples had become fully incorporated into Wendat society (Warrick and Lesage 2016).

The Wendat occupation of southern Ontario is archaeologically documented between circa AD 1000and 1650. After AD 1650, following the conjunction of epidemics and escalation of attacks by the Haudenosaunee, the Wendat chose to relocate their settlements away from this ancestral territory. Most relocated to adjacent regions, including New York State (with some populations inhabiting satellite communities within Haudenosaunee territories, Michigan, Kansas, and eventually, Oklahoma). A substantial Wendat contingent relocated to near Quebec City, where the core of the modern Huron-Wendat Nation resides today. This displacement was strategically orchestrated by Huron-Wendat emissaries who negotiated the conditions of this relocalization within the vicinity of the French Army, French civil servants, and the church (Magee Labelle 2014).

We focus on the archaeological record of the Huron-Wendat here for two reasons: First, we focus on this record because these data are more substantial than that of other Iroquoian peoples, due in part to more than thirty years of progressive cultural resource management policy that has resulted in the full excavation of dozens of village sites (Birch and Williamson 2013; Williamson 2010). The result is a more complete record of evolving village life, including the succession of village relocation and nation- and confederacy-building, than has been documented for any other area in the Northeast. Such a complete archaeological record is essential for understanding and theorizing processes of place-making and unmaking in the context of this volume. Second, we focus on this record because the Huron-Wendat Nation is actively involved in the archaeological histories of their ancestors, including the planning and shaping of academic and compliance-driven archaeological projects; orienting future research; collaborative research; and correcting misconceptions of the archaeological record based on interpretations that have not involved their perspectives (Warrick and Lesage 2016). Incorporating emic, Huron-Wendat perspectives on their ancestral histories naturally bears on the subject of place-making.

EARLY IROQUOIAN PLACE-MAKING AND VILLAGE RELOCATION

Contrary to common perceptions of the link between farming and sedentism, persistent places of habitation in the Northern Iroquoian settlement landscape are more evident prior to reliance on maize horticulture than after. Between AD 1000 and the mid-to-late 1200s, early Iroquoian sites consisted of semisedentary base camps that were intermittently occupied over a century or more by populations who continued to practice a seasonal settlement-subsistence pattern (Williamson 1990). Repeated reoccupation and rebuilding are evident in the "disorganized" nature of some early villages. At the Elliott (Fox 1986) and Calvert sites (Timmins 1997), multiple short longhouses overlap one another, indicating the repeated construction and deconstruction of structures within the same settlement footprint. In Ontario, early Iroquoian sites are most often found in clusters thought to represent subregional interaction networks of two or more contemporary communities that may have shared a hunting territory and a common resource base (Timmins 1997:228; Williamson 1990). Despite the intermittent nature of occupation at early Iroquoian settlements, these are the longest-lived habitation sites in precontact Wendat territory. However, the fact that these communities were situated in larger landscapes of resource extraction and familiarity suggests a persistent connection to the surrounding landscape that has perhaps been overlooked in settlement-focused analyses of Iroquoian archaeology and history (e.g., Creese 2012). Robert Pearce (1984) and Peter Timmins (1997) were among the first to write explicitly about the attachment of early Iroquoian communities to landscapes. More recently, John Creese (2013) has explored early village development through the lenses of place-making and assemblage theory to explore complex relational assemblages of people, places, materials, organisms, and things.

Beginning in the mid-to-late 1200s, we see the coalescence of these seasonally occupied base camps into larger village-settlements. These villages were, for the first time, occupied year-round by the entire community. The occupants of such larger settlements were likely members of the same social groups that had shared subregional territories in previous centuries (Trigger 1976:134; Williamson and Robertson 1994). This shift was accompanied by a region-wide intensification of agricultural production (Katzenberg et al. 1995; Pfeiffer et al. 2014). The formation of larger communities may have been related, in part, to the desire to maintain the year-round cohesion of social groups and bring about greater economic security through shared work parties (Trigger 1976:135–36).

Critical to the discussion of emplacement and displacement/abandonment here is the fact that concomitant with these transformations was the initiation of a shifting settlement-subsistence pattern that involved relocating villages approximately once every generation. When villages were abandoned, the community usually relocated a few kilometers away, though longer migrations were possible. Because village sites were rarely reoccupied, each represents a record of the activities of a single generation. Numerous site relocation sequences have been constructed that represent hundreds of years of occupation by contiguous groups (e.g., Birch and Williamson 2013:25–51; Finlayson 1998; Niemczycki 1984; Pearce 1984; Snow 1995; Tuck 1971).

Gary Warrick (1988) estimated that circa AD 1300–50 villages were occupied for about twenty to thirty years before being relocated. For many years, it was thought that the settlement footprint of these communities involved markedly less reorganization and reconstruction of longhouses. The Uren site (M. Wright 1986), which consisted of two clusters of longhouses, has often been held up as the type-site for the early fourteenth century. However, systematic comparison of the settlement patterns of other fourteenth-century sites suggests that some reorganization of structures within village-settlements was the norm. For example, the Antrex (ASI 2010), Meyers Road (Williamson 1998), and Gunby sites (Rozel 1979) all exhibit evidence of the addition, deconstruction, or repositioning of longhouses.

Numerous researchers have argued that declining soil productivity could not have been a primary cause of village abandonment (Mt. Pleasant and

Burt 2010; Sykes, 1980), especially for those communities with fewer than 200 inhabitants (Snow 1995), which is roughly in line with population estimates for these fourteenth-century village-communities (Warrick 2008). However, for later, larger villages such as those discussed below, population size may have been a factor influencing village relocation (Jones and Wood 2012). The process of settlement relocation would have been complex and subject to significant negotiation and decision making (Birch and Williamson 2013:87). First, an appropriate site would need to be chosen based on its environmental and topographical attributes, its soil productivity, accessibility, and so on. Then the site would have to be cleared. Ethnohistoric accounts suggest that work parties of men would have felled and girdled trees to prepare new agricultural fields. Material for the construction of new houses—suitable posts, sheets of bark, cordage for lashing—would have been stockpiled and new houses constructed. This work would have involved the cooperation of most of the community and perhaps kinsmen and friends from other communities. At the same time, the regular labors involved in the agricultural cycle and the maintenance of day-to-day domestic life would have needed to take place. Most village relocations involved movements of only a few kilometers, usually within the same drainage (Birch and Williamson 2013). In these cases, existing agricultural fields would likely have continued to be farmed as new fields closer to the new village were planted and cleared (see also Lafitau 1977:70). Longer-distance relocations may have involved significantly more travel, labor, negotiation, and planning.

As such, village relocation was not so much an "event" as a process which would have played out over a number of years, involving the cooperation and coordination of multiple households and the community as a whole. There would have been the constant need to prospect the surroundings to "produce place" (Cobb 2005:570) at new settlements, in part through the reconstruction and manipulation of the built environment.

No two Iroquoian village footprints are identical. The construction and reconstruction of new villages would have provided opportunities to (re)materialize and (re)strengthen social and political relations at each settlement (see also Birch 2012). Charles Cobb (2003:69) has written that in the Mississippian Southeast, the landscape and built environment of mound centers created "spatial crucible[s] for the reproduction of social inequality." Conversely, the practice of village relocation was one of a number of cultural mechanisms that contributed to the maintenance of equality between households and factions within Iroquoian societies (see also Trigger 1990).

MORTUARY PRACTICE AS BOTH ATTACHMENT
TO AND DETACHMENT FROM PLACE

Ethnohistoric accounts suggest that the most important event in the Wendat ceremonial calendar, the Feast of the Dead, would have taken place at the time of village relocation (Trigger 1976:85). The event involved the interment of the collective dead of a village-community in an ossuary. Ossuaries are burial features which are typically 3 to 6 meters in diameter and approximately 2 meters deep (see Williamson and Steiss 2003:table 3.1). Human remains, in various states of decomposition, would have been placed in the ossuary and commingled as a part of the funerary rites. In 1636, the Jesuit priest Sagard recounted a Feast of the Dead hosted by the Bear Nation. It included ten days of feasting, ceremony, and gift giving, including the assembly of kin and relations from across a wide social network (Wrong [1632] 1939).

The earliest Iroquoian ossuary in the archaeological record of south-central Ontario appears at the late twelfth-century Miller site, east of Toronto, and consists of a single feature containing the commingled remains of thirteen individuals (Kenyon 1968:21–23). The late-thirteenth-to-early-fourteenth-century Moatfield ossuary contained at least eighty-seven people (Williamson and Pfeiffer 2003). While most ossuaries are believed to be associated with discrete village populations, by the early fourteenth century the creation of ossuaries sometimes also involved the deceased of multiple allied villages. This was the case for the ossuaries identified at Fairty and Tabor Hills, each of which is associated with a cluster of two to four contemporary villages. At Tabor Hill, two separate pits contained the mixed remains of some 523 individuals, thought to be the result of two communities burying their dead concomitantly but choosing to inter them in separate pits (Williamson and Steiss 2003:102). Given the similarities between such precontact ossuaries and those known from the contact period, it seems reasonable to conclude that other basic aspects of the Wendat mortuary program were taking shape at the same time, including how such sites related to perceptions of and regard for sacred landscapes.

In another publication, Jennifer Birch and Ronald Williamson (2015) provide a comprehensive overview of how the process of village relocation and ossuary burial created ancestral landscapes inhabited by communities of the dead. According to seventeenth-century accounts, and still believed by contemporary Huron-Wendats, the soul is divisible, with one separating from the remains of the deceased at the time of the Feast of the Dead, and the other remaining bound to the corporeal remains, unless someone were to bear it again as a child (Thwaites 1896–1901:10:285). The final burial of the collective dead of a community allowed the souls of the deceased to travel westward to the land of the ancestors, where they would reside in villages which, during the seventeenth century, corresponded to each of the tribes, or major villages, of the Huron-Wendat (Trigger 1976:87). However, the journey to the land of the dead was perilous and the souls of those who were too old, young, or weak to make the journey were thought to remain in the realm of the living, tied to abandoned villages and planting their crops in the former clearings (Hall 1976:363; Trigger 1976:87; von Gernet 1994:42–45). Long after their creation, ossuaries, abandoned village sites, and their associated communities of the dead would have been focal points for ceremony, mourning, memorialization, and feasting (Thwaites, 1896–1901, 8:21–23; 10:269–75). Today, the funerary rite represented by the ossuary maintains the relationship between the spirits present in the bones as a reconstruction of the village and the cohabitation of those who lived in it.

For more than 200 years, processes of village relocation and the concomitant creation of communities of the dead created vast landscapes of contextual experience and social memory where both living and deceased populations were emplaced. Birch and Williamson (2015) construct a theoretical framework for how people may have experienced such landscapes that incorporates notions of experiential and referential memory (Hodder 1990; Kujit 2008). To summarize that framework here, if individuals took part in one or two village relocations within their lifetimes, then those former village locations may have been places inhabited by the familiar dead, where remembrances and kin relations could be revisited and perhaps grieved: places of experiential memory. Beyond those sites, with the passage of distance and time, a landscape of referential memory developed, including communities of the dead whose formerly inhabited villages created an extended ancestral territory (Birch and Williamson 2015:147–48). Considering processes of population circulation and the incorporation of resettled Iroquoian groups into ancient Wendat territory provides further support for the importance of such referential memory in creating ancestral territories.

POPULATION CIRCULATION AND MOVEMENT

Population Circulation

After the fourteenth century AD there was a great deal of residential mobility in the ancestral Wendat landscape. Between AD 1300 and 1500 this primarily included (1) the relocation of village-communities, as described above, (2) the short-distance relocation of house clusters between village-communities, and (3) the long-distance relocation of house clusters and entire communities to new regions. The latter two processes have implications with respect to this consideration of processes of attachment to and detachment from place.

In Northern Iroquoian society, the longhouse was the primary unit of social and cultural reproduction (Trigger 1969). Ethnohistoric records indicate that longhouses were inhabited by a matrilineal, matrilocal descent group, with the caveat that such rules of descent and residence were mutable (Richards 1967; Trigger 1978). Many fourteenth- and early fifteenth-century Northern Iroquoian villages consisted of clusters of aligned longhouses that have been interpreted as representing related households or matrilineal clan groups.

Village-level settlement pattern data indicate that both individual long-houses and house clusters were not necessarily occupied for the same amount of time. Variability in the density of house wall posts between structures has been interpreted as indicating rebuilding or repair (Warrick 1988). Where variability between longhouses or house clusters exists, this has been interpreted as indicating variable durations of occupation, suggesting some structures may have been added to a village after its initial occupation (Birch and Williamson 2013; Finlayson 1985).

Approximately half of all fully excavated village communities from the late fourteenth and early fifteenth centuries include longhouses or house clusters that were constructed after the site's initial occupation. In most cases, this has been interpreted as representing households or lineages relocating from within the region to join the community as opposed to internal growth. For example, at multiple sites—such as Alexandra (ASI 2010), Grandview (Williamson, Austin, and Thomas 2003), and White (Tripp 1978)—household clusters were added to an original core group of houses sometime after a settlement's initial establishment. Ceramic variability within these settlements suggests minor chronological variation between house clusters (ASI 2008, 2010; Williamson, Austin, and Thomas 2003) but no extraregional population influx, which would be indicated by the presence of nonlocal ceramic varieties. As such, while village relocation is a commonly recognized aspect of the Northern Iroquoian settlement landscape, the relocation of community segments—households or groups of households—between village-communities appears to have been equally common.

While it has been thought that the village-community was the maximal political unit in the fourteenth century (Williamson and Robertson 1994), the social groups represented by longhouse clusters retained a significant degree of autonomy and residential mobility. As such, despite the seemingly sedentary nature of Iroquoian village-communities, their relatively short occupations and fluid composition suggest that the ancestral Wendat settlement pattern in the late fourteenth and early fifteenth centuries more closely approximates "serial migration" (Bernardini 2005) or "population circulation" (Schachner 2012)—a pattern in which lineage-based subclans merged, split, and migrated, forming communities that persisted for a generation or so composed of groups with unique, historically informed backgrounds.

As noted above, it is clear that some ossuaries contained the commingled dead of multiple village-communities. Given the frequency of households relocating between settlements themselves, we must consider that over the long term, the locus of identity formation for ancestral Wendat peoples may not have been the village itself, but rather the landscape in which communities and subcommunity groups were situated. For every currently occupied village, there may have been multiple formerly occupied villages and communities of the dead that were important places of experiential and referential memory for coresidential populations.

Movement and Expansion

It has been estimated that between AD 1300 and 1420 the population of south-central Ontario grew from circa 10,000 to circa 24,000 people. This explosive population growth influenced the expansion and migration of Iroquoian populations into Simcoe County and the Trent Valley (Sutton 1996, 1999). Numerous village excavations in the vicinity of Kempenfelt Bay, including the Barrie (Sutton 1999), Holly (ASI 2009), Lee, and Stephen Patrick (Williamson 2014) sites have produced a rich record of pioneering Iroquoian settlement in the fourteenth century AD. These earliest Iroquoian settlements established in Simcoe County determined an ancestral Wendat presence in what would go on to become an historic-era Huron-Wendat heartland. Other sites, including Wilcox Lake (Austin 1994) and Bathurst (ASI 2017), located immediately south of this area on the Oak Ridges Moraine, provide evidence for the continuing "trickle" of population north and east during the fourteenth and early fifteenth centuries.

Recent research by John Hart and colleagues (2016) suggests that ancestral Wendat communities on the north shore of Lake Ontario, Simcoe County, and the Trent Valley were signaling with one another in previously unrecognized ways, linking both local and distant groups into social networks that persisted into the seventeenth century. This includes demonstrably close links between populations in Simcoe County and the north shore of Lake Ontario from the fourteenth century onward, suggesting continued social interactions between sending and coming populations.

In the seventeenth century, the descendants of these original inhabitants of Wendake were the Attignawantan and Attigneenongnahac nations. They were the "most populous" nations in the country (Thwaites 1896–1901:16:227–28), owing to their adoption of many "families" who originated among groups on the north shore of Lake Ontario—those groups who gradually migrated north in the years between AD 1350 and 1600 (Birch and Williamson 2015). According to the relations each "family" remained "distinct little nations, retaining the names and memories of their founders, a general name [for themselves], and a war chief and council chief" (Thwaites 1896–1901:16:227–29; Tooker 1964:11).

As such, patterns of frequent village relocation, movement, and population circulation suggest that place-making did not occur at single nodes or localities so much as it did in a vast landscape populated by shifting villages of the living, fixed communities of the dead, and the social memories and identities that recursively entangled dozens of subcommunity groups into vast ancestral landscapes. These ancestral landscapes later became politically and emotionally charged territories for aggregated villages, nations, and confederacies (Birch and Williamson 2015).

SETTLEMENT RELOCATION IN THE CONTEXT OF COALESCENCE AND CONFEDERACY FORMATION

In the late fifteenth and sixteenth centuries, an increase in violent conflict and the coalescence of village-communities into large, fortified settlements transformed processes of place-making in Northern Iroquoia. In the early fifteenth century AD, ancestral Wendat settlements in south-central Ontario had formed clusters of villages inhabiting drainages that flowed south into Lake Ontario. By the late fifteenth to early sixteenth century, these previously distinct village-communities had aggregated into a handful of larger, well-fortified settlements. This is a pattern that was repeated throughout southern Ontario and upper New York State (Birch 2012; Engelbrecht 2003; Snow 1994). Scattered and butchered human bone in middens, together with human remains bearing signs of traumatic death and trophy taking suggest that, at least initially, violent conflict was a primary motivating factor for settlement aggregation (Engelbrecht 2003; Williamson 2007). Perhaps because of this increase in violence, population circulation declined in south-central Ontario. Rather than populations regularly relocating between village-communities, settlement aggregation, and long-distance relocation are the most common patterns identified in the sixteenth century. On the north shore of Lake Ontario, coalescent communities continued to relocate northward as single large communities. The community on West Duffins Creek may have split into two smaller communities following the occupation of the Mantle site in the late sixteenth century (Birch and Manning 2016; Birch and Williamson 2013). By the early seventeenth century, the north shore of Lake Ontario was vacated, and these populations were incorporated into nations of the Huron-Wendat confederacy or their allies, the Tionontaté, notably.

Those groups that came together to form large, coalescent communities likely shared close ties engendered by the proximity of the villages they had previously inhabited. For example, the eight known groups that came together to form the Draper site had all previously occupied an area of some twenty-five square kilometers on branches of West Duffins Creek (Finlayson 1985). The proximity of their villages, field systems, and resource extraction areas—as well as shared belief systems, ties of gift giving, exchange, kinship, and intermarriage—would have engendered close connections between these populations (Birch and Williamson 2013:55). When these populations came together, their members brought with them ties to their ancestral places and landscapes. Such ties and collective memories of place may have been diverse, owing to the aforementioned processes of serial movement and population circulation in previous decades. According to Birch and Williamson (2015:147): "Shared connections to contiguous landscapes helped to unite newly-formed co-residential communities and, in turn, reinforced new, communal identities. The formation of tribal nations and political confederacies transformed ancestral landscapes into politically- and emotionally-charged territorial claims. The fact that ancestral territories were not actively occupied does not preclude their being claimed as political territories and cultural landscapes in which social memory, economic rights, and group identities were emplaced and negotiated."

The coalescent communities of the sixteenth century formed the cores of self-identifying nations that would come together into the political confederacies encountered by Europeans in the seventeenth century (Birch 2015). The connection between Northern Iroquoian nations and the landscapes they inhabited is reflected in the endonymns of each nation (Birch 2015; Birch and Williamson 2015; Hart and Engelbrecht 2012). Landscape features or natural resources became identifiers for the inhabitants of those landscapes. This practice was also the norm among the Haudenosaunee (Hart and Engelbrecht 2012:335). For example, the Attignawantan (Bear) was the longest-lived nation and inhabited the northernmost portion of Wendat territory. The Ataronchronon were a division of the Attignawantan (Bog, or "people of the swamp, mud, or clay") occupied the swampy cedar lowlands surrounding the Wye River (Trigger 1976:30). The Arendarhonon (Rock, or "people at the rock") originated in the Trent

Valley, a landscape marked by outcrops of the southern Canadian Shield and Peterborough Drumlin Fields.

By the first decade of the seventeenth century, all Wendat peoples had relocated from their ancestral territories into the historic Wendat homeland in Simcoe County (figure 4.1). However, this does not mean that they had relinquished ties to those landscapes inhabited by their ancestors, including the territories occupied by incorporated St. Lawrence Iroquoian-Wendat peoples. At this time, and for the next century, the Wendat considered themselves closely tied to the lands that stretched across the north shore of Lake Ontario from the Toronto area east to the St. Lawrence River valley. These lands encompass the total area of precontact ancestral Wendat settlement, including those territories formerly occupied by St. Lawrence Iroquoians.

CONTEMPORARY HURON-WENDAT ATTACHMENT TO, NOT DETACHMENT FROM, PLACE

For the contemporary Huron-Wendat Nation, detachment from place was a process that was never fully completed. The contemporary nation feels very strongly about their connections to their ancestral sites, deceased ancestors, and landscapes. This includes landscapes associated with sites that archaeologists have labeled Wendat and St. Lawrence Iroquoian based on material traits and taxonomic constructs.

More than three centuries of Huron-Wendat oral history identifies the St. Lawrence Valley as ancestral Huron-Wendat territory (Gaudreau and Lesage 2016; Richard 2016). According to Gary Warrick and Louis Lesage (2016:135), this ancestral connection to the lands occupied by Wendat ancestors can be viewed as extending back to at least Middle Woodland times, based on archaeological interpretations of the continuity of St. Lawrence Iroquoian-Wendat populations in the region (e.g., Gates St-Pierre 2004, 2016). For the contemporary Huron-Wendat Nation, the incorporation of St. Lawrence Iroquoian peoples into Wendat society included the incorporation of the history and memories of those peoples. As such, their ancestral places and lands are also Wendat through their inclusion in Wendat history, society, and identity. As such, what archaeologists may interpret as indications of abandonment and detachment from place by different cultural or ethnic groups may be at odds with emic interpretations about notions of identity, emplacement, and territorialization among ancestral and contemporary Indigenous populations (Gaudreau and Lesage 2016; Warrick and Lesage 2016).

The Huron-Wendat are commonly viewed by most archaeologists, historians, provincial and federal governments, and certain other Indigenous groups as a people who "abandoned" or were driven from their homeland in southern Ontario by the mid-seventeenth century as the result of seventeenth-century aggression by the Haudenosaunee and waves of epidemic diseases. For the Huron-Wendat Nation, the words *diaspora, dispersal*, and *abandonment* are "inaccurate and harmful misrepresentations of Huron-Wendat concepts of geopolitics and ancestral territory" (Warrick and Lesage 2016:138). Elizabeth Chilton (2005) similarly identifies how contemporary Algonquian populations in New England have been disenfranchised from sites they identify as ancestral on account of those groups' mobile settlement systems and informal political organization. As Chip Colwell-Chanthaphonh and T. J. Ferguson have written (2006:40) about the rejection of abandonment narratives by Hopi and Zuni attachment in the American Southwest, "these sites are not abandoned, because native peoples have not stopped using them, they have not conceded their interests in them, and they have not surrendered their claims" (see also Watkins 2006:105–6 regarding potential harm caused to Native Americans by the use of the word *abandonment* in archaeological discourse).

The Huron-Wendat know the significance of territory abandonment such as that which may follow as the result of signing a treaty with the Crown. In 1760, the Huron-Wendat signed a peace and friendship treaty with the British representatives, which later recognized their territory. However, over the last few centuries, many treaties have been signed across Canada by First Nations; the Wendat ancestors of the seventeenth through nineteenth centuries were thus the witness of other First Nations signing treaties and, in some cases, legally abandoning their territories in exchange for royalties or other benefits. At this time, these ancestors never signed such documents and thus never legally or administratively abandoned their territory.

CONCLUSIONS

For ancestral and contemporary Wendat, a lack of actively occupied villages did not mean that territories had been relinquished or abandoned by later populations. Landscapes that both recent and distant populations had formerly occupied were, and are, understood to be populated by ancestors, containing sites of pilgrimage, providing opportunities for travel, and serving as active areas for resource extraction. Importantly, these sites served as repositories for active social memories and were never deterritorialized by groups who had relocated elsewhere.

Such constructions of social memory and attachment to place continue for the modern Huron-Wendat Nation. The absence of active Wendat settlement in southern Ontario and northern New York State does not mean that they have relinquished their rights to and activities and interests in those landscapes and ancestral territories—in this way, detachment from place remains an incomplete process.

ACKNOWLEDGMENTS

Thanks to Maxime Lamoureux St-Hilaire, Scott Macrae, and Patricia McAnany for the opportunity to revisit and refine these ideas through conference sessions at the SAA meetings in 2013 and AAA meetings in 2017. Ron Williamson coauthored the 2013 SAA paper with Birch, and she is grateful for his collaboration and mentorship. Thanks to Catherine Cameron, Jeffrey H. Cohen, and Ian Hodder, the discussants from those sessions, for their helpful comments. Birch is indebted to the Huron-Wendat Nation for the opportunity to collaborate on research concerning their history, having feedback, and together building better interpretations of their past.

5

Some 3,100 years ago, a place known today as Poverty Point in northeast Louisiana (figure 5.1) was abandoned after a five-century-long history of massive social gatherings, the importation of tons of nonlocal objects, and the terraforming of over 750,000 cubic meters of earth (Gibson 2000; Kidder 2011; Ortmann 2010). We may never know why people detached from this place at this time, but the event clearly was momentous. Equally momentous was its buildup. Six concentric ridges one kilometer in outside diameter were erected in sequence after 3400 cal BP. Several conical and flat-topped earthen mounds came on line in the ensuing decades. The largest mound was built over a wetland in the century before Poverty Point was abandoned, taking only three months or less to erect by an estimated gathering of 3,000 people (Kidder et al. 2009). Not much later, large posts were emplaced in large circles in the plaza enclosed by the ridges, and a final mound was built, north of the compound (Greenlee 2009, 2010, 2013, 2015). We do not know for certain but suspect that a cache of over 250 broken soapstone vessels (Webb 1944)—from geological sources hundreds of kilometers to the east—was deposited on the eve of abandonment (Sassaman and Brookes 2017). It was, as Kidder (2011:117) suggests, something of a "reverse" history, with some of the largest public-works projects and emplacements occurring toward the end of the occupation.

Evidently, the abandonment of Poverty Point was an event involving considerable preparation and planning.

Cosmic Abandonment

How Detaching from Place Was Requisite to World Renewal in the Ancient American Southeast

KENNETH E. SASSAMAN AND ASA R. RANDALL

DOI: 10.5876/9781646420087.c005

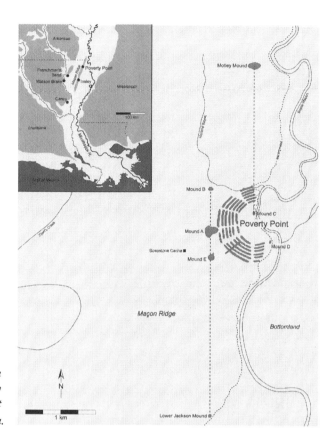

FIGURE 5.1. *Plan view of Poverty Point site in northeast Louisiana.*

To the extent that detachment from this place was in fact anticipated—and not the result of stressors (in the sense of McAnany and Lamoureux-St-Hilaire, chapter 2 in this volume) that were themselves unanticipated—we are compelled to ask how the lived experiences of those affected contributed to historical consciousness about futures. We doubt that the effective experiences trace directly to the ecological or demographic conditions of northeast Louisiana—that is, the purview of biological reproduction—but rather to the long arc of history that shaped and then challenged a cosmology of movement that is evident in the social and geographic scope of Poverty Point gatherings. Our use of the term *cosmology* is the usual sense of an understanding of the structure of the universe, but we emphasize here its intrinsic dynamic properties, essentially its moving parts and the pathways they follow. Likewise, we acknowledge that cosmologies are often reduced to a set of ideas, but subscribe to the phenomenological dictum that nothing in the mind was not first experienced in the senses (Jameson 2005:xiii). We thus strive in this chapter to situate this particular cosmology in the histories of lives lived, which, in the case of Poverty Point, transcended scales of time and space far beyond the site itself.

MATTERS OF SCALE AND CAUSE

In chapter 2 of this volume, McAnany and Lamoureux-St-Hilaire note, following Cameron (2003), that decisions to detach from places of residence "generally take place on the scale of a family or household unit." We agree, in general, but question here the applicability of the concept of *household* to Poverty Point, as we acknowledge a lack of purchase on the size, composition, and number of its residential units. We assume the count of 3,000 people inferred by Tristram Kidder et al. (2009) for the construction of Mound A was not the size of a local, resident population, but rather the scale of gatherings of persons from far and wide, consistent with its inferred purpose as a trade fair (Jackson 1991) or, more likely, a place of pilgrimage (Spivey et al. 2015).

Let us consider that the abandonment of Poverty Point—while enacted at the level of household decisions—was entangled in a social and geographic history commensurate with the scale of its imported material inventory and its pilgrims. In this regard, the history of Araucanian (Mapuche) people of Spanish-conquest Chile provides a useful analog. The Araucanians were a regional indigenous population who gathered periodically for the ritual renewal of settlements, mounds, and cemeteries, all integrated by cosmological spatial referents that extended across the region (Dillehay 2007). This regional community—what Tom Dillehay (2007) calls a *cosmunity*—endured for centuries under external threats (Spanish incursions) by mobilizing people in novel forms of resistance. In describing the spatial structure of an Araucanian gathering place, Dillehay draws on French theorist Louis Marin's (1984) notion of "utopic social engineering," in which a society's concept of utopia is expressed spatially though urban planning, settlement patterning, and other spatial dimensions of social integration. Added to this, we argue, is the potential of abandoned places to become cosmic or historical resources of time-space referencing at the regional scale.

As we open up space and time to encompass all those who participated in Poverty Point gatherings, we might ask what else the inhabitants may have had in common. In this chapter we explore the possibility that the dispersed populations of a Poverty Point cosmunity shared in histories of changing relationships between water and land, both along rivers of the lower

Southeast, but especially along the Gulf Coast, where settlements of Poverty Point affiliation were distributed as far east as present-day Florida, and arguably beyond, to the St. John River Basin of east Florida, given recent data on material transfers (Hays, Weinstein, and Stoltman 2016). The general trend along the coast, for millennia before Poverty Point, was for sea level to rise, flooding settlements and cemeteries in vulnerable places, and forcing people to detach and resettle to less-vulnerable land. We hypothesize that repeated experience with rising water and site abandonment would have led to a historical consciousness of inevitable change and that uncertainty in the periodicity and in the magnitude of change was ameliorated with reference to predictable movements, specifically cycles of the sun, among perhaps other celestial bodies.

Before proceeding, we are compelled to address the matter of cause. At face value, changing water levels would seem to be sufficient cause to explain why coastal people had to abandon sites. Perhaps this so, at least in the purely pragmatic terms of inhabitability. However, pragmatism is hardly sufficient to explain why places of inhabitation were preceded by the emplacement of burials, for instance, or later revisited for the emplacement of nonlocal objects. Places that were eventually abandoned were connected to pasts and futures that transcended the objective conditions of inhabitability at any point in time (e.g., Colwell-Chanthaphonh and Ferguson 2006), and they were not beholden to linear time. Add to this any spatial relationalities in the siting of cemeteries, villages, mounds, and caches and we have ample reason to look beyond the mundane and local to explain detachment from place. We agree with McAnany and Lamoureux-St-Hilaire (chapter 2 in this volume) that "leaving attenuates the relationship between people and place" but would add the possibility that in nonwestern logics, places existed before people arrived in the relational qualities among them, both through time (sequence/cycle) and across space (networks/movement). The history of Chacoan resettlement in the American Southwest is a case in point (Lekson 1999).

And this possibility takes us briefly to the rationale for looking skyward. Native cosmology is intrinsically astronomical, but we hasten to note that none of the celestial bodies of the sky nor movements among them is intrinsically meaningful. Although naked-eye astronomy finds purpose worldwide among people who orient their lives around cycles of the sun and moon (Aveni 2008), and among those who look to stars and planets for navigational purposes (e.g., Lewis 1994), ethnoastronomy is more than calendrics and wayfinding. We are interested here in how a cosmology that would anticipate the abandonment of Poverty Point—among other, antecedent and coeval sites—arose from the accumulated experiences of living through environmental change, in this case rising water. We are particularly interested in the way that experience with change in the material world, which is often chaotic, relates to movement that is more predictable, notably the movement of celestial bodies. We might call this relationship between earthly experience and celestial motion a matter of "mirroring," that is, an earthly microcosm of the sky, or what Gary Urton (1981) calls the "crossroads" of earth and sky. This is a matter of lived human experience, but experience that was encoded in material resources, including abandoned sites, whose cosmological significance was transmitted across generations through ritual practice, such as pilgrimages to Poverty Point. It bears repeating that our concern here is with change and thus with motion. We suspect that syncing movements of the sky with earthly movements and with moving bodies and objects was how the world was renewed as a matter of reciprocity and balance. When movements fell out of sync and could not be rebalanced through traditional practice, cosmology was challenged, which is what we suspect happened in the abandonment of Poverty Point.

A COSMOLOGY OF WATER AND EARTH

We can start to piece together a cosmology that arose recursively through centuries of living with rising water by considering how the movement of water may have been related, metaphorically, to movements of the sun. Hydrological patterns on earth are, of course, structured by surface geomorphology and underlying geology, as well as atmospheric circulation, precipitation patterns, temperature, and more. With regard to the physical attributes of the region implicated in Poverty Point history, the Gulf Coast between Louisiana and peninsular Florida—a stretch of over 500 kilometers—is a more-or-less linear contact between water and earth that is oriented along an east-west parallel roughly thirty degrees north of the equator (figure 5.2). Rivers that drain the Coastal Plain and peninsular Florida are oriented roughly along meridians, meaning north-south. These orthogonal axes—parallels and meridians—mirror cyclical pathways of the sun: the former the daily path of sunrise and sunset (and their Underworld counterparts [see below]), the latter a function of the ecliptic plane along which the sun appears to migrate from south to north over the course of six months, reversing its course after the standstill known as summer solstice, and back again six months later after winter solstice. It bears noting that the mounds of Poverty Point were arrayed along two meridians that were surveyed using a triangulation method that

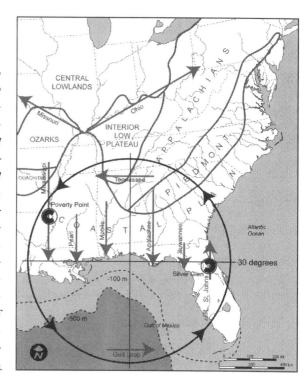

FIGURE 5.2. *Physiography of the American Southeast with directional arrows of flow of major rivers draining the Coastal Plain and peninsular Florida and modeled counterclockwise rotation of water in the greater region. Arrows following the Missouri and Ohio Rivers point to setting and rising summer solstice sun, respectively, and have reciprocal directions of flow in the direction of the rising and setting winter solstice sun, respectively.*

recapitulated solstice angles (John Clark 2004; Sassaman 2005). Moreover, solstitial alignments at Poverty Point are evident in the siting of several of its earthworks (Brecher and Haag 1980, 1983; Romain and Davis 2013).

The basic cardinality of Gulf Coast physiography mirrors movements of the sun through its movement of water. Rivers draining into the northern gulf generally flow from north to south. The Mississippi River is the western-most waterway to follow this trend, and it projects much farther north than any other gulf-draining river. Although tangential to our present argument, it is likely meaningful that far upriver the Mississippi is joined by major rivers that point to the summer solstice rise (Ohio River) and set (Missouri River). Minerals and cherts from these locations arrived in great quantities at Poverty Point via travel south, down the river. The river not only delivered large volumes of water to the gulf and lithic resources to Poverty Point, but also sediment that accumulated in a delta that has outpaced sea-level rise over much of the past 5,000 years. Over this time the delta prograded southeasterly, in the direction of the rising winter solstice sun.

At the eastern end of the northern gulf lies the peninsula of Florida. Like the Mississippi Delta, the peninsula juts below the thirty-degree parallel of the greater Gulf Coast. Moreover, just as the Mississippi River extends far to the north of other rivers, peninsular Florida extends far to the south of other land masses. In noting this feature, we qualify the term *land mass* by emphasizing how much of Florida is wetlands. The limestone bedrock of peninsular Florida is porous and it lies at very low elevation, increasingly lower in a southern direction. Comprised of vast wetlands—the Everglades prominent among them—south Florida is basically a waterscape and has been for thousands of years. Rising sea over the millennia has not only flooded low elevations, but increased the pressure of fresh water trapped in porous limestone to emerge at the surface as artesian springs (O'Donoughue 2017). Water literally flows up from the underlying rock in Florida, sometimes in spectacular "boils" of high-volume flow. In the northeast quadrant of the state, paralleling the Atlantic Coast, the channelized convergence of spring and surface water forms the St. Johns River, the only north-flowing river in the region. As we review later, settlement along the river burgeoned after becoming well watered, enabling a 7,000-year-long history of terraforming in shell and earth that would complement developments in the lower Mississippi Valley (Randall 2015; Randall and Sassaman 2017).

With the Mississippi River coursing southward and the St. Johns River coursing northward, we can posit that the metaphorical circulation of water flowed in a counterclockwise direction. This is further supported by water flows on the northern and southern margins of space commensurate with the breadth of the Gulf Coast parallel. At the north end are a series of rivers flowing to the west, the southernmost being the middle Tennessee River valley. To the south is the Gulf Loop Current far offshore, which loops from west to east. Linking all four courses, we arrive at a pattern of circulation that combines the annual and daily movements of the sun: from rising east to setting west across land, then setting west to rising east under water; and from south to north in the east, toward the summer, and from north to south in the west, toward the winter.

This inferred connection between water and sun is consistent with a non-Western cosmology that makes a distinction between upper and lower worlds, the latter sometimes described as a watery underworld. Throughout much of the Americas, indigenous informants of the recent past described a tripartite cosmos consisting of an Upper World, a Lower World, and a Middle World (e.g., Grantham 2002). The Upper World was the realm of order, stability, and permanence. In contrast, the Lower World was the realm of chaos, reversals, and fertility. The Middle World, the world of mortal beings, existed between the opposing worlds, requiring ritual interventions to keep the worlds in balance, or bring them back into balance. Emerging each day from the Lower World, the sun would travel westerly across the Upper World to descend at the end of each day into its Lower World portal, where it traveled eastward, back to its portal to the Upper World. When the Lower World is described as watery, the sun is thought to have gathered water from the Under World, or what Urton (1981:68) calls the "cosmic sea." It follows that "cosmic rivers," in this case the St. Johns and Mississippi, escorted the sun on its annual migrations north and south, respectively.

Now, if we were to rotate this vertical model of the cosmos ninety degrees on the axis of the Middle World, and align that axis with the Gulf Coast, the Upper World would consist of the terrestrial realm of the Coastal Plain, and the Lower World the watery realm of the Gulf of Mexico (figure 5.3). Noteworthy are the corresponding trends of elevation in either direction: to the north, the terrain rises in elevation to the mountains and plateau; to the south, it drops in elevation off the continental shelf into deep water. These trending surfaces are the least attenuated at the midpoint of the Gulf Coast, near present-day Choctawhatchee Bay in the panhandle of Florida. From this point east and west, the north-south rivers of the Coastal Plain are evenly spaced at about 165 kilometers apart, three rivers to each side, or six total. Incidentally, 6 is a number that recurs in the earthworks of Poverty Point and is the number of solstice triangles in a 360-degree array (6 × 60 degrees; Sassaman 2005).

The conformity between physiography and cosmos, between earth and sky, is a matter of interpretation today, as it was in ancient times. We might think of the conformity as an example of "geographic onomatopoeia," at the suggestion of Scott Ortman (personal communication, 2015), or perhaps a type of geomancy to the extent that solar movements had earthly counterparts and were thus instruments of divination in the regularity of cyclical movements. Nothing in the spatial array of rivers, gulf waters, coasts, and landforms would have been intrinsically meaningful but rather an interpretation of relevance vis-à-vis the sun, as outlined above. More revealing of cosmology, however, are emplacements of earth, shell, objects, and human bodies, and discursive practices with citations to both water and earth, as well as alignments with the sun. Conspicuous among them is Poverty Point itself, situated on the angle of the setting solstice sun from the point of intersection between the central meridian and Gulf Coast parallel near Choctawhatchee Bay, where Poverty Point–affiliated sites abound (Thomas and Campbell 1991). Emplaced in the opposite direction, on the south Florida Gulf Coast, was a 260-meter-long, U-shaped shell ridge at Bonita Bay, a bit to the south of the winter solstice line. Over 300 kilometers to the north of Bonita Bay, on the St. Johns River, was

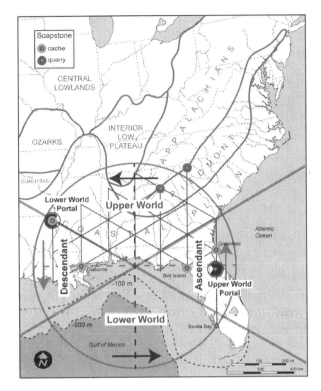

FIGURE 5.3. *Cosmogram of the American Southeast, showing Upper and Lower Worlds, portals on opposite margins of the region, solstice lines emanating from south of Choctawhatchee Bay, locations of soapstone caches, and locations of two major soapstone quarries of the Upper World.*

Silver Glen Springs, a shell ridge of comparable size and orientation. Little is known about Bonita Bay, other than its fifth millennium B.P. age, but the other two places (Poverty Point and Silver Glen) are demonstrably locations of social gathering involving both terraforming and the importation of objects from afar. We elaborate later the argument that these two locations on opposite sides of the physical world were portals that enabled virtual travel between the Upper and Lower Worlds.

Other types of emplacements involved movements of objects and human bodies in response to changes in the relationship between land and water, which is to say between the Upper and Lower Worlds. In the cosmology modeled earlier, rising sea may have been reckoned as the Lower World overtaking the Upper World, presumably an imbalance in need of intervention. In practical terms, sites at the coastal interface of land and water had to be abandoned and relocated as places of residence. This occurred repeatedly over the millennia, so much so that we suspect that the anticipation of change—the inevitable future of abandonment and relocation—was codified in cosmology. In the section that follows we illustrate this point with examples of abandonment and emplacement along the northern Gulf Coast.

COASTAL SETTLEMENT, SEA-LEVEL RISE, AND THE FUTURE AS PLACE

The archaeological record of settlement on the northern Gulf Coast is truncated at about 5,000 years ago because of postglacial sea-level rise. With the exception of those on high dunes and other raised landforms, coastal settlements predating this benchmark are now underwater (e.g., Faught 2004). As is the case with low-gradient coastlines such as the Gulf Coast, transgressions of the shoreline can be dramatic even with modest increases in sea level, but mitigating factors such as marsh aggradation, oyster reef accretion, and even human interventions (i.e., terraforming) preclude a direct correlation between sea-level and shoreline transgression. The complex relationship between land and water is evident in the ongoing work of the Lower Suwannee Archaeological Survey (Sassaman et al. 2017). Centered on the delta of the Suwannee River and extending about forty kilometers along the northern Gulf Coast of Florida, the project area contains a robust record of human land use on the extant coastline punctuated by periods of abandonment and resettlement. The most intensive settlements date to the Middle Woodland period (ca. 1800–1300 cal BP), when large civic-ceremonial centers were established by the emplacement of cemeteries and mounds. Three millennia earlier, at a time when the rate of sea-level rise decelerated to enable productive estuarine conditions, including the formation of oyster reefs, communities of the Late Archaic period (5000–3000 cal BP) flourished. The extant terrestrial record of settlements of this age exist today on elevated landforms, and we presume that shoreline settlements at lower elevation were long ago inundated because sea level continued to rise, albeit at subdued rates compared to the early Holocene (Donoghue 2011) and generally in overstep events (Goodbred, Hine, and Wright 1998; McFadden 2016; Wright et al. 2005) that would have devastated coastal communities. The record of Late Archaic settlement is admittedly cryptic, but ongoing shoreline erosion attending recent overstep events has exposed cemeteries of this age and an intriguing pattern between the emplacement of graves and site abandonment.

In late 2012, human burials dating to the Late Archaic period began to reveal themselves in the eroding shoreline of a Florida gulf-coastal island (Sassaman et al. 2015). The tidal erosion of cemeteries has become a recurring theme in recent decades. In March 1993 an assemblage of Late Archaic

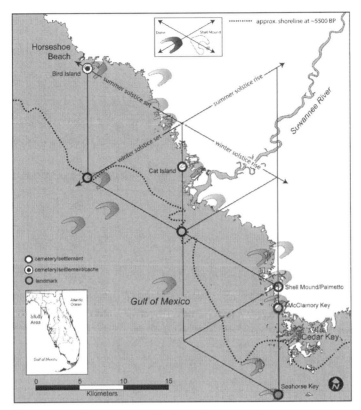

FIGURE 5.4. *Futurescape of the Lower Suwannee Region, ca.*
4,000 years ago, showing locations of three cemeteries and the meridians
that structure a solar grid connecting the past to the future with respect
to the rising sea.

burials was exposed on another island (Stojanowski and Doran 1998), and since about 2000, several burials of presumably similar age have emerged from the shore of a third. These three cemeteries (McClamory Key, Bird Island, and Cat Island) are evenly distributed across the study area of Lower Suwannee Archaeological Survey (figure 5.4).

Cemeteries and sites of Late Archaic age were established when sea level was as much as two meters below present levels. Those that are now washing out of the intertidal zone were therefore established back from the shoreline, an estimated five to ten kilometers landward. The three eroding cemeteries are all remarkable for their consistent elevation and orientation. All appear to have been emplaced on the northern arms of parabolic dunes that were open to the southwest, toward gulf water. Details of the treatment of individuals in the cemeteries are sketchy, but at least two consisted of shore-parallel rows of interments, and all three cemeteries included secondary, bundle burials.

Cemeteries were not randomly emplaced, nor were they apparently associated with settlements at the time individuals were first interred. Rather, they appear to have been emplaced back from the now-submerged shoreline at a relatively fixed distance. In this regard, it is not likely coincidental that one of the cemeteries (McClamory Key) lies on a meridian that connects the highest dune crest in the area to another cemetery (Palmetto Mound) that was initiated no later than 2,750 years ago. Currently at approximately sixteen meters amls (above mean sea level), Seahorse Key is the highest coastal elevation in Florida. Throughout most of the early to mid-Holocene, Seahorse Key was attached to the mainland, but it would have been the first of many islands to form as sea level rose.

Using the Seahorse Key meridian as a baseline for extrapolation, additional north-south lines through the other two Late Archaic cemeteries shows them to be separated from each other by a little more than ten kilometers on the parallel. Extrapolating the distance between Seahorse Key and the McClamory cemetery (a little less than ten kilometers) to the other two cemeteries puts us in proximity to the submerged coast ~5000 cal BP. The meridian emanating southward from Cat Island is especially noteworthy for its association with the submerged Suwannee Delta. Although drowned shorelines await better documentation, it would appear that prominent physiographic features (e.g., Seahorse Key) occupied southern points for sighting northern lines over substantial distances to emplace cemeteries back from the coast when sea level was down.

Late Archaic surveyors may have employed a variety of methods for sighting straight lines, but it must have involved some measuring standard if the distance between the coast and interior cemeteries is nonrandom. A clue may be seen in the orientation of sand dunes on which cemeteries were emplaced (figure 5.4). The parabolic dunes that once covered the landscape, and whose remnants remain, are open to the southwest at an azimuth of ~240° and closed to the northeast at angle of ~60°. These are the respective angles of the setting winter solstice sun and the rising summer solstice sun. Worldwide the solstices provide calendrical points of reference, but they also provide a means for surveying space through the simple process of triangulation. Solstice triangles are equilateral triangles, with 60° vertices. Once oriented to a meridian, a solstice triangle can be used to not only sight the rising and setting sun of the solstices, but also follow a straight line by triangulating off of a parallel line. Moreover, solstice triangles can be standardized to a length constant for a measurement system, much like John E. Clark (2004) documented for Poverty Point and earlier mound complexes of the lower Mississippi River valley.

To the extent that a solar grid gauged the movement of bodies (human and celestial) through space, it materialized cyclical time. A variety of time scales can be imagined. Tides and the sun operate at subdiurnal and diurnal scales, while the migration of the sun from south to north and back again gauges subannual and annual cycles. Even larger scales of time may be implicated in the practice of siting cemeteries back from the coast. As noted, the long-term experience of coastal dwelling was one of punctuated change. Over the course of many generations, during the Late Archaic period, sea level rose significantly enough to overstep shorelines repeatedly. Thus, settlements established at low elevation on the coast had to be abandoned and relocated landward, or removed to elevated landforms. Emplaced when sea level was down, cemeteries were among the places of landward relocation, suggesting that they may have anticipated, indeed afforded relocation. In this sense, the solar grid was a *futurescape* that enabled the relocation of communities without disrupting "traditional" living, making change appear changeless (Sassaman 2016). Put another way, the dead led the living into a certain future.

UPPER WORLD OBJECTS AT THE SHIFTING INTERFACE OF WATER AND EARTH

The chronological relationship between cemeteries and associated Late Archaic settlements is cryptic, but we suspect that relocated cemeteries preceded relocated settlements by as much as two centuries. What is less ambiguous is the timing of the emplacement of nonlocal objects in or near cemeteries after coastal settlements were abandoned. At the Bird Island site, where 32 individuals were interred, at least 18 soapstone vessels were emplaced in proximity to the burials, apparently postdating the habitation period by a century or two. The closest sources of soapstone were ~450–500 kilometers distant, to the interior north, at elevations in excess of 250 meters amsl. Soapstone vessels were distributed widely outside of source areas, but caches along the coastal margin of the Southeast are spaced rather evenly (~165 km apart) at sites located at the mouths of major river drainages or embayments, coincident with the meridians marked in figure 5.3.

We have independent radiometric dates for soapstone caches at two locations outside the Lower Suwannee study area. At the Greenfield site near the mouth of the St. Johns River, four soapstone vessels were recovered in proximity to human remains (Johnson 1998). Dating to circa 3500–3400 cal BP, the vessels were apparently deliberately broken before being emplaced near the grave(s). Incidentally, Greenfield lies on the St. Johns meridian connecting Bonita Bay and Silver Glen, the two U-shaped shell ridges we imagine to have served as portals to the Upper World.

The second well-dated cache is on the western margin of the northern Gulf Coast, a mirror image of the Bird Island location. At the Claiborne site near the mouth of the Pearl River in Mississippi, a cache of twelve whole soapstone vessels was emplaced near the apex of a 200-meter-wide sand-and-shell ridge open to the west (Bruseth 1991). All but two of the vessels were emplaced upside down in a sand deposit that amateur excavators surmised was a mortuary facility, though bone preservation was too poor to substantiate their claim (Roberts Satchfield, and Lowry 1968). Irrespective of the ambiguous mortuary context, the vessels were emplaced at the end or after the occupation of Claiborne, no earlier than 3200 cal BP (Sassaman and Brookes 2017).

Claiborne was a site of Poverty Point affiliation (Gagliano and Webb 1970), considered by James Bruseth (1991) to be a waypoint or gateway in the westerly movement of nonlocal materials and objects from geological sources to the East. Soapstone vessels were indeed among the common items of importation at Poverty Point, where a cache of sherds from over 250 vessels was emplaced in a pit to the west of the mound complex (Webb 1944).

Although soapstone vessels were used over fire for presumably mundane cooking tasks, they were not necessary for cooking, because earthenware pottery was widely available. For decades regional specialists assumed that stone vessels predated pottery and were thus a prototype of the durable cooking pot. Recent AMS assays on the soot from soapstone vessels dispels this myth (Sassaman 2006) and encourages us to find alternative explanations for the importation of such heavy objects to locations hundreds of kilometers from geological sources. The emplacement of soapstone vessels in mortuary caches along the coast provides our best lead. Originating from Piedmont and Appalachians of Alabama, Georgia, and the Carolina, soapstone is a material of the Upper World. Cached at the interface of land and water, at the boundary between Upper and Lower Worlds, soapstone vessels may have been an intervention against the encroachment of sea, an effort of the part of coastal dwellers to rebalance the two worlds. Considering that caches were emplaced at or after the time of coastal abandonment and relocation, soapstone caches were something of a closing ritual, a necessary rite to renew life in a new location whose direction relative to past places of dwelling was predetermined by a grid that mirrored the northern migration of the sun, the direction of increasingly longer days.

Remarkably, the largest cache known for the Southeast resides at the greatest distance (>1,300 kilometers by water travel) from geological sources of soapstone, and some 400 kilometers north of the modern Gulf Coast, up the Mississippi River. Like those of the Gulf Coast, the Poverty Point cache likely occurred at the end of the occupational sequence, on or after site abandonment at circa 3100 cal B.P. We do not have independent dates for this caching event, but can infer a late date because the cache consists of not whole vessels or whole vessels broken in the act of caching, but rather of sherds collected from across the expansive site, according to Clarence Webb (1944:394). One gets the impression that the site was "cleansed" of surface finds of soapstone before people detached for good. As far as we know, the Poverty Point cache was not associated with human burials (indeed, burials have never been found at Poverty Point), and it obviously could not have mirrored coastal caches insofar as those were emplacements at the interface of earth and water; the cache at Poverty Point was located over one kilometer from the nearest bayou, seemingly away from water. It bears noting that the Poverty Point cache was emplaced in a pit connected to one of the principle mounds at an azimuth of 240°, the winter solstice set (Sassaman 2010). This and other qualities of the site provide affinity to the coastal alignments noted above, but there is clearly more to the story of Poverty Point to suggest its construction, use, and abandonment departed from what came before. In the balance of this chapter we explore some of these other discursive practices of Poverty Point and suggest that they coincide with changes in physical movements of the greater Southeast, including the coast, that presented contradiction between the cosmos of earth and water that crystallized over previous centuries of sea-level rise. It was, we argue, a contradiction that required, as a novel mode of rebalancing, the abandonment of Poverty Point.

POVERTY POINT AS COSMIC ABANDONMENT

Coupled with a massive inventory of other nonlocal materials (Gibson 2000), soapstone at Poverty Point connects this place to a network of other places stretching from the Atlantic Coast to the edge of the Great Plains and far north up the Mississippi Valley to the Great Lakes. Researchers debate the level of sociopolitical integration signified by the movement of nonlocal materials, but beyond the objects themselves are attributes of the orientation and sequencing of mounds at Poverty Point that reveal some underlying themes shared with Gulf Coastal communities stretching from Florida to Louisiana. The mounds at Poverty Point were aligned on a meridian, with the oldest elements to the south and the youngest to the north. As noted earlier, lines connecting major mounds at the site follow solstice angles (Romain and Davis 2013), and the measurement system used to site mounds (Clark 2004) bears affinity to the triangulation of the coastal solar grid.

It is tempting to infer that Poverty Point was the penultimate intervention against rising sea, literally the refuge of displaced coastal dwellers. There is much to recommend that coastal people visited Poverty Point (Hays, Weinstein, and Stoltman 2016), likely through pilgrimages (Spivey et al. 2015), and contributed to the labor pool of public works projects. Others must have been involved too. One of the last constructions at this site, Mound A—the second-largest earthen mound in North America—required at least 2,000 and more likely closer to 3,000 people to erect in the three-month timeframe Anthony Ortmann and Kidder (2013) surmise from their recent fieldwork. The resident population of Poverty Point was too small to have accomplished this feat on their own, in this short a period, and thus participants must have been drawn from the larger network of communities with which they interacted.

Whether soapstone vessels arrived at Poverty Point directly from pilgrims coming from source locations to the east, or more indirectly through enchained communities of the coast and Coastal Plain, their agency as an Upper World material may have had special power at this particular place. To the extent that Poverty Point served as a western portal to the Lower World, soapstone afforded renewal in the manner that the sun entered the Lower World on the western horizon to replenish itself before emerging the next day on the eastern horizon. In this sense, the westerly movement of so much soapstone renewed not simply the place, but the entirety of its network, the cosmos. Still, the caching event at Poverty Point was different, a break from former practice. Under what circumstances did this peculiar event take place?

One possible answer lies in climate changes that elapsed over the late fourth millennium B.P., change that was not anticipated by the collective experience of scores of previous generations. The trend of rising sea that spanned millennia of the Holocene had one prolonged reversal or standstill that is poorly documented for the Gulf Coast but known from studies of the Atlantic. Between about 3,400 and 3,200 years ago, the sea level stopped rising and may have reversed in some locations for several centuries. Better detail on the scope of this multicentury regression awaits geoarchaeological attention in the gulf, but we know enough from the inventory of sites, collections, and radiocarbon assays to suggest that communities dating from about 3200–2500 cal BP either followed the coastline southward with falling seas or abandoned the coast altogether. Either way, the reversal of such a long-standing trend may have posed something of an existential crisis for coastal dwellers, as it did for the community of Poverty Point. Region-wide, this was a time of great upheaval, with abandonments across both Atlantic and Gulf Coasts, as well as stretches of major rivers (Kidder 2006; Thomas and Sanger 2010).

The construction of Mound A at Poverty Point offers a window into the rationale for abandoning the site, if not also the cosmos. Kidder (2011) interprets the act as the materialization of the widespread cosmogonic myth known as the Earth Diver. In brief, the Earth Diver myth involves a turtle or bird that dove into the primordial sea to retrieve earth that was brought to the surface to beget land on which humans could dwell. Around 3,200 years ago, not long before Poverty Point was abandoned, Mound A was constructed over a patch of wetland to the immediate west of the six concentric ridges that were emplaced over the previous two to three centuries. After infilling the wetland with earth, a thin layer of light-colored silt was emplaced, followed by a heterogeneous mantle of silt in the shape of a bird flying westward. Other constructions at the site followed, but by about 3100 cal BP, it was no longer a place of residence. If it continued to be a place of pilgrimage, it did not involve the deposition of abundant nonlocal objects, as was its history.

The cache of soapstone vessels at Poverty Point must have come late in its history too. Gathering up objects of traditionally Upper World provenance and emplacing them in a pit to the west of the mound—in the direction of the flying bird and setting sun—brought closure to a history of synchronization between rising water and solar cycles. It may not have been a reversal or standstill of sea that disrupted practice at Poverty Point as much as increased river flooded attending cooler and wetter weather (Kidder 2006; Kidder et al. 2017). No matter the particular circumstances, change was afoot and we see in the abandonment of Poverty Point not only detachment from place, but a rethinking of the cosmos. For the next 500 years, until the dawn of Early Woodland mound building, native people of the greater Southeast would forfeit the practices of terraforming, and for another 500 years avoided investments in place that tethered daily practice to the infrastructure of ritual.

CONCLUSION

Over the course of millennia in the Lower American Southeast, indigenous people were in constant negotiation with a world of changing water. As their predecessors knew, oceans overstepped shorelines, rivers changed course, and groundwater rose and fell. Many of the abandoned sites of their history clearly were vulnerable to such change, but detachment was necessary to renew the world as they knew it. The uncertainty of localized changes was ameliorated by reference to movements of the sun, both daily and annual. If the tripartite native cosmology of the ethnohistoric Southeast bears relevance, the sun traveled from the Upper World of order to the Lower World of disorder, reappearing the next day as the cosmos rotated from east to west. Likewise, the sun migrated from south to north as the spring turned to summer, then back to the south as autumn turned to winter. One can imagine that long before physical bodies were detached from places, the souls or spirits of persons embarked on journeys with the sun through terraformed portals at the west and east edges of the world, in this case Poverty Point in Louisiana and Silver Glen in Florida. All of this experience with change was challenged after about 3,400 years ago, when reversed climatic trends disrupted synchronicity between cosmic and earthly movements, stimulating widespread regional abandonment. Considering the long arc of Native history, places or regions were never abandoned, only repositioned along continua of motion involving more than the coming and going of physical human agents.

The perils of inferring cosmology from the residues of material practices are not lost on us, but we are confident that historical consciousness can be discerned from emplacements of objects, ritual infrastructure, and persons in relation to astronomical and earthy movements of collective experience (e.g., Pauketat 2013; Pauketat, Alt, and Kruchten 2017). Earth and sky meet in the practices people undertake in cyclical fashion both timed and sited with reference to predictable motion. Since the end of the Ice Age, people living along the northern Gulf Coast of the American Southeast, as elsewhere, had to contend with rising water. Change came in fits and starts and at varying rates and magnitude. As is our experience today—even with the instruments and logic of science—the ancients were not able to predict with certainly the timing and magnitude of the next watery encroachment. We may accept that sea will rise at some point in the future, but not knowing when, we still gamble on an uncertain future by emplacing valuable assets in vulnerable places. If instead we referred the inevitability of an unpredictable change to cycles of predictable change, we would, as did the ancients, be ahead of the curve. We would abandon the coast, before it is inundated, to renew the world as we know it.

In the tripartite native cosmology that we refer to in this chapter the interface between sky and earth, This World, was the locus of ongoing efforts to balance the Upper and Lower Worlds. As materialized in the region of the northern Gulf of Mexico, that margin shifted with rising sea for millennia and we can observe residues of the ritualized practices that enjoined the movements and cycles of the sun, to balance the worlds. When conditions on earth changed and led to contradictions in the imposed synchronization between earthly and solar movements, cosmology was challenged as a rationale for collective action. The basic structure of a tripartite cosmos may not have been fully rejected, but its substances and earthly points of reference indeed must have changed to accommodate new conditions. After a long history of water encroaching over land—of the Lower World overcoming the Upper World, requiring emplacements of Upper World objects at the interface of water and earth—the denizens and pilgrims of Poverty Point repurposed the cosmos to emplace earth over water, much as aggrading shorelines, notably deltas, would have done with a standstill of sea.

Much remains to do to determine how earthly and celestial movements were calibrated to render daily and annual cycles into longer-term trends; to examine cosmic substances other than soapstone, such as marine shell, which was exported far into the interior; and to explain how the Poverty Point community was dissolved and then redistributed into social formations of the ensuing Woodland period. Detachment from place was integral to the renewal of society and the cosmos for people who experienced and thus expected change routinely. Given projections for sea-level rise attending climate change that too many are reluctant to accept, a sea change in cosmology like the one that materialized at Poverty Point may be in our collective future.

6

A Historical Ecological
Approach to the Differential
Abandonment of the
Minanha Agrarian
Population

*A Case Study from the
Southern Maya Lowlands*

Scott Macrae,
Gyles Iannone, and
Pete Demarte

DOI: 10.5876/9781646420087.c006

The Late Classic (AD 675–810) Maya polity of Minanha was located within the North Vaca Plateau of west-central Belize. This small kingdom was maintained by the accumulated efforts of a large support population and a series of administrative minor centers. The agrarian population that endeavored to sustain the expanding social hierarchy and ambitious construction projects of the Minanha royal court invested heavily in the geointensive agricultural practice of terracing. However, despite the efforts of the Minanha ruling elite and support population, the polity went through a prolonged period of decline and abandonment across the Late to Terminal Classic transition (AD 810–900). This chapter addresses the differential abandonment processes associated with the rural support populations that once resided in the Contreras Valley—located about 15 kilometers to the southeast of the Minanha epicenter, as well as the minor center of Waybil, situated about two kilometers to the south-southwest. The extensive excavations and study of Minanha's settlement units and agricultural terrace systems, as well as a detailed regional climatic change sequence, provide an excellent archaeological case study to address abandonment in relation to changing socioecological systems from a historical ecology perspective. In doing so, the concepts of *landesque capital* and *sense of place* are utilized to test their efficacy in discussions of abandonment, as well as to gain a more nuanced understanding of the differential abandonment of the North Vaca Plateau.

THEORETICAL PREMISE

Historical ecology provides a unique approach to understanding the complexities of human-nature relationships. Focusing on the *landscape* as the medium of interaction between both society and the environment facilitates a different perspective when addressing abandonment. Further, the use of the historical ecology research program, a landscape-focused approach, provides an avenue for the application of two theoretical concepts: landesque capital and sense of place. These concepts will be used to examine the differential abandonment experienced by the Minanha support population. However, prior to its implementation, a cursory review of this theoretical premise is required.

HISTORICAL ECOLOGY

The research program of historical ecology is based on the study of the complex and intertwined relationship between humans and their environments. Research involves the study of the reciprocal roles that nature and culture play in the creation and maintenance of the unique and complex history embedded in the landscape (Balée and Erickson 2006:6). This concept has a long past in the discourse of history, ecology, geography, and anthropology (see Conway 1948; Deevey 1964; Deevey et al. 1979; Grainger 1946; Rice 1976). However, a more focused interest in historical ecology as a research program developed during the mid-1990s (see Balée 1998; Crumley and Marquardt 1987; Crumley 1994; Scoones 1999). As a result, historical ecology was developed as a multidisciplinary research program that explores the dynamic and synergistic interrelationship between humans and the environment they live in—a human-nature relationship that is conceived as a dialogue rather than a dichotomy (Balée 1998:14; Crumley 2006:388–89; Ingerson 1994:64). These early works addressed the importance of multiscalar approaches to spatial and temporal research (Crumley 1993:377–78). The incorporation of these temporal and spatial scales was viewed as imperative for defining the parameters for the study of human-nature relationships, degrees of interaction, and consequences. Many researchers who apply a historical ecology approach focus on landscapes as a medium for recording changes in the human-nature dialectic relations over time (Balée and Erickson 2006:74; Crumley 1993:378; Crumley 1994:6, 9; Erickson 2008:158). These discussions follow closely the perspective of landscape as defined by Bernard Knapp and Wendy Ashmore (1999). Drawing on a history of landscape discourse, landscape is understood as a relative term, with its conceptual transformation being based on historically contingent human preconceptions or viewpoints (Fowler 1995:100–101). Due to the shifting conceptions of the concept, there is no "absolute landscape" but rather a medium imprinted with specific historical and cultural contexts (Hirsch 1995:23; Tilley 1994:37). It is within this broader understanding of landscape and its implications for the premises of historical ecology that the two theoretical concepts used in this chapter, landesque capital and sense of place, can be further explored.

LANDESQUE CAPITAL

The theory of *landesque capital* has a long history, with early applications of the term directed toward differentiating between investing in either labor productivity or land productivity among underdeveloped economies (Sen 1959:279–80). Harold Brookfield (1984) can be credited with one of the first applications of landesque capital in anthropological discourse, redefining and expanding its use as an outcome of innovation to include resulting changes and interdependencies within the social systems that implement them (Brookfield 1984:16, 20, 36; Brookfield and Stocking 2001:79). These early discussions diverged from the previous dichotomy of labor and land productivity to describe landesque capital as an investment of labor in long-lasting improvements of the landscape, with the goal to reduce labor and increase production (Brookfield 1984:36). While these initial discussions hinted at the social ramifications associated with the widespread adoption of innovation and the development of landesque capital, it took the broader application of this concept by anthropologists and archaeologist such as William Balée (Balée and Erickson 2006), Clark Erickson (Erickson 2006a; 2006b; 2008), and N. Thomas Håkansson and Mats Widgren (2016) to refine the concept of landesque capital (i.e., landscape capital or domesticated landscapes) in terms of the insight it can provide into social organization and political economies. Our discussion of abandonment is framed by this incorporation of landesque capital into the purview of historical ecology.

SENSE OF PLACE

The concept of sense of place follows the idea that landscape, in a historical ecology perspective, is a combination of the natural and human condition. More specifically, individuals and communities develop a sense of place through the experiences of interaction that occur between society and the environments they inhabit, a process that includes histories, memories, and symbolic meanings, through which landscapes are transformed, identified, and endowed with social importance as meaningful places (Anschuetz, Wilshusen, and Scheick 2001:161; Feld and Basso 1996:xiv; Knapp and Ashmore 1999:20–21; Lozny 2008:15). Through this sense of place, the landscape becomes a strong form of identification for the people who inhabit it, and it in return structures and patterns the occupation of the environment (Anschuetz, Wilshusen, and Scheick 2001:182; Lozny 2008:22). The concept of sense of place has been applied broadly throughout academia and between disciplines, resulting in a multitude of divergent and occasionally conflicting perspectives (Graham, Mason, and Newman 2009:14). In this chapter, we draw loosely on Martin Heidegger's (1977) dwelling concept, but more applicably from the writings of Keith Basso (1996) and Ted Jojola (2006). Heidegger (1977) describes how dwelling develops a lived experience and consciousness within which people perceive and interact with a place and the related aspects of its surrounding landscape. This is further elaborated by the process of interanimation, which is related to the fact that familiar places develop an inherent value and meaning within the minds of the people who experience them (Basso 1996:54). These meanings and values are created by the actions of the people within the landscape and are often reinforced by community-related activities (57). In this manner, the landscape becomes internalized as a fluid sense of place, constantly reconstructed by the actions of the community. Over time, these mentally created places can play a greater role in community unity and identity than does the actual geographical location (85). This development can act as an anchoring mechanism between people and space. Clearly, such conceptions are also relevant to abandonment processes.

BACKGROUND

The discussion of abandonment from a historical ecology approach requires an understanding of the dialogue that occurs between society and the inhabited environment (Balée 2006). Below, the two interrelated case studies are situated through a broader discussion of the geographic and paleoclimatic conditions of the North Vaca Plateau, as well as the political and economic history of the Minanha polity.

The North Vaca Plateau

The North Vaca Plateau is located in west-central Belize and eastern Guatemala. Geologically, the North Vaca Plateau is a karst limestone landscape (Miller 1996:110) with rainfall providing the majority of above- and belowground hydrology (Reeder, Brinkmann, and Edward Alt 1996:127). As a result of these geological and hydrological processes, this is a region of exaggerated topography with irregular valley networks of hills and ridges (Miller 1996:111; Reeder, Brinkmann, and Edward Alt 1996:121, 128). The physical landscape creates thin and often nonexistent soils on the tops and sides of the steep residual hills, while accumulating deep soil beds along the valley bottoms and gentle slopes (Pollock 2007:103; Macrae 2017:71). Generally, the soils are high in clay content and stony, though they have been described as highly fertile and, given proper agricultural management, extremely productive (Baillie et al. 1993; Macrae 2017:155–67; Pollock 2007:103–4; Reeder, Brinkmann, and Alt 1996:122; Wyatt 2008:71). However, the soils' natural characteristics and local environment create crop production issues, making the management of soil moisture and erosion the largest constraint for agricultural productivity.

PALEOCLIMATIC RECONSTRUCTION

Over the last decade, collaborative studies in the North Vaca Plateau have focused on geologic, geomorphic, and speleologic data to reconstruct past local weather conditions that are linked to regional climate trends (see Northern Vaca Plateau Geoarchaeology Project; Brook and Akers 2010; Polk 2010; Reeder, Brinkmann, and Alt 1996; Webster 2000; Webster et al. 2007). Recently the MCO1-E stalagmite from the Macal Chasm, located within ten kilometers of Minanha, has been resampled targeting the period of ancient Maya occupation in the North Vaca Plateau (Akers 2011; Akers et al. 2016; figure 6.1).

Results have identified six major dry events (MDE) across the period of Maya occupation that correlate well with reconstructions from other parts of the Maya world. Major dry events are defined as mulitdecadal periods of dryness that maintain levels of δ18O and δ13C of 1–3‰ greater than the eras before and after the dry period, coinciding with both lower UVL values and petrographic evidence of dryness (Akers et al. 2016:274). It is important to note that MDEs are not necessarily singular periods of sustained dryness, but rather an average preponderance of dryer years, often punctuated by brief wet years (278).

Results indicate that the transition from the Early Preclassic to the end of the Middle Preclassic (900–400 BC) in the North Vaca Plateau was relatively wet. However, a slow increase in dryness began after 1000 BC, culminating to a dry period during the last 250 years. The transition into the Late Preclassic (400 BC–AD 100) witnessed a return to wet conditions in the region, following which the shift from the Late Preclassic into the Early Classic (AD 250–550) exhibited an MDE that continued until the early part of the Early Classic

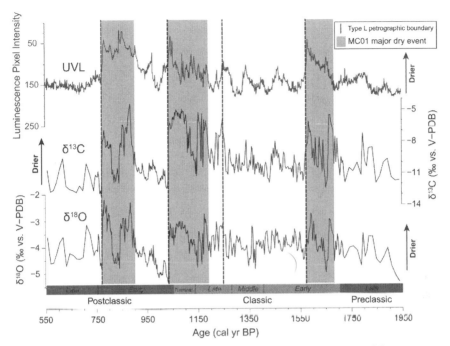

FIGURE 6.1. *Climate proxy data from stalagmite MC01 covering the major Maya occupation on the Vaca Plateau: (A) ultraviolet-stimulated luminescence, (B) δ13C, and (C) δ18O (modified from Aker et al. 2016:fig. 11).*

(Akers et al. 2016:282; Iannone et al. 2014:286–89). This MDE period exhibited two peaks in intensity at the beginning and end of the event, though given the dating difficulties for this period, ascribing specific dates for these MDE's remains problematic. During the later Early Classic and into the early facet of the Late Classic (ca. AD 675–750) the climate demonstrated a relative equilibrium between wet and dry, though it still exhibited some fluctuations (Akers et al. 2016:284; Iannone et al. 2014:289). The late facet Late Classic exhibited a MDE period that began in AD 750 and continued through the Terminal Classic (AD 810–900), ending shortly after the onset of the Early Postclassic, circa AD 925 (Akers et al. 2016; Iannone et al. 2014:290). This 175-year-long MDE was punctuated by a brief wet period between circa AD 800 and AD 825, with intensity peaks directly before and after it (Akers et al. 2016:281). This climatic sequence highlights how the North Vaca Plateau climate was neither stable or consistent for very long, as even MDEs witnessed climatic fluctuations.

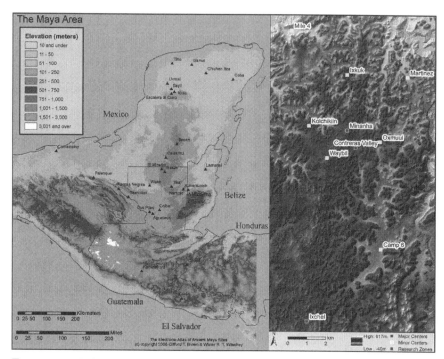

FIGURE 6.2. *Left: Important archaeological sites of the Maya world (modified from Walter R. T. Witschey and Clifford T. Brown, The Electronic Atlas of Ancient Maya Sites, 2008); right: archaeological sites of the North Vaca Plateau.*

MINANHA POLITY

Minanha is situated in the North Vaca Plateau (figures 6.2 and 6.3). The center of Minanha is referred to as a small polity capital, composed of an epicenter and surrounding residential site core settlement zone (see Hills 2012; Iannone 2005; Longstaffe 2010). At its height, Minanha can be referred to as a "full-service" center with a complete set of architectural features that accommodated residential, ritual, civic-ceremonial, and service functions (Iannone 2005:29–30). The site core, immediately surrounding the epicenter, is composed of administrative, ritual, and residential features (Longstaffe 2010:8, 207–8). The evidence for occupation at Minanha dates from the Middle Preclassic (600–400 BC) to the Early Post Classic (AD 900–1200; Schwake and Iannone 2016:135).

Minanha's epicentral community experienced relatively humble beginnings during the Late Preclassic / Terminal Preclassic (400 BC–AD 250) with the first construction projects and associated ritual deposits being established both

FIGURE 6.3. *The settlement groups found within the Minanha Epicenter and Site Core.*

inside the epicenter and its periphery (Hills 2012:67, 205). The epicenter continued to grow during the Early (AD 250–550) and Middle Classic (AD 550–675), as the site core settlement zone was also established and expanded (Hills 2012:203; Longstaffe 2010:168–69). However, the most significant expansion of the Minanha epicenter and adjacent site core did not occur until the Late Classic (AD 675–810), at which point Minanha emerged as a key center in the North Vaca Plateau and the home of a petty royal court (Carleton, Iannone, and Conolly 2010; Iannone 2005:29; Schwake and Iannone 2016). During this expansion period, the royal court complex was created—henceforth defining the Minanha epicenter—and this complex hereafter served as a tangible manifestation of the institution of kingship and presence of a royal court, thus constituting the physical and conceptual seat of power for the Minanha polity (Iannone 2005:29–30).

The late facet of the Late Classic (AD 775–810) period represents a tumultuous time for the Minanha royal court and its epicentral community, as it is marked by a series of destruction and rebuilding events (Iannone and Longstaffe 2010:72; Schwake and Iannone 2016:142–44). The first destruction event likely occurred shortly after AD 775. After this first destruction event a new building program was instituted that both modified and added to the existing epicentral complex. The Minanha epicenter experienced its second destruction event between AD 800 and AD 810. This was a targeted destruction event that signals the dissolution of the royal court at Minanha (Iannone 2005:32, 37; Schwake and Iannone 2016:146–49). Iannone and colleagues (Akers et al. 2016:284; Iannone 2005:40; Iannone et al. 2014:293–94) posit that the final abandonment of the Minanha royal court was likely due to the combined stress of local inefficiencies of the rulers to combat climatic change and declining agricultural productivity, while on a regional scale the maneuvering of the surrounding polities attempting to secure resources added additional sociopolitical pressures. Although void of a royal presence a more modest occupation, likely by commoners, continued during the Terminal Classic and Early Postclassic (AD 900–1200; Hills 2012:189, 203, 206; Iannone and Zehrt 2005:12–14; Longstaffe 2010).

CASE STUDIES

In the following section, two case studies are presented: the minor center of Waybil and the Contreras Valley support population. After a brief description of each case study, their occupational history will be addressed in concert with the broader background of the North Vaca Plateau. The reasoning for presenting these case studies is to define how the inhabitants developed landesque capital through the investment in geointensive practices that transformed the landscape to increase its production potential. Following the discussion of their occupational histories—including longevity, changing settlement patterns, and land use, as well as connections to the larger sociopolitical and socioeconomic sphere—insights into the developing sense of place that occurred at both loci will be considered. Our understanding of both landesque capital and sense of place will be utilized to assist in deciphering the differential abandonment processes that characterized these two components of the broader Minanha support population.

Contreras Valley

Situated one kilometer from the Minanha epicenter is a study zone referred to as the Contreras Valley (figure 6.4; table 6.1). This peripheral community is

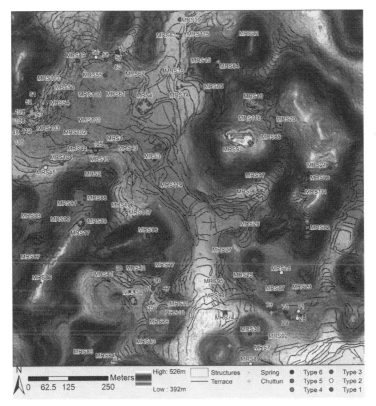

FIGURE 6.4. *The Contreras Valley survey zone representative of the Minanha support population. Surveyed archaeological structures and GPS recorded groups.*

representative of the residential and agricultural zone that was home to some of Minanha's support population. This hinterland zone exhibits extensive terracing and 100 settlement units, including both groups and solitary structures (Macrae 2010). Excavations in the Contreras Valley were based on a 15 percent stratified random sample of all settlement units discovered during reconnaissance (Iannone, Phillips, and McCormick 2006; Iannone et al. 2007; Iannone, McCormick, and Conolly, 2008).

Analysis of the settlement groups within the Contreras Valley suggests that they exhibit some of the longest-lasting settlements at Minanha, with occupation beginning in the Terminal Preclassic (AD 100–250) and enduring into the Early Postclassic (AD 900–1050; Lamoureux-St-Hilaire et al. 2015; Macrae

TABLE 6.1. Settlement Type Classification (see Ashmore et al. 1994)

Type	
I	Isolated mound (less than 2 m high)
II	2–4 mounds (informally arranged; all less than 2 m high)
III	2–4 mounds (orthogonally arranged; all less than 2 m high)
IV	5 or more mounds (informally arranged; all less than 2 m high)
V	5 or more mounds (at least 2 arranged orthogonally; all less than 2 m high)
VI	1 or more mounds (at least 1 being 2–5 m high)

and Iannone 2010; McCormick 2007). Agricultural terrace construction and use within the Contreras Valley began during the Late Terminal Preclassic (AD 100–250) and ended in the Late Classic (AD 675–810; Macrae 2010:112–13; Macrae and Iannone 2010:189–90; Pollock 2007:158, 197–200).

During the Terminal Preclassic, inhabitants of the Contreras Valley initiated the construction of tamped earth floors at the settlement unit MRS4, which would become one of the valley's most complex and largest settlement groups; it would persist as an occupation locus until the valley's abandonment. Further evidence of settlement is the penultimate building at MRS96 (Macrae 2010:112–13; Macrae and Iannone 2010:189–90). The initial settlement pattern in the Contreras Valley is indicative of a decentralized organization, potentially following the concept of principle of first occupancy (see also McAnany 2013). The first evidence for agricultural terracing also appears during the Terminal Preclassic, as revealed by two terrace planting surfaces exposed beneath later architecture (Macrae 2010:112–13; Macrae and Iannone 2010:189–90). These initial settlement units, MRS4 and MRS9, were expanded with the construction of additional structures during the Early Classic. The gradual construction and development of terraces during this period were carried out by pioneering and established households in a piecemeal fashion, in an attempt to conserve and improve their local agricultural lands (Macrae 2010:127; Pollock 2007:222–23). Prime agricultural lands witnessed the development of isolated pockets of denser, more complex, and higher-quality terraces within the interfluvial valleys near the established house lots (Macrae 2010:129–30).

During the Middle Classic (AD 550–675), settlement patterns in Contreras Valley changed abruptly; not only were there more settlement units, but many increased in size, and most were oriented toward the maximization of agricultural lands by targeting less productive areas such as hilltops and slopes (Iannone et al. 2007:154; Iannone, McCormick, and Conolly 2008:152; see also

Fedick 1995:31). There is also an increase in isolated structures, or *trojas* (field houses), suggesting that the use of fields further away from primary residences had become a necessity (Iannone et al. 2007:154; Iannone, McCormick, and Conolly 2008:152). Increasing troja prevalence over time may imply increasing competition and stress on agricultural resources, as well as the in-migration of landless peoples. Elsewhere in the Contreras Valley, other lineages and extended families expanded into more marginal lands and improved their agricultural productivity by using intensive terrace production (Macrae 2010:123–37). These terrace systems underwent an expansion, as evidenced by terrace excavations that have revealed Middle Classic ceramics (Pollock 2007:158, 197–200). In response to the growing population, farmers may have expanded agricultural terracing to maximize the arable lands, potentially using these to lay claim to shrinking land resources (Macrae 2010:139; Macrae and Iannone 2010:191). Terraces were produced uniformly and developed into clear sets based on topographical situations and association with settlement units. The interconnectivity with surrounding terrace subsystems, their high numbers, and the protracted length of several of these terraces suggest a suprahousehold level of interaction, beyond the household, involving large-scale construction processes (Macrae 2010:123–37).

The expansion of both settlement units and agricultural terracing continued into the Late Classic, when both population levels and the development of agricultural infrastructure reached their peak. The increase in population is not surprising, given the "gravitational pull" of the full-service center that Minanha had become. The spread of settlement units appears to correlate with the majority of the visible terraces, suggesting a considerable investment, which is supported by the evidence that all terraces excavations exhibit a Late Classic component (Macrae 2010; Pollock 2007). At this point, settlement units are found throughout the entire Contreras Valley with associated terracing transforming vast stretches of the landscape into an agricultural anthropogenic landscape.

During the Terminal Classic (AD 810–900), some of the larger founding settlement units continued to flourish, including the long-standing MRS4 courtyard (Macrae 2010:114; Macrae and Iannone 2010:193). New construction did occur within the fledgling MRS63 settlement unit, while MRS15 also experienced an episode of development and expansion (Macrae 2010:140). However, all but these three settlement units and two trojas were abandoned, which may indicate that the majority of landless and land-controlling groups of the Contreras Valley were either pushed out or left with the influence and wealth of the royal court. During the Early Postclassic (AD 900–1200), all the structures within MRS4 were in use, attesting to the longevity of this primary settlement (Macrae 2010:141). The only other settlement unit still in use was MRS15, which by this time was reduced to the occupation of a single structure, indicating a contraction in population levels.

It appears that the Early Postclassic occupation exhibits a return to a decentralized settlement pattern, with a smaller population, similar to that exhibited by the Terminal Preclassic and Early Classic periods. During this time, there is no evidence for additional agricultural terrace construction or development. That said, the location of the enduring settlement groups in areas adjacent to improved terraced lands suggests a continued use of the anthropogenic landscape.

WAYBIL

Waybil is a subsidiary site of the Minanha polity, located 1.92 kilometers southeast of the Minanha epicenter (figure 6.5). This site is representative of a middle-level settlement (Iannone and Connell 2003:1–6), often referred to as a minor center (Bullard 1960:360–61). The epicenter and surrounding settlement zone are composed of 15 settlement groups, 8 isolated structures, and 587 agricultural and 4 water management features. The Waybil epicenter comprises Group A, with adjacent Groups B and C considered as part of the greater site core settlement zone. Surrounding the epicenter and site core are a series of smaller settlement units, isolated structures, and agricultural terraces. Waybil's settlement chronology has been determined by 100 percent settlement sampling through courtyard and patio-focused excavations in settlement units and strategic structure excavations within the epicenter and large settlement groups (Demarte et al. 2013). Excavation and subsequent ceramic analysis revealed an occupational history for Waybil stretching from the Late Preclassic (400 BC–AD 100) to the Terminal Classic (AD 810–900; Demarte et al. 2013; Hills et al. 2012; Schwake et al. 2013). Agricultural terrace construction and use at Waybil began during the Early Classic (AD 250–550) and ended during the Late Classic (AD 675–810; Macrae 2017).

Waybil lacks evidence for permanent residential settlement during the Late Preclassic. However, it did exhibit a significant investment in Group A, the ceremonial epicenter. Evidence for this is provided by the construction of a large plastered shrine structure and associated stucco mask that were later carefully entombed with a dedicatory cache beneath the penultimate structure in the Terminal Preclassic (Hills et al. 2012:47–52; Iannone et al. 2011:101–7). Additional circumstantial evidence for growth during this latter period

FIGURE 6.5. *The settlement groups found within the minor center of Waybil, located in the North Vaca Plateau.*

is found within the floor fill of what would become a small settlement unit, Group N, the construction fill of a terrace wall, and a terrace planting surface (Demarte et al. 2013:84; Macrae and Demarte 2012:94). While evidence suggests a growing community in this microregion of the North Vaca Plateau, there still is no solid evidence for long-term occupation at Waybil dating to this early time. Iannone (2017) has suggested that the site held the significant ritualistic role of a ceremonial center that served dispersed populations in the surrounding region, including the rural populations surrounding the site of Minanha.

During the Early Classic, Waybil experienced an increased investment in the epicenter. This is shown by the penultimate construction of a large range structure (Str. AV) and the construction of the Group A courtyard with an associated burial. The penultimate range structure provided no evidence for the multiple superstructures or masonry footing that would be indicative of multiple rooms used for administrative/ceremonial functions (Schwake et al. 2013:140). Rather, the large open platform atop the structure, potentially enclosed by a single perishable superstructure, may have functioned as a storage facility (Iannone 2017; Schwake et al. 2013:140), perhaps representing the first nonritual architecture constructed at Waybil. Excavations have identified that the first terrace walls were constructed at this time. This building indicates a shift in the identity and role of the inhabitants of Waybil within the larger sociopolitical and socioeconomic organization of the North Vaca Plateau at this time. During this period, the site's identity shifted from a ritual and ceremonial site to an agricultural focus aimed at providing food security for the surrounding community. It can be argued that climatic shifts caused stress on the newly established role of Waybil as an agricultural and administrative enclave, which spurred the initial use of terracing to disperse and capture limited precipitation (Macrae 2017:265). Further, the use of terraced and nonterraced fields in both the nearby Contreras Valley, and potentially at Waybil as well, likely increased the susceptibility to erosion within the cultivated fields, a factor escalated by sporadic wet periods. The lack of permanent settlement at Waybil at this time suggests that the agricultural systems were strongly interconnected with remote farming populations who aimed, if not to increase production, to at least stabilize it during the extreme dry and wet phases of the associated MDE (Macrae 2017:262).

During the Middle Classic, Waybil residents constructed the first architectural features in what would become the site's first and longest-occupied residential unit, Group B, indicating that the settlement housed a permanent and invested resident population by this time. It is at this time that subterranean chambers in the limestone bedrock, or *chultun(ob)*, within the Waybil site were used (Iannone et al. 2011:108–11). The lack of ritual or burial material found during the excavation of a sealed chultun suggests that some of these features were likely used to store perishable materials (108–11). A decrease in environmental pressure to a more pleasant climate likely prompted an increase in the agricultural potential of Waybil. However, it is possible that the simultaneous increase in social-political tensions applied by the larger and developing Minanha polity could have amplified the pressures placed upon Waybil, requiring its residents to both maintain agricultural surpluses, heighten production levels, and initiate the development of storage facilities, while simultaneously navigating a complex patron-client socioeconomic relationship.

There is a drastic change in occupation during the Late Classic (AD 675–810). At this time Waybil experienced its most dramatic growth with construction and expansion in all settlement units (Demarte et al. 2013:106). In addition, all but one of the five excavated terrace walls and two of the thirteen investigated planting surfaces exhibit a Late Classic component. Thus, it can be confidently stated that all terrace systems were constructed and/or in use in use during the Late Classic. The site core exhibited the construction of a new shrine structure (Hills et al. 2012:53–54) and the terminal construction at the original epicentral shrine structure and large storage building (Iannone 2017; Schwake et al. 2013:130–41). Further, the continued use of chultunob indicates the importance of food storage at this time. This increased development and investment in agricultural infrastructure represent the first true full-time occupation of the settlement.

During the Terminal Classic the construction and occupation at Waybil virtually ends, suggesting a significant contraction within the Waybil population. Only the epicenter and Group B exhibit evidence of Terminal Classic occupation. This evidence is provided by ceramics, all of which were found within the uppermost stratigraphic excavation levels (Hills et al. 2012:47–52; Schwake et al. 2012:67, 71, 80; Schwake et al. 2013:133–34, 140). The only exception at Waybil are two dedicatory caches and two burials placed within structure BIII, the easternmost structure of Group B (Schwake et al. 2012:79). The radiocarbon dating of the BIII-B/1 burial provided a relatively weak signal for the Late to Terminal Classic (775–885 [68 percent]). Additionally, two terrace walls or planting surfaces revealed a few ceramics from this period, but in severely reduced numbers. This presence of Terminal Classic ceramics suggests that at least some of the terraces surrounding Waybil were being maintained at this time. After the Terminal Classic, however, there is no evidence for enduring occupation or extended visitations at Waybil.

DISCUSSION

At the onset of this chapter, the concepts of landesque capital and sense of place were defined and presented within the framework of historical ecology. Two case studies, embedded within the larger background of the North Vaca Plateau, were presented to address how these concepts may inform us about abandonment. The history of settlement and investment in the in the Contreras Valley and the Waybil was outlined. We now return to the concepts of the landesque capital and sense of place; identifying how they are internalized by the case studies will provide a basis for discussing the differential abandonment of Waybil and the Contreras Valley.

Landesque capital describes an investment in landscape that ultimately increases long-term productivity. This investment carries with it subsequent consequences for the social structuring of the groups involved. The minor center of Waybil and the Contreras Valley support populations, both subsidiaries groups within the greater Minanha polity during the Late Classic period, invested heavily in the geointensive practice of agricultural terrace development, expansion, and maintenance. Over centuries of occupation, this intensive agricultural practice transformed the North Vaca Plateau into an agriculturally productive anthropogenic landscape. However, the adoption of this labor-intensive agricultural strategy occurred in two distinct sequences and under changing social conditions (figure 6.6).

Within the Contreras Valley, the decision to invest in agricultural terracing began by AD 100–250, in an accretional fashion with lower levels of investment (Macrae 2010:139–40; Macrae and Iannone 2010:190–91). Despite the early decentralized approach to household agricultural production, the strategy became more centralized and encompassed a community-level management by AD 550–810. At Waybil, there is limited evidence for experimentation with agricultural terraces between AD 250 and AD 550, with expedient terrace construction increasing between AD 675 and 810. The rapid transformation of the Waybil landscape would have involved a significant labor investment and commitment to agricultural terracing, as the entire site became occupied and oriented toward the production and storage of agricultural surplus. Agricultural terracing in both the Contreras Valley and the minor center of Waybil appear to have peaked by AD 810. The Contreras Valley took circa 425 years to reach the peak of terrace use, while this occurred within circa 125 years at Waybil. Despite the differing start dates, both case studies exhibit near total transformation of their surrounding landscapes through terracing, albeit a more aggressive topography not appropriate for terracing reduced the coverage in the Contreras Valley. Further, through the development of landesque capital, which included the beneficial qualities of increased production, in conjunction with the increasing social pressure exerted by the developing Minanha polity, both case studies exemplify hinterland populations that underwent significant social and organizational changes as a result of their immediate environmental, socioeconomic, and sociopolitical interactions. In the Contreras Valley, this social change is represented by the centralization of the agricultural strategy, while at Waybil this represents the whole-scale change in site identity from an original civic ceremonial function to one of agricultural an enclave with storage and administrative capabilities.

Returning to the discussion of abandonment within the Contreras Valley (AD 900–1200) and Waybil (AD 810–900), consequences in both resource production and social changes brought on by the development of landesque capital

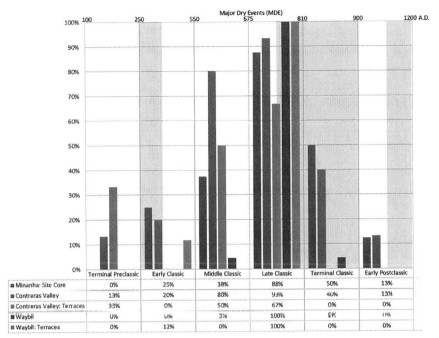

	Terminal Preclassic	Early Classic	Middle Classic	Late Classic	Terminal Classic	Early Postclassic
Minanha: Site Core	0%	25%	38%	88%	50%	13%
Contreras Valley	13%	20%	80%	93%	40%	13%
Contreras Valley: Terraces	33%	0%	50%	67%	0%	0%
Waybil	0%	0%	3%	100%	0%	0%
Waybil: Terraces	0%	12%	0%	100%	0%	0%

FIGURE 6.6. *Percentage of occupied residential settlement units and agricultural terraces, in association with Major Drought Events (MDE).*

require attention. When considering the role of landesque capital in terms of abandonment it is obvious that even the accumulated infrastructure, increased agricultural productivity, minimized effects of the fluctuating climate, and combated erosion were not enough to tether the people to the landscape when the Minanha polity began to lose its integrative powers. However, the study of production benefits may not be what best informs us about abandonment processes, but rather the social ramifications of developing landesque capital.

The process of constructing the agricultural infrastructure that forms the basis of the landesque capital in both cases studies would have developed strong ties to the landscape, resulting in the development of a strong sense of place. This connection would have been reinforced by household or community-based activities, such as terrace-building (see Basso 1996:85). When considering the two case studies, it is possible that the extended period of time that the inhabitants of the Contreras Valley spent not only farming within the landscape, but also investing and building agricultural terraces would have developed in them a stronger sense of place than in the case of the inhabitants of Waybil. The latter community, while exhibiting a similar degree of terracing in the landscape, spent considerably less time building and planning their terrace systems.

A sense of place develops as individuals and communities experience and interact with the environment they inhabit, developing histories, memories, and symbolic meanings, during which landscapes are transformed into meaningful places (Anschuetz, Wilshusen, and Scheick 2001:161; Feld and Basso 1996:xiv; Knapp and Ashmore 1999:20–21; Lozny 2008:15). It is unlikely that this study, or most archaeological studies, will be able to explicitly state what sense of place an individual or community develops. However, it is possible to consider the variables involved in the creation of a sense of place and to use these to discuss the connections developed with the inhabited landscape. Within the case study these variables relate to the longevity of occupation, changes in settlement patterns and land use, as well as connections to the larger sociopolitical and socioeconomic spheres.

Simply stated, both the activities and length of time a community interacts with a particular landscape can influence the experiences developed and memories constructed. Comparing the two case studies, the Contreras Valley exhibits circa 950 years of continuous occupation, while the Waybil minor center demonstrated circa 1,300 years of use, but only circa 350 years of actual agrarian settlement. During their occupations both case studies exhibited significant changes in settlement patterns. Early settlement organization in the Contreras Valley centered around lineage-based households. By AD 550–675 the settlement pattern took on a much more centralized, top-down organization with a dramatic increase in the number of settlement units. During this period 80 percent of excavated residential settlement units were in use, 30 percent of which were trojas. Shortly after AD 810 the settlement pattern shifted once again to an organization similar to the initial occupation of the Contreras Valley, with a degree of persistence of some of the founding settlement units. Waybil experienced a different occupation history and settlement pattern. While initially the minor center acted as a civic-ceremonial locus for the surrounding community, it was only between AD 675 and 810, and potentially as early as AD 550–675, that the center changed to a production and administrative enclave for the developing Minanha center and Late Classic polity with a significant influx of residents. This pattern was relatively short lived, with nearly all the households abandoned by AD 810.

Not only did the Contreras Valley have an extended period of occupation, but it was initially occupied by settlement nodes that would persist until the final abandonment of the valley. These nodes would have experienced life as a much smaller community prior to the Minanha royal court, and when the classic kingship institution declined and the pull of the Minanha epicenter waned, the groups inhabiting these founding settlement nodes returned to a similar social and settlement organization as that which had been the norm prior to the Classic period. It is possible that the inhabitants of the Contreras Valley took advantage of the ability to remember a previous time, or retain a sense of place, and this may have facilitated or eased their transformation in social and economic restructuring in community akin to what had existed prior to the Minanha royal court's appearance. In contrast, the short-term residential occupation at Waybil did not allow for a true sense of place to develop out of what existed prior to the influence of the Minanha royal court taking hold. This may have left the Waybil inhabitants poorly equipped to carry on in the new sociopolitical and socioeconomic circumstances that took hold during the Terminal Classic and Early Postclassic periods.

CONCLUSIONS

Abandonment is not always the uniform social process it appears to be; it may be gradual, affecting distinct parts of the same site in a differential fashion and at a different pace (Lamoureux-St-Hilaire et al. 2015:550).

As described by Lamoureux-St-Hilaire and colleagues, the study of abandonment and detachment from place is a complex process. To adequately address the complexity of abandonment, studies need to meet certain criteria. First, the resolution of data needs to be fine enough to recognize the subtle changes that occur over time at a household level, all the while placing it within the larger dynamics of regional studies. Second, these studies need to be placed within a framework capable of including multiple datasets while identifying the interconnections between multiscalar variables. For this reason, our study has adopted the approach of historical ecology.

By outlining the history of occupation and changing agricultural strategies in relation to the concepts of landesque capital and sense of place, we were able to discuss the differential abandonment sequences associated with our two case studies. This study describes how, over time, agrarian populations developed an intimate and connected relationship with their landscape and sense of place. This sense of place not only defines the relationships people develop with the landscape, but it can also play an important role in the timing, sequence, and degree of landscape abandonment. The results presented in this chapter identify how the investment in landesque capital, in the form of agricultural terracing, provided the capability to persist through climatic fluctuation, environmental stressors (i.e., erosion), and, to an extent, social pressures and demand. Further, it testifies to the important social implications that landesque capital can have. Through the continued long-term investment and use of agricultural terracing by segments of Minanha's agrarian population, a powerful sense of place was developed. In the cases of the Contreras Valley, a sense of place, which persisted in some form despite a changing landscape and through social and economic upheavals, ultimately assisted in offsetting the stressors to which the Waybil community fell subject. Throughout this chapter, it has been suggested that the building and maintenance of landesque capital in concert with a developed sense of place played an important role in differential abandonment exhibited across the North Vaca Plateau and potentially in the broader discourse of abandonment.

ACKNOWLEDGMENTS

We would first like to thank all the Social Archaeology Research Program (SARP) staff members, who dedicated countless hours excavating and surveying all over the North Vaca Plateau. We especially want to thank the dedicated Belizean excavators and surveyors who have worked with us over the years. The continued support of SARP provided by the Belizean Institute of Archaeology and all their devoted staff made working in Belize not only possible, but also an amazing experience. Our gratitude goes also to Dr. Kitty Emery for her support and guidance, Dr. Augusto Oyuela-Caycedo for the initial introduction of historical ecology and support throughout our preliminary theoretical studies, and Dr. Nate Lawres for providing a sounding board for our exploration of place-making. Finally, we would like to thank all the reviewers who provided both suggestions and support. The research reported in this chapter was possible only thanks to funding awarded to Dr. Gyles Iannone by Trent University, the Social Science and Humanities Research Council of Canada, and the Alphawood Foundation, and to Scott Macrae by the University of Florida, including the Department of Anthropology, Florida Museum of Natural History, and the Latin American Studies Program.

7

As a social phenomenon, detachment from place involves negotiations between people and a landscape that is either being abandoned or nearing that stage—a discursive process that generally leaves physical traces. Detachment-related behaviors take a mundane form when we lock our doors, water houseplants, take out the trash, or leave a note on the counter for house sitters. Alternatively, these may take critical proportions when communities perceive a departure as final, such as in the case of a fleeing population burning down houses to avoid looting from invaders. These contrasting examples highlight the breadth of the spectrum of detachment-related behaviors, which are defined by the degree and nature of entanglement between people and their landscape (Hodder 2016a) and by the natural and sociocultural conditions associated with processes of abandonment (McAnany et al. 2016). As the context of detachment varies in nature, so does its duration; it may take as little as minutes and as much as decades, or may never be completed. When studying detachment from place in the archaeological record, we must thus pay attention to contextual and chronological variables by examining abandonment behaviors (see Cameron 1993; Inomata and Webb 2003b; Schiffer 1987). In other words, to adequately study interactions between abandoners and landscapes, we must examine landscape modifications and artifactual assemblages left during detachment from both a contextual and chronological standpoint. The detachment-related behaviors responsible for these

Detachment from Power

*Gradual Abandonment in
the Classic Maya Palace of
La Corona, Guatemala*

Maxime Lamoureux-
St-Hilaire,
Marcello A. Canuto,
Tomás Q. Barrientos, and
José Eduardo Bustamante

DOI: 10.5876/9781646420087.c007

physical traces may document many dimensions of social (dis)entanglement (see Lamoureux-St-Hilaire et al. 2015). Civilizational collapse, resulting in the widespread abandonment of geopolitical landscapes, obviously represents an enlightening window to study variability in processes of detachment from place.

DETACHMENT FROM PLACE DURING THE CLASSIC MAYA COLLAPSE

The Classic Maya collapse took place in the southern Maya Lowlands over a period of roughly a century, between 800 and 900 CE—leading to the abandonment of scores of urban centers. There are different adequate ways to define this collapse, all of which address the end of the institution of divine kingship, which had thrived since at least the Late Preclassic period (300 BCE–250 CE; Aimers 2007; Freidel 2008; Iannone, Houk, and Schwake 2016; Rice, Demarest, and Rice 2004). Scholars have used dates inscribed on the last hieroglyphic monuments erected by many lowland royal courts to date their demise from a *terminus post quem* standpoint (Bove 1981; Ebert, Prufer, and Kennett 2012; Lowe 1985; Neiman 1997; Premo 2004). The end of the practice of dedicating public monuments reflects when royal courts lost the political ability—or legitimacy—to self-promote in urban centers. While this approach is a good starting point, it yields three major flaws: (1) Some polities did not erect those kinds of monuments, while, in other cases, monuments were not spared by natural and cultural formation processes: two equifinal processes making this terminus post quem method irrelevant for many Classic Maya centers; (2) in many instances, penultimate monuments preceded last ones by quite some time, suggesting that royal courts had lost most of their power earlier than suggested by the last recorded date; and (3) this approach tackles but a single dimension of civilizational collapse, as Classic Maya governments did far more than erect public monuments.

Before they collapsed, Classic Maya royal courts were anchored, within urban centers, in a monumental architectural landscape epitomized by regal palaces. The political and economic power of royal courts was both manifested and embedded—or entangled—within these landscapes. Since Classic Maya regimes ranged from small principalities to large hegemonic kingdoms, these political landscapes greatly varied in form and size. As governments collapsed, these distinct landscapes were abandoned in varying fashions: "Sometimes the kings and their institution[s] appear to have been suddenly extinguished and in other instances they seem to have faded away slowly and gradually" (Taylor 2016:xv). The study of these processes of detachment from power, beyond helping us date the collapse of individual centers, can shed light on how distinct institutions collapsed, and on how political power was detached from its seat.

This chapter presents a case study of detachment from power during the Classic Maya collapse, complementing similar studies (e.g., Child and Golden 2008; Inomata 2016; Schwake and Iannone 2016; Yaeger 2010), by examining the gradual abandonment of the regal palace of La Corona, Guatemala. We believe our study of political disentanglement to be interesting not just because of its rich dataset, but also because La Corona was uniquely situated in the Classic Maya geopolitical world. Sak Nikte' (its Classic Mayan name) may only have been a small urban center, but it was intimately tied to the most powerful Classic Maya regime: the Snake Kingdom, Kaanul.

We first address how the development of the political institution of Sak Nikte' was overseen by Kaanul, after which we discuss its transformation following the implosion of that hegemonic kingdom in the early eighth century. The presented dataset reveals how this royal court adapted to its new political reality and endured for a century, but inevitably reduced its activities and was gradually abandoned.

POLITICS AT LA CORONA

La Corona (figure 7.1) was a center of modest size located at the western edge of the central karstic uplands of the southern Maya Lowlands, in the northwest corner of modern Petén, Guatemala. This small urban center comprised two major architectural groups: the Main Plaza and the Coronitas Group (figure 7.2). These two groups, some smaller complexes, along with dozens of surrounding elite and nonelite household groups, were all built on elevated terrain nestled among the string of rain-fed lakes characterizing the region. The Main Plaza, covering one hectare, is particularly notable for the large palatial acropolis, Str. 13Q-4, that occupies its western flank—dwarfing all other constructions on site. This acropolis, built in five major phases, today has an area of 80 by 55 meters and is between 7 by 13 meters in height; moreover, as the regal palace, it was the political heart of La Corona (figures 7.2 and 7.4).

Our understanding of Sak Nikte' relies on its unusually rich historical record narrating the long relationship between its rulers and the mighty Kaanul kings based initially at Dzibanche and later at Calakmul, Mexico (figure 7.1). This historical record was beautifully inscribed in a series of hieroglyphic monuments—mostly sizable paired panels and smaller "portable" blocks—located in the site's two major groups, consisting one of the longest continuous Classic Maya inscriptions (see Stuart et al. 2014).

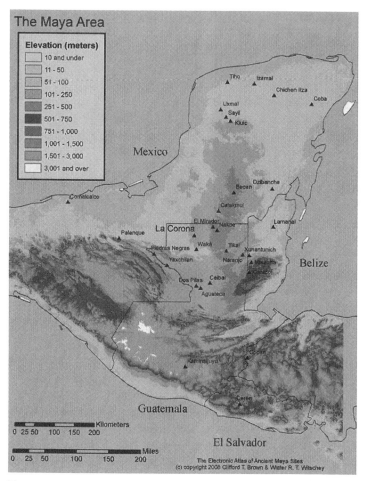

FIGURE 7.1. *Map of the Maya world with important archaeological sites (modified from Walter R. T. Witschey and Clifford T. Brown, The Electronic Atlas of Ancient Maya Sites, 2008).*

We know from this record that the Sak Nikte' royal court and its regal palace were transformed in 520 CE, when the Kaanul king Tuun Kab Hix, then ruling at Dzibanche, made a political alliance with a Sak Nikte' ruler, betrothing him to a Kaanul princess named Ix Naah Ek' (Canuto and Barrientos 2011, 2013a; Stuart et al. 2014). Stratigraphic excavations in the palace indicate that the arrival of this Kaanul lady transformed the La Corona regime and prompted the first monumental expansion of the regal palace, corresponding

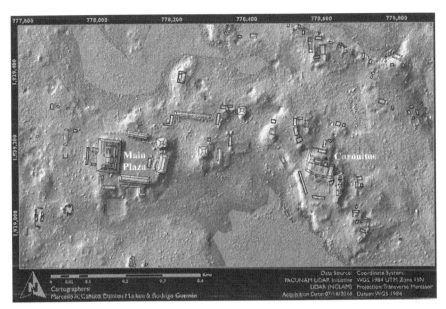

FIGURE 7.2. *Map of the La Corona epicenter.*

to the Colibrí construction phase (Lamoureux-St-Hilaire and Bustamante 2016). This palace was occupied during the expansion of Kaanul, its relocation at the site of Calakmul, and the reign of Yuhknoom Ch'een II—perhaps the greatest Classic Maya king (Martin and Grube 2008; Stuart 2012). This period is also when La Corona became the capital of a key client-state, or a colony, of Kaanul, corresponding to the reigns of several known Sak Nikte' rulers, who all bore the title of *sak wahyis* (Canuto and Barrientos 2013b). This asymmetric alliance endured for over two centuries and was punctuated by interactions recorded on the La Corona hieroglyphic monuments. These fine limestone monuments portrayed different sak wahyis interacting with Kaanul kings, or addressed this alliance by portraying the Kaanul queens of La Corona (see Stuart et al. 2014).

The most important palace construction phase, Halcón A, took place just before 700 CE, corresponding to Kaanul's apogee and to the reign of Yuhknoom Yich'aak K'ahk', who ruled most of the Southern Maya Lowlands (Canuto et al. 2017). Empowered by this alliance, which clearly increased the economic success of Sak Nikte', the sak wahyis Chak Ak' Paat Kuy built a truly monumental palace for his court, comprising four architectural groups (the Northeast, Southeast, Southwest, and Northwest Groups) surrounded by corbel-vaulted masonry buildings decorated with elaborate stucco friezes. It even appears that Kaanul owned a few rooms within the palace's Southwest Group, dubbed "Halcón South," which had mixed residential and administrative functions and likely consisted of an embassy at La Corona (see figure 7.4).

While this relationship continued into the early eighth century, during the reign of Yajawte' K'inich, this was a time of decline for Kaanul and for its king "Spangle Head"-Ti' K'awiil, who struggled and saw his hegemonic kingdom rapidly shrink (Martin and Grube 2008). This period was marked by another change in regime at La Corona, around 750 CE, when Halcón South was terminated and when major modifications to the Northeast Group restructured palatial politics. This new era of rulership was brought to fruition at the very end of the Late Classic period, circa 800 CE., when the Northeast Group became the clear focus, bolstering a newly assembled hieroglyphic staircase, a throne room, exterior meeting spaces, and a new temple-pyramid (Lamoureux-St-Hilaire 2017, 2018). This new order was to prevail, and for a century, Sak Nikte' took on its own, postcolonial institutional form of rulership—one that embraced its hegemonic past (Lamoureux-St-Hilaire 2018). Yet, this court progressively reduced its activities, beginning processes of gradual abandonment and detachment from power that lasted until circa 900 CE.

RENOVATIONS AND TRANSFORMATIONS IN THE REGAL PALACE

The 150-year-long process of detachment from power and place of the La Corona royal court is presented in five chronological periods below, corresponding to two construction phases, two occupation phases, and an abandonment phase. This discussion is not exhaustive, leaving many details aside to focus on the most relevant architectural and artifactual features.

HALCÓN B (750 CE)

The Halcón B construction phase occurred circa 750 CE and was the first renovation after the monumental circa 700 CE Halcón A Phase that created the large acropolis still standing today (Lamoureux-St-Hilaire 2018). The Halcón B Phase transformed the regal palace in two significant ways by (1) terminating "Halcón South," the Kaanul embassy; and (2) modifying every building in the Northeast Courtyard.

Halcón South was composed of a few rooms in the palace's Southwest Group. These large rooms were well built, with tall corbel-vaulted ceiling, massive platform-benches, and red-painted walls and floors. Two of these,

FIGURE 7.3. *Photo mosaic of Room 1 of Str. 13Q-4P, located in Halcón South, featuring some of the archaeological correlates of its reverential termination (photos by Lamoureux-St-Hilaire).*

Rooms 1 and 2 of Str. 13Q-4P, were ceremonially terminated around 750 CE (Bustamante 2017; Canuto et al. 2017). Room 1 (figure 7.3) was the theater of an elaborate, five-step reverential termination ritual during which

1. the backrest of its massive bench was methodically destroyed;
2. an individual was intrusively interred into its floor, in front of the doorway;
3. nine uncarved, fine limestone monuments were placed on the floor: seven medium blocks and one large column were placed in the center, and another column was placed over the burial;
4. fifteen ceramic tablets, three vessels, and a shell ornament were placed on and in front of the damaged bench;
5. the room's access was hindered in two ways: (1) an approximately one-meter-tall masonry feature was built in the doorway, partially blocking it and creating a window opening onto the terminated room; and (2) another large uncarved column was placed in front of the staircase leading to the front platform of Str. 13Q-4P.

The buried individual, who had for only grave offering a small bowl, was radiocarbon dated to 686–[730]–774 CE, providing a date for this termination ritual. The ceramic tablets were quite unusual—they were all unslipped, of portable format, and may be divided into seven technological categories, the majority of which are either quadrangular or ovular (Lamoureux-St-Hilaire 2019). While this type of ceramic artifact is unreported, depictions of analogous items in ceramic figurines and painted media are associated with priestly figures holding a stylus (Freidel, Masson, and Rich 2016). These tablets, sometimes confused for, or resembling, mirrors, could have been covered in beeswax or another substance and traced upon for matters of tallying and accounting (Freidel, Masson, and Rich 2016; McAnany 2010) and likely had scribal, administrative functions. It is noteworthy that benches with a backrest appear to have had—at La Corona, at least—administrative functions. The combined destruction of the administrative feature of the bench and the discard of accounting tools suggest that this ritual aimed at deactivating the administrative functions of Str. 14Q-4P. This complex reverential termination decommissioned an important administrative building and transformed it into an enshrined testament to the colonial heritage of Sak Nikte'. While Halcón South was terminated, the elaborate neighboring Str. 13Q-4O, overlooking the West Plaza along the west edge of the acropolis—a probable administrative building or a residence for priests—remained in use.

The termination of Halcón South was coeval with transformations in the regal-political functions of the court, whose center was relocated to the Northeast Group (Lamoureux-St-Hilaire 2018). There, the south gallery of Str. 13Q-4G was subdivided into five smaller rooms, and three new large rooms were added on the east and west flanks of the courtyard, Room 2 of Str. 13Q-4B1, and Rooms 1 and 2 of Str. 13Q-4F. A dedicatory burial was placed in the construction fill of Room 1 of Str. 13Q-4F, providing the radiocarbon date of 738–[750]–768 CE for these transformations. The creation of the small rooms in Str. 13Q-4G and Room 2 of Str. 13Q-4B1 indicates increased residential and administrative functions for the group. Meanwhile, Room 1 of Str. 13Q-4F was a passageway that articulated the Northeast and Northwest Group—an ancillary group dedicated to supporting the domestic and political activities of the court (Lamoureux-St-Hilaire 2018; Lamoureux-St-Hilaire et al. 2019). The Northwest Group further led to the West Plaza—another ancillary area—through Str. 13Q-27, a large platform abutting the acropolis. Abundant evidence for ancillary economic activities was unearthed in the nearby, massive midden located north of Str. 13Q-27 and dated to 700–800 CE—including many fragmentary cooking, storage, and fine serving vessels, along with great many faunal remains, but featuring limited evidence for craft production (Lamoureux-St-Hilaire 2018:342–52).

This new political order at Sak Nikte' involved the creation of the royal Northeast Courtyard and its ancillary Northwest Group, the enshrinement of the Kaanul embassy, and was probably orchestrated by the sak wahyis Yajawte K'inich. This political shift was also associated with new hieroglyphic

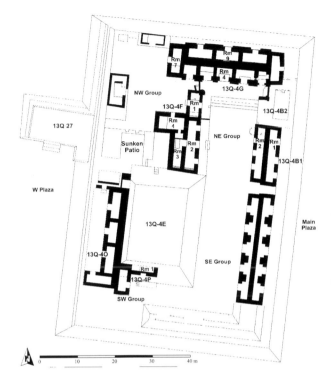

FIGURE 7.4. *Top plan of the Tucán Phase of the La Corona palace with features mentioned in the text labeled—note that most architectural features of the Halcón B Phase are also visible on this map (by Lamoureux-St-Hilaire and Bustamante).*

monuments of a distinct style: large altars and stelae mostly found in the Main Plaza (Stuart et al. 2014:441). Yet, the court's political memory remained associated with Kaanul, as evidenced by the enshrined embassy. This should not come as a surprise, since Yajawte' K'inich was married to Ix Ti' Kaan, the daughter of the last major Kaanul king, "Spangle Head"-Ti' K'awiil (Stuart 2013). While this new La Corona regime would endure for over a century, the termination of Halcón South by this government also represented the first step in its disentanglement from Classic Maya divine kingship.

TUCÁN (800 CE)

The Tucán Phase is the last-documented for the palace (figure 7.4), but was not a single event, rather consisting of a series of renovations and constructions spanning circa 800–850 CE. These modifications focused on the Northeast and Northwest Groups, which had by then become the heart of the royal court. The renewed Tucán Northeast Courtyard was notable for the addition of a hieroglyphic step, two hieroglyphic benches, a large stucco frieze, a new throne room, and a new small pyramidal temple, Str. 13Q-4B2 (Lamoureux-St-Hilaire 2018:100–181).

The hieroglyphic step from the Northeast Courtyard consisted of the upper, fourth step leading to Str. 13Q-4G, the largest building in the group. This upper step was unfortunately entirely destroyed by looters circa 1960, who, however, discarded two broken and two eroded monuments (Elements 57, 58, 60, and 61; Lamoureux-St-Hilaire 2017, 2018:126–34). The hieroglyphic blocks found as part of this step were all *spolia*; that is, they were in a secondary location, having been translocated from their original context (Barrientos et al. 2016). In addition to these, at least one (but probably two) exterior benches also boasted spolia hieroglyphic monuments in the courtyard (including Elements 55 and 56; Lamoureux-St-Hilaire 2018; Lamoureux-St-Hilaire and Morales Forte 2016; Stuart et al. 2015). The step and benches featuring hieroglyphic monuments were complemented by the modeled stucco friezes that covered most walls surrounding that courtyard. Together, these decorative elements would have conferred this exterior space a strong elite, political overtone. Notably, indications are that most of these monuments dated to the late seventh and early eighth centuries, addressing the tight relationship the Sak Nikte' rulers entertained with Kaanul (Barrientos et al. 2016).

In addition to these exterior monuments, Room 4 of Str. 13Q-4G was also transformed into a throne room with a massive C-shaped bench and a lintel-sized, red-painted hieroglyphic monument (Element 59) portraying Chakaw Nahb Chan by himself wearing a traditional period-ending Kaanul costume and wielding a royal K'awiil scepter (Diedrich 2019; Lamoureux-St-Hilaire 2017, 2018). Thus, this new throne room featured a reset panel portraying the sak wahyis Chakaw Nahb Chan, a prominent dynastic foundational figure of La Corona. Meanwhile, this throne room was also framed by the hieroglyphic step and benches, consisting an elaborate political tribute to La Corona's Kaanul-affiliated past. The juxtaposition of this throne room dedicated to a La Corona king who ruled during the apex of Kaanul and of a Kaanul-themed political stage reflects a clear attachment to this glorious past. While this may seem surprising because Kaanul had by then imploded, this political aesthetic was seemingly effective, as it succeeded in helping this government endure for a century.

At the onset of the ninth century, the Northwest Group played a dual role as an ancillary group and an important pathway, connecting the Northeast Group to the Southwest Group, Str. 13Q-4E, and the West Plaza (Lamoureux-St-Hilaire et al. 2019). This important traffic-oriented function coalesced in the transitory Sunken Patio, which led to all those different spaces.

Early Tucán Occupation (800–850 CE)

Beyond its political aesthetic, the success of the Tucán royal court may have been related to the industrious character it took during the ninth century. At this time, the Northwest Group had probably shifted from a primarily ancillary group to one geared toward craft production and storage. This functional shift is visible in the fate of Str. 13Q-27, which was decommissioned and buried under a thick midden by 850 CE. This midden yielded evidence for crafts involving the use of many stonecutting, drilling, incising, carving, and polishing implements; the crafting of jewelry; and the making of figurines, pigments, and textiles (Lamoureux-St-Hilaire 2018:324–31). This increase in craft production and reduction in the support-oriented functions of the palace—embodied by the closure of an access point to the West Plaza—followed in lockstep with the termination of Halcón South. This trend suggests that, by then, the royal court had reduced its food-related, domestic, and likely reception-oriented activities, while augmenting its role as a center of craft production and probable distribution. The midden that buried Str. 13Q-27 also featured a surprising range of sherds from diagnostic Terminal Classic vessels, especially fine-gray and fine-orange types of the Chablekal Grey, Tres Naciones Grey, Altar Orange, and Balancán Orange ceramic groups.

Late Tucán Occupation (850–900 CE)

The second half of the ninth century witnessed the continuation of the trend away from courtly receptions and toward economic activities. Indeed, the Sunken Patio, which had been a traffic node, was also decommissioned soon after 850 CE and became the receptacle of a sizable midden. This midden yielded the same kinds of craft-related implements as those covering Str. 13Q-27, very few polychrome sherds, and a high proportion of Terminal Classic diagnostics (Lamoureux-St-Hilaire 2018:309–22). The closure of this patio isolated the Northwest Group, which, by then, only communicated with the Northeast Courtyard. A third midden was found tucked against the front of Str. 13Q-27, in the West Plaza, indicating that while this place was still in use, it was in an informal fashion that allowed for refuse to be left exposed on its fringes—reflecting further detachment from formerly institutional space.

It should be highlighted that the archaeological encounter of large middens, which likely took decades to accumulate, over previously salient spaces within palatial context, is unusual and contrasts with the Halcón B Phase midden that was located off-architecture. This refuse-disposal practice, which negligibly decommissioned whole swaths of the court, reflects an informality that is hardly reconcilable with the exalted regal space that was the Northeast Courtyard. This shift in practices was probably related to a decrease in royal ceremonialism in the Northeast Courtyard and, incidentally, of the quantity of active palatial retainers (Lamoureux-St-Hilaire 2018).

The decommissioning of these ancillary spaces was probably associated with the reverential, ritual termination of the large Str. 13Q-4O, which previously connected with the Northwest Group through the then-defunct Sunken Patio. Two intrusive burials—comprising a human and a jaguar skeleton—were placed in the central axis of the two central rooms of that large corbel-vaulted building (Bustamante 2016). Following this, the corbeled vault of the building was purposefully collapsed, completely closing off this administrative structure. While distinct from the reverential termination of Str. 13Q-4P, this ritual deactivation reflects a concerted ceremonial practice.

The combined closure of this administrative building, of the West Plaza it overlooked, and of the traffic-oriented Sunken Patio, suggests that at least half of the royal court had been decommissioned by the mid-ninth century. This gradual discontinuation of the administrative, ceremonial, and ancillary functions of the palace indicates a detachment from arguably important dimensions of the royal court's authority. Yet, this court kept using the exquisite Northeast Courtyard and its attached Northwest Group, indicating that considerable domestic, economic, administrative, and ceremonial activities still occurred in the palace at that time.

THE ABANDONMENT PHASE (CA. 900 CE)

While this curtailed political institution endured for decades, the process of detachment from place eventually extended to the entire north section of the palace. However, this final abandonment did not involve the same kind of formal reverential termination behaviors that characterized the southern section. Several abandonment-related, on-floor assemblages found in the north section indicate that the members of the court vacated the palace in a gradual fashion that allowed them to carry most of their valuables away with them. Three categories of materials were left behind in the palace: (1) several bulky pot-stands were left on the front platforms of buildings, (2) some serving vessels and other goods were left in storage, and (3) two discrete ceremonial assemblages were left in eccentric locations (Lamoureux-St-Hilaire 2018:243–362; 437–41).

The most common artifacts found on the northern groups' floor were the broken mouths of medium-to-large unslipped jars, which were left in front of

Str. 13Q-4G and -4F. These bulky recycled jar mouths, seemingly used as pot-stands, were left behind at the time of abandonment. The placement of these near the facade of large range-structures was probably pragmatic: jars or other vessels with a rounded base placed on these pot-stands could have been used to collect rainwater running off roofs (Lamoureux-St-Hilaire 2018:257). This water could then have been used for domestic activities within the courtyard, suggesting that domestic activities had by then superseded the political functions of the Northeast Courtyard.

The second-most-common context for abandonment-related artifacts was serving vessels and other artifacts that were apparently left in storage on wooden furniture such as shelves or in attics (Lamoureux-St-Hilaire 2018:244–95). As the buildings eventually collapsed, those artifacts tumbled down and broke in on- or above-floor contexts. Several such assemblages were found in Str. 13Q-4B1, -4F, and -4G. Above-floor material in Room 1 of Str. 13Q-4B1, thought to be primarily used for storage, mostly consisted of large basins and jars of the Cambio Unslipped, Encanto Striated, Tinaja Red, and Chaquiste Impressed types. Above-floor material from Room 3 of Str. 13Q-4F, thought to have been the ruler's residence, included some finer ceramics, such as a large incense-burner of the Pedregal-Modeled type and a small bowl of the Pabellon Modeled-Carved type. A large amount of on-floor material was recovered in the closet located in Room 4 of Str. 13Q-4F, including a large biface, two blocks of raw lithic material for making bark beaters, a partial jar mouth, and a partial, small double-drum of the Carmelita Incised type. Finally, above-floor material from Rooms 7 and 9 of Str. 13Q-4G included serving vessels from many types, mostly Nanzal Red, Infierno Black, and Tinaja Red, but also rarer Terminal Classic types such as Anonal Orange polychrome dishes and a Caribe Incised fine orange bowl. The presence of these vessels in storage context either suggests that abandoners could not be bothered to carry them away or, more likely, that they anticipated to return.

The third abandonment-related context consists of two assemblages associated with Room 2 of Str. 13Q-4B1 (Lamoureux-St-Hilaire 2018:273–75). The first one was found inside the niche of a bench (featuring a backrest) that was seemingly used for an abandonment-related ritual involving the combustion of wood and many artifacts: five sherds, nine chert fragments, and many faunal bones. The sherds came from two vessels, including a small bichrome Provincia Plano-Relief bowl. The combustion of materials in this niche—which clearly was not designed as an oven—was sufficiently intense to crack the cut stones above the niche. It is possible that the reuse of this administrative space to perform this ceremony aimed at terminating its

FIGURE 7.5. *Close-up photo of the on-floor figurine cache during excavation, after the sherds covering it had been removed (looking southeast; photo by Lamoureux-St-Hilaire).*

original function. The combination of fine-orange sherds of the Balancan ceramic group with a radiocarbon date of 836–[851]–866 CE, which came from a charcoal sample found near the niche, indicates that the palace's abandonment occurred late during the second half of the ninth century.

The second ritual assemblage consisted of twenty-five fragments of ceramic figurines found "cached" on the floor of the Northeast Courtyard, tucked in the corner formed by the west wall of Str. 13Q-4B1 and the north edge of its exterior bench (figure 7.5; Lamoureux-St-Hilaire 2018:267–73). These figurine fragments were found in different states of preservation, primarily consisting of heads, but also limbs and other body fragments that were originally part of 17 anthropomorphic and 8 zoomorphic figurines. This unique on-floor cache, which did not include a complete figurine, was informally covered by fourteen sherds. Figurine fragments of this type were common in the palace, especially in the later middens, where their crafting was documented. We suggest that these figurine fragments—as "autonomous" artifacts—served a ceremonial function, perhaps as divining tokens (Freidel, Masson, and Rich 2016) and were thus placed there by a ritual specialist who planned to eventually recover them. The close spatial relationship between this cache and the burned offering suggests that they were both associated with an abandonment-related ceremony. That said, this ceremony was far less formal than the reverential termination rituals that closed off Halcón South and Str. 13Q-40.

These on-floor and above-floor assemblages are the latest evidence available for the La Corona regal palace, which had been fully abandoned by circa 900 CE. These discrete assemblages reflect a gradual abandonment during which abandoners carried most of their valuables away, while leaving some behind because they probably planned to return. While anticlimactic, this abandonment pattern aligns perfectly with the gradual detachment from power characterizing the Sak Nikte' royal court.

SUMMARY AND DISCUSSION

We began this chapter by contextualizing and characterizing the political institution of the Classic Maya center of La Corona, which was physically anchored in the site's regal palace: a large acropolis built under the auspices of the most powerful monarchs of the era, the Kaanul kings. We then addressed the fate of the Sak Nikte' royal court during the next 150 years by describing five sequential chronological events: the Halcón B and Tucán Phases of construction, the Early and Late Tucán occupations, and the Abandonment Phase. These periods were discussed by addressing the archaeologically detected interactions between the members of the court and their architectural landscape. These five facets of the late Sak Nikte' government may be summarized in three phases of detachment from power:

1. Following the implosion of Kaanul, the Sak Nikte' government transitioned out of its traditional form of colonial governance. This reformulation of rulership was first marked by the decommissioning of the Kaanul embassy, circa 750 CE, which somewhat disentangled the local rulers from their overlords. These events were followed by the expansion and transformation of the palace's north section, from 750 to 850 CE (comprising the Halcón B and Tucán Phases of construction). This successful institutional adaptation to a changing geopolitical landscape retained ideological ties with Kaanul, created a beautiful royal courtyard, and expanded the economic production of the court.
2. Throughout the ninth century, transformations in the regal palace indicate that the Sak Nikte' government progressively reduced its political activities. This downscaling was discernible by the increasing disuse of

areas surrounding the Northeast Courtyard, beginning with the West Plaza, followed by Str. 13Q-4O and the Sunken Patio. This process of decommission reflected a shift away from the ancillary activities supporting the ceremonial and political gatherings of the royal court, and away from administrative activities associated with priesthood. Beyond the reduction in political activities, this process resulted in the accumulation of large quantities of refuse over previously high-usage areas (i.e., preabandonment middens), indicating a trend away from an orthodox use of palatial space. Additionally, these shifts in palatial practices indicate a reduction in the ancillary labor force required at court.

3. After a century of contraction, the nobles occupying this late palace probably hardly consisted of a royal court. The final abandonment of the palace occurred around 900 CE, but was not led with the same flourish that characterized the termination of its southern section. Instead, the act appears to have been done with little ceremony and probably with the anticipation that this small court was to eventually bounce back, which it never did.

CONCLUSION

The detachment by the Sak Nikte' governing elite from their palace was a decidedly discursive process. This disentanglement between government and institutional architecture was so long and involved that it resulted in multi-faceted physical alterations, or detachment-related behaviors, ranging from the enshrinement of a room to the burial of pathways under refuse. It was challenging to synthesize this process in a short chapter. Yet, we hope that our discussion of this resilient, yet ultimately failed government highlights the importance of closely examining architectural institutions while addressing questions of civilizational collapse. Beyond the Classic Maya, this case study addresses the broader question of detachment from power among client states, or colonies of hegemonic states, and the practices adopted by the rulers of these polities to disentangle from their overlords—a postcolonial process that transformed their geopolitical world.

ACKNOWLEDGMENTS

We would like to thank the IDAEH for continuously supporting research by PRALC over the past decade. None of the PRALC discoveries would be possible without the work of the talented archaeological workers of San

Andrés and Dolores, Petén. Rubén Morales-Forte (Tulane University) was also instrumental in some of the archaeological work behind this paper. Excavations in the La Corona palace were funded by an NSF-DDIG (Award ID: 1623787), Tulane University, PACUNAM, the Alphawood Foundation, and the Louisiana Board of Regents. Lamoureux-St-Hilaire would also like to thank the two amazing research libraries that supported him during the authoring of this chapter: Dumbarton Oaks (2017–18) and the Boundary End Center (2018–19). In particular, the work of the late Bridget Gazzo of Dumbarton Oaks was truly appreciated during the writing of this chapter.

8

Detachment and Reattachment to Place in the Bassar Region of Northern Togo

Phillip de Barros

DOI: 10.5876/9781646420087.c008

HISTORICAL BACKGROUND

This chapter discusses site abandonment or detachment from place in the context of West Africa, specifically the Bassar region of northern Togo, where the author has studied the history of traditional ironworking and its sociocultural context since the 1980s (de Barros 1985, 1986, 1988, 2000, 2001, 2012, 2013a, 2013b, 2016, 2017). Bassar ironworking occurred during the Early Iron Age (400 BC to AD 150) and Later Iron Age (AD 1200 to AD 1950). This chapter will focus on the Later Iron Age, especially from the sixteenth century onward. Following up on research by Cameron (2013), Glowacki (2015), Lamoureux-St-Hilaire et al. (2015), McAnany and Lamoureux-St-Hilaire (2013), and others in the New World, as well as Gerard Chouin (2009), de Barros (1985), and Stéphan Dugast (1992) in West Africa, the author will discuss the following topics to the extent the data permit: (1) the reasons for site abandonment, including stressors affecting the site abandoned, and enablers that attracted migrants to settle in a new place; (2) what signatures of site abandonment were left behind, if any; (3) the migratory routes that led the migrants to eventually establish a new, permanent settlement; (4) the processes involving accommodation with the new host and the rituals associated with settling in a new place; and (5) the material, spiritual, and ritual relationships between the new place and the abandoned site.

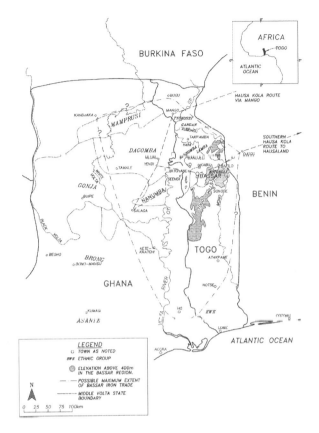

FIGURE 8.1. *Bassar and Bassar iron trade in relationship to states of the Middle Volta Basin and Hausa kola routes ca. 1800; village migration sources also shown, e.g., Meung.*

THE BASSAR REGION: ENVIRONMENT AND CULTURE

The Bassar region is bisected by the Katcha, a tributary of the Mô, which flows into the Oti River, where it joins the Volta in Ghana to the west. It is bordered by iron-rich hills and mountains, including the nearly pure hematite ores of Bandjeli (figures 8.1 and 8.2). The climate has alternating dry and rainy seasons, with an average annual rainfall of fifty-five inches. The savanna-woodland vegetation has been significantly impacted by deforestation and cultivation. Subsistence is based primarily on shifting horticulture focused on sorghum and yams with millet and *arachides* (groundnuts) as major secondary crops. For centuries Bassar have exported foodstuffs and iron products for cloth, charcoal, slaves, and cattle.

Since circa 1800, most Bassar have lived in the four population centers of Bassar (65,000), Kabu-Sara, Bandjeli, and Bitchabe (figure 8.2). The Bassar represent

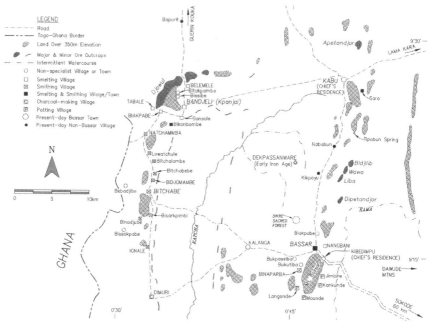

FIGURE 8.2. *Bassar region showing iron ores, chiefdoms centered on Bassar and Kabu, and specialist villages at contact (1890s).*

a mixture of indigenous Paragourma-speaking groups and immigrants over the centuries from the north (Lamba, Gangan, Konkomba, Tyokossi, Gurma), west (Gonja and Dagomba), and east (Tem or Kotokoli, Tchamba, Kabiye). These immigrants came seeking a place of refuge from regional slave-raiding, for its farmlands, and in some cases because of its iron industry (Cornevin 1962:24–44; de Barros 1985:57–58, 2012; Dugast 1992:107–209; Martinelli 1982:3–10; Martinelli 1984). The neighboring Kabiye, despite using some of the most intensive farming techniques in West Africa (Sauvaget 1981:72), suffered from famine due to high population densities, forcing residents to sell some children to the Bassar to feed the remaining ones (Dugast 1992:202–4; Lucien-Brun 1987:23–25, 75–76). Enslaved males were used for field labor and enslaved females as domestic servants who sometimes became their owners' wives. Over time, most of these immigrant and slave populations were assimilated into existing, often heterogeneous Bassar clans (Cornevin 1962:115–16).

Bassar communities are composed of a localized exogamous kin group or clan or *kitingban* (an amalgam of several residence groups) belonging to one or more clans. Some clans are split among different communities, such as the chiefly

Nataka clan and the ironworking Bissib and Koli clans. Upon the arrival of the Germans (1890), several villages specialized in smelting, smithing, charcoal making, or potting, while often farming as well (figure 8.2). At contact, Bassar political organization consisted of the Bassar and Kabou chiefdoms in the east, which arose circa 1780–1810 and 1850, respectively, and the relatively autonomous groups to the west presided over by the most senior lineage or *ukpil* (clan elder).

BRIEF HISTORY OF THE BASSAR REGION
SINCE THE LATER IRON AGE

IMPACT OF LARGE-SCALE IRON PRODUCTION AND
THE RISE OF LONG-DISTANCE TRADE

The Later Iron Age begins with the introduction of induced (natural) draft furnace technology in the thirteenth century with iron products traded to neighboring populations (de Barros 1985, 1986). The emergence of the Dagomba, Gonja, and Mamprusi states in the Middle Volta Basin of neighboring Ghana (figure 8.1) during the fifteenth and sixteenth centuries greatly increased the demand for iron weapons, horse paraphernalia, and chain mail for their cavalries, along with the demand for iron hoes and axes for basic subsistence activities. These states, along with Bono-Mansu and then Asante, stimulated long-distance trade into the Middle Volta Basin by the Hausa (see below). Bassar responded with a spectacular growth in iron production between the later sixteenth and eighteenth centuries (de Barros 1986, 2001, 2016:91–106; Levtzion 1968:5–6). Major iron production centers developed north of Mount Djowul, north of Kabu near Apetandjor, and near Tipabun Spring south of Kabu (figure 8.2). Bassar iron markets (e.g., Natchamba) and Bassar blacksmiths organized trading parties to adjacent areas. Bassar iron was traded throughout most of Togo and much of eastern Ghana (de Barros 1986, 2001). This period was also a time of marked population growth due to better living standards, the importation of Kabiye slaves as field laborers, and the immigration of peoples fleeing regional strife and/or seeking new opportunities.

The growth of the iron industry led to larger, more sedentary villages; a population shift closer to major ore deposits (de Barros 1988); specialization within the iron industry; and a rising standard of living for ironworkers, especially lineage elders who could trade their iron products for food, cowrie shells (special purpose money), cattle, sheep/goats, slave labor, and imported goods, such as Kirotashi agate beads from the Niger River and European glass beads (de Barros 1986; Klose [1899] 1964:162–63). A new regional settlement pattern developed between 1600 and the later eighteenth century consisting of larger villages with satellite hamlets, which may have resulted in incipient big men or simple chiefdoms (de Barros 1988), but oral traditions do not mention chiefdoms prior to the late eighteenth or nineteenth century.

In present-day Ghana, the rise of the Middle Volta Basin states, as well as Bono-Mansu, and Asante (figure 8.1), led to the rise of three major Hausa caravan routes from Nigeria (Levtzion 1968:24): the first through Niger and Burkina Faso (not shown); the second through Niger to Mango in northern Togo, both continuing southward to Yendi and Salaga; and a third through northern Dahomey (Djugu), Kotokoli country, the Bassar region, and onward to Yendi and/or Salaga (Barbier 1982; de Barros 1985:325–29, 2001:68; Norris 1984; see figure 8.1). For much of the 1800s, most of the trade between Hausaland and Salaga passed through Bassar, with caravans of close to 1,000 people and as many pack animals (Clapperton 1829:68; Levtzion 1968:25). This southern route became popular due to a major rise in the demand for kola nuts in Hausaland after Uthman dan Fodio's 1804 jihad, which forbid alcoholic beverages. Kola became a major substitute, and due to its perishable nature, the route through Bassar was preferred as it was the shortest (de Barros 2001; Norris 1984).

Because of intensive raiding of the Bassar region during the later eighteenth through later nineteenth centuries by the Dagomba and Tyokossi cavalry-led forces, most populations fled the Bassar peneplain, leaving it deserted of any major village or hamlet. The end result was the rise of communities beneath major mountains where they could take refuge (de Barros 1985:439, 653–61, 1988, 2001; see figure 8.2).

Regional Slave Raiding by the Dagomba and the Tyokossi

The rise of the transatlantic slave trade, especially during the seventeenth and eighteenth centuries, and the growth of the Asante State, saw slaves flowing increasingly from Kumasi to the coast. The Asante obtained their slaves through war, tribute from conquered states, such as the Dagomba and Gonja, or from the sale of gold, with surplus slaves sold to European coastal markets (de Barros 2001:68; Wilks 1995:76–78, 223–29). Beginning in the later 1700s, the Bassar region was subjected to major slave raiding by the Dagomba from the west and the Tyokossi Kingdom from the north (de Barros 2001:68–70).

The Dagomba. Since at least the seventeenth century, both the Dagomba and Gonja States had occasionally raided acephalous peoples for both slaves and cattle, including the Konkomba and the Bassar (Tait 1961:9). In the mid-eighteenth century, the Asante invaded and conquered the Gonja and Dagomba States, but tribute did not begin until the 1770s, under the reign of

Asantehene Osei Kwadwo (Wilks 1975:21–23). While accounts vary (Dugast 1992:66), Ivor Wilks (1975:432) affirms that in the early nineteenth century, the annual Dagomba tribute was 2,000 slaves, 800 cattle, and 1,600 sheep, which were often paid through slave raiding. The most violent periods occurred 1856–60 and 1867–76, especially 1873–76 (de Barros 1985:653–56; Dugast 1992:66). In the first case, the Asante demanded the Dagomba pay the tribute the Asante had been largely ignoring or the Dagomba's capital would be destroyed, which led to immediate Dagomba raids in 1856, with several hundred captives taken away (Tamakloe 1931, cited in Dugast 1992:67; see also Cornevin 1957:85; and Froelich and Alexandre 1960:259–60). After 1867, the Dagomba under Ya Na Abdullah (ca. 1864–76) led a series of raids against the Bassar that culminated in the Great Dagomba War of 1873–76 and the siege of the Bassar agglomeration beneath Mount Bassar, which finally ended with the death of the Ya Na Abdullah (Cornevin 1962:57; de Barros 1985:655–56; Wilks 1975:67–68, 305–6). The Bassar were beaten but took refuge at the farms and water sources on Mount Bassar (Dugast 1992:67; Klose 1964:173). While the Dagomba never conquered Bassar, there is some evidence that Bandjeli may have periodically paid tribute or gifts and possibly Bassar itself (Dugast 1992:63; Rattray 1932:580). Interestingly enough, the western Bassar were also perceived by the Dagomba as their economic partner, especially in Bitchabe, which has been populated since the sixteenth or seventeenth century by Dagomba blacksmiths who emigrated from Meung north of Yendi (Dugast 1992:68).

The Tyokossi. The Tyokossi (Anufom) came from the Kong Kingdom in east central Ivory Coast and later became mercenaries who successfully fought for the Gonja State circa 1750. The Tyokossi were composed of three elements: *donzom* (Mande cavalry warrior lineages), led by the Ouattara of the Kong royal family; their Muslim advisors/merchants, the Djula (Dioula), also of Mande origin; and a large group of foot soldiers of Akan (Agni-Baoule) origin. After Gonja they continued to serve as mercenaries and/or by pillaging local villages for booty and slaves. They later settled at Sansanné-Mango in circa 1764 along the Oti River, 125 kilometers (75 miles) north of Bassar (de Barros 2001; Dugast 1992:70; Norris 1984). The Tyokossi first established authority over local Gangan villages and then spent a decade or more destroying the former capital of the Gurma confederation in southern Burkina Faso.

In the 1790s, they turned their attention southward pillaging Djugu and Aledjo Kura in western Benin, as well as the Kotokoli in Bafilo and Dawude, and the Bassar (de Barros 1985:656–57, 2001). These attacks usually had two goals: to obtain slaves and to defeat the local populations to force them to pay tribute, largely food (de Barros 2001:70; Norris 1984:164). According to E. G.

Norris (1986), Tyokossi tactics and society underwent major changes in the nineteenth century. What began as local pillaging among the Gangan led to an ostentatious warring prestige competition after 1850 among the donzom lineages as part of an ever-widening circle of predatory pillaging. As long as villages paid their tribute they were left alone, but the donzom expanded their raids beyond these villages to wreak havoc in more remote settlements. Different village groups were dominated and extorted by different donzom lineages (Dugast 1992:71–73; Norris 1986:127–31).

Bassar oral traditions say little about such Tyokossi raiding. Some speak of attacks in the northern portions of the region, such as Bandjeli, Bapuré, and Kabou (de Barros 1985:657–58; Dugast 1992:719; Klose 1903:309). Informants in Bitakpambe and Belemele believed the Tyokossi attacked them when they lived at Bitakpambe Tapu and Titur north of Mt. Djowul (de Barros 1985:658), but Bandjeli informants speak more commonly of Dagomba attacks. Heinrich Klose (1903:309) thought Bandjeli and Bapuré were still paying tribute (usually hoes) to either the Dagomba or the Tyokossi in 1897, but local informants deny this ever occurred (cf. Rattray 1932:580). To the southwest, Bitchabe does not recall such Tyokossi raids, but in the town of Bassar, early German observers Klose (1903:309) and von Zech (1898:131) believed the Tyokossi held sway over the region, and Norris (1986:128) says Tyokossi oral traditions confirm this. However, late nineteenth-century Tyokossi settlements in Bassar (Kodjodumpu) and in Bandjeli (Sansale) were actually the result of attempts by the Tyokossi to create a temporary alliance with the Bassar against expanding Dagomba incursions to the east that were disrupting the Hausa caravan trade route through their home base in Mango (Dugast 1992:20–725).

EFFECTS OF SLAVE RAIDING ON BASSAR
REGION SETTLEMENT PATTERNS

The significantly increased tempo of slave raiding during the later eighteenth and early-to-mid-nineteenth centuries led to the near total abandonment of the Bassar peneplain on either side of the Katcha River by the early nineteenth century and a regrouping of populations in mountain refuge areas as shown in figure 8.2 (excluding the modern villages of Nababoun and Kikpayu). These migrations resulted in the rise of the Bassar agglomeration containing at least forty different village neighborhoods or communities (Dugast 1987). Major ironworking centers moved to new locations: to south of Djowul Mountain near Bandjeli; to Sara near the newly founded (ca. 1850) Kabou chiefdom; to north of Nangbani near Bassar; and closer to the mountains at Bitchabe. Populations also left from the Dikre sacred forest area and settled near Mount Bassar at Nangbani, Bukpassiba, Wadande-Bassar, and Kibedimpou. The intensive slave raiding leading to this major settlement shift is also associated with the rise of the Bassar Chiefdom circa 1780 and 1810 (de Barros 1985:723–27; 2012:80; Dugast 1992). As raids again intensified in the second half of the nineteenth century, especially by the Dagomba, additional smaller-scale migrations took place either to other nearby mountain areas or closer to, or up onto, mountain terraces or mountain tops, as was the case during the Dagomba siege of the town of Bassar. These migrations solidified a settlement pattern of villages near mountain slopes and farmers' fields and clan territorial sacred sites up to 10–12 kilometers (5–7 miles) out onto the plain where they had formerly lived.

ESTABLISHING OR CREATING AN ATTACHMENT TO PLACE

Before discussing the process of site abandonment and links between new settlements and places abandoned, it is necessary to provide some basic information about how the Bassar find and create an attachment to a new place. Each Bassar clan has its *diwaal* (principal spirit or force) that occupies a place central to clan identity and territory. This sacred place is usually associated with a sacred grove where the clan's principal collective diwaal resides within the ground. It is thought to be a spirit or powerful force that embodies and controls a specific locality of earth or land. Annual or periodic sacrifices of renewal are made to this diwaal at the place where it resides, a place called *ditangbandi* in eastern Bassar and *litaŋbanli* in western Bassar, due to dialectical differences. In Bassar culture and in many other related Voltaic cultures (Dugast 2004; Liberski-Bagnoud 2002), when people create a new settlement, it is necessary to "capture the land" in a given locality where a diwaal is "discovered" to reside, often through divination. These cultural groups do not use the classic conceptual dichotomy typical of many parts of sub-Saharan Africa between the secular chief and the earth chief or priest. Instead of an earth priest, there is a person responsible for ritually serving and maintaining the sacred place that was captured, the litaŋbanli, where the diwaal resides. This individual is called *utandaan* in Bassar, and he is always chosen through divination (Dugast 1992:645). He is responsible for maintaining and protecting its location, that is, keeping it spiritually healthy and free of bad spirits, as well as keeping away enemies, such as the Dagomba or Kotokoli—keeping it "beautiful" for both firstcomers and latecomers who will make the village grow and be successful (Dugast 2004:210–15). The utandaan is also responsible for other types of clan (collective) diwaals. The utandaan and elders are in charge of offering them libations in the form of sorghum beer made from the first maturing sorghum sheaf or grains, prior to the actual harvest (Dugast 1992:643). According to local informants, sometimes a diwaal renewal ceremony may include the sacrifice of a cow, but it may also be a goat or sheep. In cases where fire has damaged the sacred forest or grove where the litaŋbanli is located, a goat, a bird, and red palm oil may be required to clean and dress the wounds of the litaŋbanli (de Barros and Assouman 2017). Such rituals also help maintain land tenure rights on formerly inhabited ancestral lands.

There are two groups of people associated with a settlement and its locality: the *bitindambi* (possessors of the locality or clan territory) and the *binikɔkab* (strangers or those who entered later; Dugast 2004:210). They are often referred to as firstcomers and latecomers (de Barros 2013b; Kopytoff 1987). To be a firstcomer in Bassar (and in many other Voltaic cultural groups), one has to be a part of the group involved in the founding of clan territory in a new, unoccupied area by "capturing" it. Such new territory is inhabited by beasts and genies and other hostile spirits, both visible and invisible, which need to be kept at bay to render the land hospitable. So to "capture the earth or locality" means to tame or civilize or humanize it. This is accomplished by placing a powerful medicine, usually an object prepared by a "specialist" or "powerful person" who will become part of the bitindambi, which is buried in a place that becomes the "principal place" of the new settlement or litaŋbanli. A set of taboos are associated with this founding, which if violated, can rent the fabric of the protected space. Once such a place is created, it is important to keep it "beautiful," or free of potential evils. The institution of the Bassar fire dance is one of the primary ways that such potential evil forces can be detected and removed from the locality. It is often performed after a series of bad events or bad omens, and it reveals what bad forces or spirits are present and how best to remove or avoid them. Once performed, these arrangements or acts called *sala*—which can include libations, sacrifices, and/or the fire dance—are believed to restore equilibrium and restore the "beauty" of the locality (Dugast 2004:210–13). Each group has its principal collective or clan diwaal, but other, less powerful and all-encompassing diwaal may be "discovered" or be associated with powerful ancestors, ancestral heroes, or those associated with bringing rain, for example. Diwaal may also be associated with "strong natural places," such as a stone in the ground or a tree(s) associated with key food resources or key water sources. Finally, some powerful men escape death and simply disappear into the ground; later such a place may be elevated to the status of a diwaal (de Barros and Assouman 2017; Dugast 1992:638–88).

SITE ABANDONMENT OR FORCED DETACHMENT
FROM PLACE: STRESSORS AND ENABLERS

Several regional examples of site abandonment during the sixteenth and eighteenth centuries that led groups to eventually settle in the Bassar region will be discussed, with migrations ranging from thirty to seventy-five kilometers (18–45 miles). In some instances, later smaller migrations of the same groups of less than a mile are included. The emphasis will be on the stressors and enablers leading to such migrations. The author has not seen or heard of any evidence in Bassar oral traditions that site abandonment rituals were practiced (Stéphan Dugast, personal communication 2017), and the author has not detected obvious vestiges of such rituals in major excavations at the four-hectare Later Iron Age smelting village of Titur (de Barros 2016) or at the twenty-eight hectare Early Iron Age ironworking village of Dekpassanware (de Barros 2013a).

Migrations from Meung near Yendi (Ghana) to Bitchabe

Meung is just north of Yendi, the former capital of the Dagomba State, and Bitchabe is about seventy kilometers southeast of Meung. Several migrating groups are involved, all now living in Bitchabe: the former settlers of nearby Kpacaanli (site BASSAR- or BAS-379), who now live in Bitchabe-Kpandjal; and the former occupants of site BAS-323, who now live in Bitchabe-Tapu, Paapu Jool, and Naataaku (figures 8.1–8.3). Bitchabe means "the blacksmiths" in Bassar. Archaeological data and oral traditions suggest Bitchabe was founded in the sixteenth century. Informants from all groups concerned agree that they are descended from Dagomba blacksmiths once living in Meung, though the data suggest that those at Kpacaanli probably preceded the other three. Local informants state they came directly from Meung to Kpacaanli just north of today's Bitchabe, whereas the other three groups first settled between Tabale and Biakpabe in the Bandjeli smelting zone (figure 8.2), all linked to a common ancestor, Gbampul. Later, disputes forced the groups to head south with a brief stop near the smithing village of Natchamba before settling in Bitchabe (BAS-323). Lands were provided to these incoming migrants by the inhabitants of Bidjomambe, who claim indigenous status. A fifth group came later from Meung to Bandjeli (also called Kpandjal), but accusations of sorcery forced them to leave. They eventually joined groups who had left Kpacaanli to settle in what is known as Bitchabe-Kpandjal (figure 8.3) (de Barros and Assouman 2017).

Based on oral traditions, the primary stressor that led these groups to abandon Meung was warfare and/or raiding. Other stressors during their

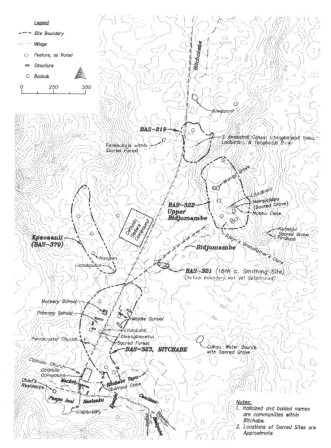

FIGURE 8.3.
*Bitchabe region
with key village,
archaeological, and
sacred sites.*

migrations included accusations of sorcery and an inability to get along with
the host region in Bandjeli. Large-scale iron production arose in the Bassar
region in the mid-sixteenth century (de Barros 1986, 2016:1, 2017). Eventually
the Bandjeli zone would become known for smelting and the Bitchabe zone
for its smithing. The primary enabler that led to migration to the western
Bassar region was the presence of a major ironworking industry, where these
Dagomba smiths might find opportunities to conduct their profession. Some
tried the Bandjeli area first, but all eventually settled and helped to develop
the smithing zone of Bitchabe. Later, in the mid-to-late-nineteenth century, raiding by the cavalry-led Dagomba looking for slaves and cattle to pay
Asante tribute led to the abandonment of BAS-323 and Kpacaanli as groups
took refuge on the mountain slope, where Bitchabe exists today.

Migrations from Seendi (Seni) in Ghana to Bitchobebe

Seendi appears to correspond to the village or town of Sheini in the Bassar-speaking area of eastern Ghana about thirty kilometers (eighteen miles) southwest of present-day Bitchobebe (figures 8.1 and 8.2). When asked about their origins, local informants focus on the mythical story about how the people of Bidjomambe and Bitchalambe were being attacked by a monstrous bird that preyed upon children and livestock. They called upon a great hunter among the peoples of Seendi named Naabaasi to slay the "monster." He was successful, and in gratitude, the *utandaan* and elders from the two local communities gave them ownership of part of their lands, which led to migrations from Seendi and the creation of Bitchobebe, which was initially at site BAS-319 (figures 8.1–8.3). Archaeological data from BAS-319 indicate this move occurred in the later seventeenth or possibly early eighteenth century. This story provides an enabler, the offer of good farmland, but it does not explain what stressor would have pushed members of the communities to migrate. One possibility includes Dagomba raids. Oral traditions from the present-day potting village of Langonde beneath Mt. Bassar (figure 8.2) speak of fleeing their original homeland at Seendi to avoid such raids (Dugast 1987). BAS-319 itself is located at the foot of a linear, north-south mountain that also abuts Bidjomambe (figure 8.3). Another enabler, not present in the Meung migrations, was the common Bassar language. Once at Bitchobebe, these farmers became blacksmiths through apprenticeships with those in Bitchabe (de Barros and Assouman 2017).

Migration from the Tyokossi Region to Titur and Later to Belemele

The village of Belemele is in the Bandjeli region, where many villages practiced smelting for centuries until the mid-twentieth century (figure 8.2). Belemele migrations include a trek of about 70–75 kilometers (42–45 miles) from south of Mango in the Kumongou River valley to the site of Titur (BAS-295) north of Bandjeli, followed by short migrations of less than a mile to the Belemele of today (figures 8.1, 8.4, and 8.5). No specific village site is known as the place of origin, but the area was inhabited by the indigenous Gangan and the Bicakob (Tyokossi), the latter of whom exploited and taxed the former beginning in the mid-eighteenth century. The primary stressor for site abandonment thus appears to have been violence inflicted by the Tyokossi with their constant pillaging and tribute-seeking. As a result they fled—men, women, and children—packing their belongings on their donkeys (de Barros

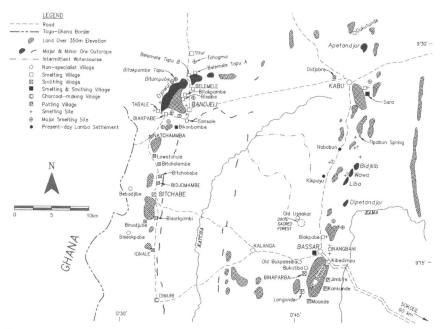

FIGURE 8.4. *Bassar region at contact, including villages/sites from 1825 to the 1890s, especially north of Bandjeli.*

and Assouman 2017). After a short stay in Bapuré, they settled at Titur, first as farmers. They state they learned smelting from neighboring groups in the area and did most of their smelting at Tchogma 1 (BAS-4) 500 meters to the southeast, the largest accumulation of slag of the Bassar region (figure 8.5) (de Barros 1986, 2016). No clear enabler emerges but the land was sufficiently fertile to remain, and learning a new trade in a thriving economic region was clearly a motivation for staying. Later, due to serious slave raiding by both the Dagomba and Tyokossi in the late eighteenth and early nineteenth centuries, they abandoned Titur exposed on the plain, migrating less than a mile to Belemele Tapu A (BAS-366) at the foot of Tchogma Mountain, eventually moving to their present-day location via Belemele Tapu B during the German and French colonial periods (figure 8.5). Thus, violence and warfare/raiding were the primary stressors for both migrations; the enabler once they arrived was probably the potential to make a better living in smelting than one could at farming.

The only discordant note about the above scenario is chronological. Recent archaeological excavations and C14 dates show Titur was settled by at least

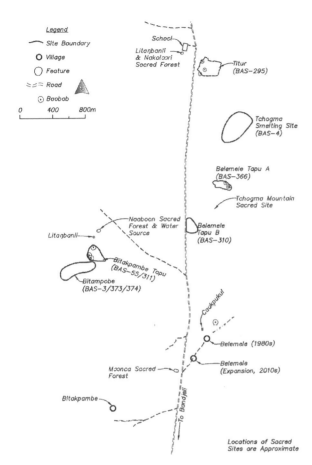

Legend
— Site Boundary
○ Village
◯ Feature
≋ Road
⊙ Baobab

0   400   800m

School
Litaŋbanii
& Nakolaari
Sacred Forest

Titur
(BAS–295)

Tchogma
Smelting Site
(BAS–4)

Belemele Tapu A
(BAS–366)

Tchogma Mountain
Sacred Site

Naaboon Sacred
Forest & Water
Source

Belemele
Tapu B
(BAS–310)

Litaŋbanii

Bitakpambe Tapu
(BAS–55/311)

Bitampobe
(BAS–3/373/374)

Caukpukui

Belemele (1980s)

Belemele
(Expansion, 2010s)

Moonca Sacred
Forest

Bitakpambe

To Bandjeli

Locations of Sacred
Sites are Approximate

FIGURE 8.5. *Northern Bandjeli region with key village, archaeological, and sacred sites.*

the sixteenth century with evidence for smelting in the fourteenth through fifteenth centuries (de Barros 2016:94). However, if the Tyokossi were the cause of the migrations toward Titur, this activity could not have taken place earlier than the mid-eighteenth century, when the Tyokossi first arrived at Mango. This suggests that there were people living and smelting at Titur when the migrating group arrived, something oral traditions do not explain.

Migration from Takpamba to Bitampobe/Bitakpambe Tapu

Bitakpambe is also in the Bandjeli smelting zone (figures 8.2 and 8.5). The place of origin of Bitakpambe's ancestors was the present-day village of

Takpamba situated 15 kilometers (9 miles) north of the Kara River and about 57 kilometers (34 miles) from its ultimate destination known as Bitampobe, then Bitakpambe Tapu (figures 8.1, 8.4, and 8.5). The primary stressor was the violence and strain of living under Tyokossi domination as farmers forced to pay tribute. They migrated with their "brothers," the Bitampoobi (Dugast 2016:8) or Bitampobe (de Barros 1986) and settled near the northern edge of Mount Djowul (figure 8.4), as early as the mid-sixteenth century according to surface pottery (de Barros 1985:741). No C14 dates are available. The migrants came as farmers but learned smelting from unidentified neighboring populations. After initially living together, they quarreled and eventually split apart (Dugast 2016:8), perhaps in the late eighteenth / early nineteenth centuries (de Barros 1985:693–96), into two separate habitation and associated smelting areas: Bitampobe (BAS-3/373/374) and Bitakpambe Tapu (BAS-55/311). As with the ancestors of the Belemele, the primary stressor for site abandonment was again violence and raiding, and enablers may have included land that was sufficiently fertile and the ability to make a good living by adopting smelting. Again, the same chronological problem regarding the Tyokossi as an explanation for site abandonment presents itself here, given that archaeological data indicate settlement at Bitampobe as early as the sixteenth century.

With the advent of Dagomba and possibly Tyokossi raiding in the late eighteenth or early nineteenth century, the people at Bitakpambe Tapu did not flee as they were already at the foot of Mount Djowul (figure 8.4) and could easily take refuge on the mountain slopes. In fact, an old informant spoke of how their fathers showed them where they had killed the biggest of the Dagomba cavalry men and noted that spurs still show up while cultivating (de Barros and Assouman 2017). They dwellers of the mountain slopes gradually migrate south to present-day Bitakpambe between the later nineteenth century through the 1920s (de Barros 1985:698–99; 2016:9). During roughly the same period, the Belemele migrated to Belemele Tapu B and then onto their present-day location, as did those at Bitampobe who eventually settled at Tabale (figures 8.2 and 8.5).

RELATIONSHIPS MAINTAINED WITH ABANDONED LANDSCAPES
Sacred Groves and Diwaal/ litanbanli

Chouin (2009:150–55), in his discussion of the ecological, historical, political, social, and ritual significance of sacred groves in Africa, uses the following typology to distinguish types: "sacred groves associated with burial grounds (and fortuitously with old settlements); sacred groves associated with abandoned settlements (and fortuitously with burials); and, sacred groves that are not associated with any archaeological remains, with the exception of those on the surface, eventually produced by ritual practices (155)."

A sacred grove that is associated with the principal diwaal linked to clan identity and territory would fall into the third category, as this diwaal/litaŋbanli is always situated outside of habitation zones (Dugast 1992:643), ranging from a considerable distance to relatively close proximity. Often its location corresponds to a distinctly noticeable element of the natural environment (a prominent rock outcrop, a hilltop, a cave, a tall tree, or a section of a stream), and it is surrounded by dense vegetation of shrubs and trees. The presence of the dense vegetation is the result of the strict application of certain taboos or requirements, such as no wood cutting, no gathering of dead wood, no burning, the clearance and maintenance of a fire break around the forest, and sometimes the creation and maintenance of a secret, low entrance and passageway used to access ceremonial areas known only to the utandaan and clan elders (643). The total lack of human exploitation makes it appear to outsiders as if it were a remnant of primeval forest (Gnon 1967:30). Finally, the apparent pristine nature of the sacred forest, free of human exploitation and elements of the world of the present, is critical for the maintenance of the privileged relationship between the diwaal/litaŋbanli and the primeval earth, a world essential to human survival because from it come the seeds of all things existing on earth; in fact, one must enter the forest for such ceremonies without any clothing or at least with no modern clothing or technology (de Barros and Assouman 2017; Dugast 2008:21 22). If a clan abandons their original site and does not migrate too far away, its utandaan and key elders will revisit this sacred grove to perform periodic or annual renewal rituals to keep the place beautiful. Note that other collective (clan) diwaal of lesser importance may be associated with a sacred grove situated within abandoned settlements (Chouin's second type).

EXAMPLES OF RITUALS ENTERTAINED WITH ABANDONED LANDSCAPES

BITCHABE AND KPACAANLI

The peoples living in the Bitchabe Tapu, Paapu Jool, and Naataaku sections of Bitchabe captured the land at their principal diwaal/litaŋbanli situated in a large sacred grove or forest in the heart of site BAS-323, within 50–100 meters or more from former habitation and smithing areas to the north and south (figure 8.3). Prior to the creation of the Bitchabe-Bandjeli road, a fire break was regularly created to prevent fire damage to the grove; this is still done today but only to the south and southwest. Annual renewal ceremonies take place at the litaŋbanli that may involve the sacrifice of a cow or goat or bird(s) and libations of beer made from the sorghum's first fruits. When a cow is to be sacrificed, all three communities contribute to the cost as do their daughter communities who settled in Binadjube and Bisarkpimbi to the south (figure 8.2). Other ceremonies take place at four other sacred trees situated within a few tens of meters of the litaŋbanli on both sides of the road, including a Dinaŋgbansitul (baobab) that has a major beehive said to contain the "soldiers" of litaŋbanli and, close by, a group of five Dinaakpɔkɔwaal (fruit trees) that is the locus of a diwaal associated with one of the wives of litaŋbanli (de Barros and Assouman 2017; figure 8.3). Ancestral burials exist in former habitation areas of BAS-323, especially near the Catholic Church and near the *dikumpool* (ancestral cone) of their common ancestor, Gbampul. Such a cone is an earthen butte reinforced with a cement layer to make it last longer (Dugast 1992:658, 666; Szwark 1981:94–95). Some families continue to bury old men in some of these old habitation areas.

What about links with Meung? According to Stéphan Dugast (personal communication 2017) links to abandoned sites are often not maintained to any significant degree if they are far away. In the case of Meung, some families have occasionally visited to maintain contacts with relatives, specifically at a place called Yaajooyi, but rituals are not maintained with former litaŋbanli. In fact, the migrants from Meung appear to have taken all important rituals with them to Bitchabe, a complex process that is beyond the scope of this chapter. However, it was recently learned that when a new chief is installed at Bitchabe, the dean of the elders that advise the chief must go to Meung to obtain a certain "power" (*puissance*) necessary for this process (Lantame Assouman, personal communication 2019).

North of BAS-323 is the site of Kpacaanli (BAS-379), 750 meters north of where its descendants live today in Bitchabe-Kpandjal (figure 8.3). It contains habitation middens, smithing slag deposits, baobabs, sacred sites, and a large *likumanjool* (iron bloom crushing mortar) used to break up the bloom prior to forging it into iron ingots and tools (de Barros 1985:166–73; Dugast 1986). The site probably goes back several centuries, and C14 dates are pending.

According to informants among the descendants of Kpacaanli, periodic or annual libations are offered at Licaakpukul (figure 8.3), a term associated with the difficult installation of a forge and its anvil and best translated as "person of the old forge" (Stéphan Dugast, personal communication 2017). In addition, old men continue to be buried in the vicinity of Licaakpukul, but only from Bitchabe-Kpandjal and not from the other three neighborhoods. The site of

Naajeen is within a sacred grove associated with a baobab tree where ceremonies and sacrifices are performed (figure 8.3).

Finally, informants from Kpacaanli and the three other groups state that vestiges left behind by libations and other rituals associated with litaŋbanli can include buried cattle bones, a few flat stones seats, piles of stones to identify its location, and/or overturned pots (or fragments thereof) used during rituals (de Barros and Assouman 2017).

BITCHOBEBE AND ABANDONED SITE BAS-319

The principle collective *diwaal* (clan) of Bitchobebe is located at Faŋkpukuja within a large forested area, whose northern part is a sacred grove (figures 8.2 and 8.3). This spot marks where a "strong stone," a stone associated with powerful forces, is now recognized as a diwaal because it provided the power necessary for the hunter Naabaasi to rid the area of the monstrous bird of prey. Fankpukuja's location is typical of a clan's principal diwaal in that it is away from inhabited areas. However, the principal diwaal or litaŋbanli for Bitchobebe is on a small mountain ridge in a sacred forest to the east (figure 8.3).

The former smithing site of Bitchobebe (BAS-319) contains other diwaal associated with three ancestral cones under a few trees in the center of the site. Sacrifices and libations supervised by the utandaan and elders are performed here, often on an annual basis. These include Utaŋgbankpil Yalko, along with his wife, Lombimbɔ, whom one asks for help to find a woman to marry, as well as the ancestral cone, Taŋgbanja Bɔki, which was formerly near Bidjomambe to the southeast, but which land disputes led to be moved to its current location (de Barros and Assouman 2017). Vestiges of these ceremonies include ceremonial pots and coins. It is not clear whether people bury their dead within BAS-319 today, but there is a ritual burial site for old men (Kuwaannii) associated with a tall tree and a few other smaller trees just twenty-five meters north of BAS-319 (figure 8.3), suggesting it may have been used well into the past.

UPPER BIDJOMAMBE

Bidjomambe is one of several indigenous villages in the Bassar region (Cornevin 1962:34). There are two important sacred groves associated with the village. The first represents its principal collective diwaal, Kutaajul, on top of Jooman, the mountain just to the east (figure 8.6). The second is called Nampajalpu, which means "sacred dwelling" and is associated with Bidjomambe's

FIGURE 8.6. *Sacred grove Kutaajul on top of the mountain (Bidjomambe).*

creation story, where God created the first man and his wife, Saba Bɔmbɔnli and Kalikambi, who multiplied to create the people of Bidjomambe (figure 8.3). Nampajalpu is up on a lower terrace of Jooman Mountain and is referred to as Upper Bidjomambe. When intensive Dagomba raids struck the Bassar region during the third quarter of the nineteenth century, an important part of the people of Bidjomambe took refuge on the terrace and did not leave until circa 1980. In part because of the creation story and in part because it represents an abandoned settlement, the area is frequently the site of various rituals, including the burial of Bidjomambe's utandaan (pl. *bitindambi*) well into the past. The grove also contains a diwaal/litaŋbanli and ancestral cones of the son of Saba Bɔmbɔnli, called Naabu, and, a few meters away, his aunt, Kibɔɔli. An enormous cone with embedded coins was constructed for Naabu in 2016 and important rituals are associated with Kibɔɔli, who is seen as bringing rain in her wake when she travels. Finally, there is an ancestral cone (diwaal) associated with a recent chief's grandfather, who avoided death and disappeared into the ground. In addition, since the author first mapped the site in 2013, at least five old men have been interred at Upper Bidjomambe, a sacred area where only male ancestors are buried. Both sacred groves, especially Kutaajul, are subject to animal sacrifices and the libations of sorghum's first fruits by the utandaan to keep the place beautiful. At Kutaajul, the animal sacrifices are not consumed as food, and numerous animal skulls are eroding down from the east side of the forest. There are also abandoned libation pots and numerous ball point pens left by students who have asked for help to succeed in school. Finally, fire breaks are maintained around both sacred groves (de Barros and Assouman 2017).

BELEMELE AND TITUR

While informants do not recall the specifics, they emphasized how the land at Titur was captured and civilized to become an integral part of clan identity and territory and how the diwaal either revealed itself to a person or persons in the founding group or via divination (Dugast 1992:645). This is how the litaŋbanli situated west of Titur in the sacred grove Nakolɔɔri was created (figure 8.5). Since Titur was abandoned circa. 1825, the people of Belemele periodically return to the litaŋbanli to pour libations of sorghum beer made from sorghum's first fruits and to make animal sacrifices when they can. The utandaan and elders conduct these sala (ceremonies), sometimes accompanied by younger people aged thirty-five to fifty, to eliminate any bad spirits or genies that might be present and to ask the diwaal for protection (de Barros and Assouman 2017). In 2015, sacrifices were made to the litaŋbanli prior to our excavations at Titur, asking that we succeed in our efforts. Aside from a sorghum beer libation, a ram was sacrificed and cooked on the spot and then distributed to the families represented by the elders. A small amount was provided to the author and his team. No photos were permitted (de Barros 2016:10). It is also important for the people of Belemele to maintain the litaŋbanli, instead of moving it to their present location, as it helps maintain their land tenure rights at Titur, an area now farmed by the Konkomba and traversed by herds of cattle managed by Fulani pastoralists. Belemele informants also affirmed that old men were and continue to be buried at Titur, and the author noted a new burial mound in 2016. Vestiges left at the litaŋbanli are similar to what has been recorded at other sites, but the chief noted that one could also bury a large bar of iron (de Barros and Assouman 2017).

BITAKPAMBE AND BITAKPAMBE TAPU

Bitakpambe informants essentially described the creation of a new settlement in the same way as did those from Belemele. When asked whether they perform ceremonies for their principal diwaal/litaŋbanli at Bitakpambe Tapu or in their former location at Takpamba, an informant said their ancestors had taken all of their diwaals with them when they left Takpamba and implied the same was true for Bitakpambe Tapu. A visit to the site did confirm that their former litaŋbanli had been transferred to the present-day village from its former location northeast of Bitakpambe Tapu. It is apparently associated with the sacred grove of Mɔɔnca northeast of Bitakpambe, but this needs to be confirmed (figures 8.2 and 8.5). There is also a sacred site north of the former litaŋbanli of Bitakpambe Tapu called Naaboon. It is surrounded by a sacred grove, as well as a small thicket of bamboo, and consists of a water hole that never dries up. Informants said this water hole was used for drinking, cooking, and the making of furnaces and tuyeres when they lived there. It is also the spot where all the ancestral souls of the people of Bitakpambe reside, except for those of married women who are buried under the courtyard of their husband's house. About forty to fifty meters away are two other waterholes where there is evidence of recent ceremonial sacrifices. Informants confirmed that they still farm in this area and go to Naaboon to perform sacrifices. However, the chief said they do not bury their dead there, but rather in their current village. Finally, today's Belemele is situated on lands owned by Bitakpambe (figure 8.5). When schools and other structures were built on these lands in the past, it was the utandaan and elders from Bitakpambe who conducted the various ceremonies to keep their land beautiful (de Barros and Assouman 2017), including the important site on a small hill north of Belemele called Caakpukul, referring to an ancient blacksmith or forge (figure 8.5).

SUMMARY AND DISCUSSION

Reasons for Site Abandonment

If we look at stressors, a state of warfare and/or raiding are paramount, especially Dagomba and Tyokossi slave and cattle raiding and demands for tribute. If we look at enablers, several factors might have made migration ultimately attractive. For those leaving Meung, this would include the potential for continuing one's profession as blacksmith in the Bassar ironworking region, especially in the Bitchabe region. This area was also attractive to smiths because of the presence of high-quality quartzite stone for quarrying and making anvils (de Barros 1985; Dugast 2013). Once the first group of Meung blacksmiths was established, such as at Kpacaanli, this would have encouraged others to migrate due to their professional and kin connections. These blacksmiths were part of a transethnic clan, the Koli clan, whose identity was indissolubly linked to their work as blacksmiths (de Barros 2017:81; Dugast 1992:174–79; Tcham 2009). The presence of good farmlands may also have been a factor for some groups. For the farmers from Seendi who settled in Bitchobebe, the common Bassar language would also have served as enabler. While the Koli blacksmiths came with their ironworking skills, the other groups studied (Bitchobebe, Belemele, and Bitakpambe) came as farmers but soon adopted ironworking, probably because it provided a higher standard of living.

Creating a New Settlement or Attachment to a New Place

An important aspect of Bassar culture is the ability to assimilate migrating individuals and groups into existing clans, along with the adoption of the Bassar language and many of its cultural traditions and religious practices, including how a group settles in a new territory by capturing a locality and its associated diwaal, thus creating a litaŋbanli. This process would be especially true of numerous Voltaic cultural groups with similar practices (Liberski-Bagnoud 2002). A litaŋbanli is inseparable from clan identity and territory, ensuring that relatively short migrations would lead to a continuing relationship between the abandoned site and the new settlement.

One aspect only indirectly discussed thus far is the question of how a migrant group manages to negotiate permission to settle and to sufficiently integrate itself into the host population. We have seen that migrants were often given permission to settle nearby, and in one case (Bitchobebe) they were even given ownership of the lands. For the migrations from Meung, it is possible local inhabitants saw it as advantageous to have blacksmiths in their area. For migrants fleeing the Tyokossi-dominated area, little is yet known about how they were received when they arrived. There is the perplexing problem of the timing of the Belemele and Bitakpambe migrations, where archaeological data show smelting was already taking place at the sites they settled! In terms of migrant settlement patterns, in most cases migrants appear to have formed their own settlements, rather than joining an existing village. However, in the case of Bitchabe, the Koli blacksmith groups (Kpacaanli, Bitchabe Tapu, Paapu Jool, and Naataaku) eventually coalesced into the village or town of Bitchabe.

Links between Abandoned and New Settlements

First, there is no evidence in oral traditions or at archaeological sites that the Bassar practiced site abandonment rituals. Second, we have seen that if the migration is a long one, people may not return to continue rituals at their former home. In many cases, rituals practiced in the original homeland are brought to the new location and operate autonomously from those in the former settlement. This is not to say that ritual links with more distant communities do not happen, as in the case of the role of Meung in the installation of the Bitchabe chief. In addition, there is the case of the Bissib clan lineage that founded the chiefdom at Bissibe in Bandjeli during the later nineteenth century. The last two Bissibe chiefs (Maniébo and Sérétchi) told the author they made periodic pilgrimages to their place of origin at Dukuntunde north of Kabou, a distance of at least twenty-five kilometers (fifteen miles) (figures 8.2 and 8.4), to participate in ceremonies associated with a key clan diwaal, Kpandjal, a name that was later transformed into "Bandjeli" at contact.

In short, if sites are not too far apart, ritual ties between the abandoned and new settlements can be very strong. Ties are most strongly focused on the principal collective (clan) diwaal or litaŋbanli in its sacred grove outside habitation areas, but ties can also be strong with other types of sacred sites, some of which are also in a sacred grove or a group of trees. In either case, these groves develop as the result of a set of taboos and requirements that encourage their growth and protection. They may be associated with creation (Bidjomambe) or migration (Bitchobebe) stories or with powerful and protective ancestors or even key natural resources, such as water. With the exception of Bitakpambe, it is also common to bury old men within the confines or near the abandoned settlement. But even at Bitakpambe Tapu, the sacred water hole of Naaboon is said to be the resting place of the souls of the Bitakpambe people. In the case of Belemele, there was talk of moving the litaŋbanli to present-day Belemele, but residents of present-day Belemele decided against it to ensure their land tenure rights in the vicinity of Titur.

Based on local informants' and the author's observations, material vestiges left at abandoned sites due to annual renewal libations and sacrifices at litaŋbanli and other sites include buried or surficial animal bones, skulls, and/or feathers of cows, rams or birds; stone seats; a pile of stones to mark the ceremonial place; whole and/or fragmented jars or bowls used for libations; and even an large iron bar (Belemele) or perhaps ancient stone or clay artifacts (Licaakpukul at Kpacaanli).

Material Links to Abandoned Sites

Abandoned sites may have important material links with new settlements, such as the reuse of slag and potsherds for small game slingshot hunting and the making of potsherd pavements within family compound courtyards, respectively (de Barros 2016:34–37). Abandoned sites are often seen as excellent places to cultivate because of their rich organic soils produced by long-term human occupation as witnessed today at BAS-319 near Bitchobebe. Finally, in the case of abandoned sites largely forgotten, as is the case of the sixteenth-century smithing site, BAS-321 (figure 8.3), borrow pits have been recently dug into the habitation middens containing potsherds, bone and slag, which provide excellent soil for making unfired adobe bricks for house construction. Finally, it is very likely that once the inhabitants of present-day Bidjomambe realize the historical importance of this sixteenth-century site, they may very well discover or rediscover a clan diwaal through divination, thereby renewing religious ties with a long-abandoned settlement.

Linguistic Notes

Two non-Latin letters are used in Bassar: ɔ = 'aw' and ŋ = 'ng'. Long vowels are doubled (*aa*); *u* is pronounced as in 'who', *c* as in 'tch', *j* as in 'dj' as in 'job', and *w* as in 'week'.

ACKNOWLEDGMENTS

This research was made possible by a 2013 CIEE Senior Fulbright Scholar grant. Thanks go to cultural anthropologist Stéphan Dugast, interpreter Lantame Assouman of Bassar, and to the traditional chiefs, utandaan, and elder informants from Bitchabe, Bidjomambe, Bitchobebe, Belemele, and Bitakpambe. Thanks also go to the cartographer Joel Paulson, for the maps.

9

Detachment as a Cultural Response to Climate Fluctuations in Early Bronze Age Northern Mesopotamia

The Enabling Role of Pastoralism

MICHAEL D. DANTI

DOI: 10.5876/9781646420087.c009

The cultural impacts of the 4.2–3.9 ka BP climate event in the ancient Near East, interpreted by some scholars as a "megadrought" that marks the end of the Early Bronze Age (Weiss 2015, 2017), have received much attention and debate since the 1990s, especially in relation to sociopolitical decentralization and reduced hierarchy and, arguably, widespread settlement abandonment and "nomadization" across northern Mesopotamia (Hole 1994; Issar and Zohar 2004; Kuzucuğlu and Marro 2007; L. Cooper 2006; Schwartz 2017; Schwartz and Miller 2007; Staubwasser and Weiss 2006; Weiss 2000; Zettler 2003). A significant increase in the published proxy datasets of regional and global climate patterns and improved archaeological coverage have driven this trend (for an overview, see Weiss 2015:36–38, 2017: 132–34). Still, much remains to be done to understand the stressors and enablers at the household level that drove detachment, settlement refounding, or long-term abandonment in the late third and early second millennia and thereby shaped the Early Bronze Age-Middle Bronze Age transition. To this end, I have previously argued that we turn our attention to developing better understandings of regional subsistence economies over the *longue durée* and look to the regions that seem to defy the trend of "collapse," for it is in these areas that important lessons were learned regarding how to cope with the changing environment (Danti 2010). For the sake of argument, I assume herein that the 4.2–3.9 ka BP climate event was in fact a sudden and prolonged period of heightened aridity.

The Middle Euphrates region of northern Syria, especially the Early Bronze Age (EBA) site of Tell es-Sweyhat (possibly the ancient kingdom of Burman) and its surrounding area, provides one of several archaeological datasets that invalidate the hypothesis that the megadrought necessitated sudden, wholesale settlement abandonments over vast areas. In this area, and across much of western Syria (see esp. Schwartz 2017), an emphasis on balanced agropastoral economies, a lack of imperial extraction of surplus production, and the smaller scale of sociopolitical systems provided a more resilient socioeconomic base for sustaining urbanism during the climate fluctuations of the later Middle Holocene. The sudden and heightened impact of the climate event on the Khabur region in northeastern Syria, while well documented at larger urban centers, is anomalous, and was perhaps due to an imbalanced production strategy of intensive dry farming related to the region's incorporation into the Akkadian Empire centered in southern Mesopotamia. This created a brittle socioeconomic system, weakened by policies mandating surplus production for a hegemonic power. In contrast, in northern Mesopotamia at Sweyhat and other sites outside the control of southern Mesopotamia, local adaptive responses are apparent in the late third millennium BC, particularly an increasing shift toward transhumant pastoralism and a concomitant *gradual* decline and restructuring of urbanism, while in southern Mesopotamia the successor of the Akkadian Empire, the Ur III "empire" or territorial state, tellingly exhibited an obsessive preoccupation with controlling pastoral production in the piedmont and mountains of its eastern hinterland (Steinkeller 1991) during the climate event. The population of the Sweyhat area and those of other urban centers unquestionably withstood the megadrought, but settlement and agropastoral production in this region of the Euphrates Valley were gradually reorganized with large parts of the population disentangled from sedentary households and reattached to regional landscapes through transhumant pastoralism. Early Bronze Age patterns of regional settlement would return to the Khabur region in the Middle Bronze Age (2000–1600 BC), but the Sweyhat area would not see a similar proportionate attachment to permanent settlements until the modern era (Wilkinson 2004). The greatest weakness of the megadrought hypothesis is its inability to reconcile the evidence that Sweyhat and other urban centers survived and *often flourished* during the climate event only to experience widespread detachment from settlements *at or near its termination* without a subsequent recovery to predrought conditions after the event, as is seen in the Khabur region.

"MEGADROUGHT" AND LATE THIRD AND EARLY SECOND NORTHERN MESOPOTAMIA

Scholars of the ancient Near East have long turned to droughts and attendant famines and nomadization to explain abandonment, often with little evidence. Advances in paleoclimatological methods and the availability of proxy datasets covering long time spans and diverse regions have improved our ability to incorporate climate in archaeological models of cultural systems. Over the last twenty-five years, several Near East experts and other Old Word archaeologists have developed theories to explain periods of instability and abrupt cultural change that elevate catastrophic climate events to the role of megastressors and even monocausal prime movers. These climate events are dated to 8.2, 5.2, 4.2, and 3.2 ka BP (see most recently Weiss 2017). The 5.2 and 4.2 ka BP events, characterized by extreme aridity and lower temperatures, mark the beginning and the end of the Early Bronze Age (3100–2000 BC). The 5.2 ka event is often interpreted as contributing to the collapse of the Uruk period (4000–3100 BC), the world's first known civilization (Brooks 2006; Staubwasser and Weiss 2006; Weiss 2003). The 4.2–3.9 ka BP event is believed by some to have brought down the world's first experiment with empire, the Akkadian Empire (2350–2150 BC), and instigated a widespread decline in urbanism and a wave of societal collapses throughout northern Mesopotamia and much of the wider Near East and Mediterranean region (Arz, Lamy, and Pätzold 2006; Cullen et al. 2000; deMenocal 2001; Drysdale et al. 2006; Staubwasser et al. 2003; Staubwasser and Weiss 2006; Weiss et al. 1993). The intervening period was marked by relatively mild and stable climate and the "Second Urban Revolution" in northern Mesopotamia. Understanding the cultural responses to these putative climate events is no easy task, and the advocates of the 4.2–3.9 ka BP megadrought hypothesis have not convincingly demonstrated that their theory can be reconciled with a significant number of regional archaeological datasets outside the Khabur region (e.g., see Schwartz 2017 for western Syria). Moreover, from a methodological standpoint, the hypothesis has not adequately addressed decision-making processes at the agent- and household-levels of analysis and is weakened by a lack of excavations at small rural sites and by simplistic models of agropastoral subsistence economies. This author does not doubt the climate model—the increasing resolution of proxy data generally supports the prevailing interpretation of the timing and magnitude of the 4.2–3.9 ka BP event—but rather questions the interpretation that this incident triggered such a limited range of simultaneous cultural responses.

CULTURAL RESPONSES TO THE 4.2–3.9 KA BP
EVENT IN NORTHERN MESOPOTAMIA

Since the publication of the first versions of the megadrought hypothesis, the catalyst for the supposed catastrophe has changed in various models and included a volcanic eruption, a bolide, and most recently periodic interruptions in the North Atlantic Oscillation. Changing interpretations of the triggers aside, the local and global proxy data for these events appear robust, but the catastrophic cultural impacts and responses posited for Greater Mesopotamia—widespread detachment, mass migrations, and "nomadization"—are problematic and unproven. It is important to note that *nomadization* is something of a misnomer in reference to Early Bronze Age economies, since true nomadism did not appear in the Middle East until much later.

In the period immediately prior to the onset of the climate event (2350–2200 BC), parts of the rainfall agriculture plains of northern Iraq and Syria were incorporated into the Akkadian Empire of southern Mesopotamia. To say that our understanding of the internal dynamics of this hegemonic polity is superficial would be an understatement, but compelling evidence exists for direct Akkadian rule of the Khabur drainage basin from the reign of Sargon's grandson, Naram-Sin, onward (see summary of evidence in Weiss 2015:40). One working assumption in all versions of the megadrought hypothesis is that the Akkadian dynasty regularly extracted and depended on surplus grain from conquered Khabur city-states. In his earliest writings on this topic, Harvey Weiss argued for a staple-finance model, with surplus Khabur grain shipped overland by caravans to the Akkadian heartland, a region characterized by high-yielding irrigation agriculture. Setting aside the "carrying-coals-to-New-Castle" ramifications of this supposition, this method of surplus extraction has been shown to be unfeasible and historically unattested (Zettler 2003:21). Weiss has since backed away from such assertions with little explanation (2015:40), making passing references to possible river-borne shipment of grain based on slim and ambiguous evidence (40). Weiss views Akkadian imperialism as a stressor on the city-states of the Khabur, citing "effective intimidation, terror, and large military forces" (2015:40), and I would add periodic imperial extractions of agricultural produce would also qualify as a stressor for the Khabur area and other regions under the Akkadian yoke. Yet, to fully understand the impact of this stressor for the populations of the Khabur region, we must interpret the objectives behind surplus extractions through the lens of agropastoral production as documented over millennia. The Akkadian State would far more likely have collected, controlled, and redistributed surplus grain and straw to support large-scale state-managed sheep and goat production in the Khabur plains. Live animals and their byproducts—such as preserved dairy products, wool, and textiles—would have been far more readily exportable to distant markets. Surplus pastoral production in surrounding regions expanded and diversified the economy of southern Mesopotamia—both in terms of production and the incorporated climatological zones—boosting economic resilience and stability. In addition, there is an added incentive to such activity: in ancient and modern times in northern Mesopotamia, state control of local fodder production provides an effective means of controlling both sedentary and transhumant agropastoral populations since winter fodder is required for effective herd management (see below).

The reasons behind and the timing of the collapse of the Akkadian Empire remain shrouded in mystery. There is little direct archaeological evidence or contemporary historical documentation from southern Mesopotamia (Weiss 2015:42). The Akkadian capital city of Agade has never been located, and much of what we know of this nebulous empire comes from limited excavated exposures within provincial cities on its peripheries. Weiss believes the megadrought is to blame, interpreting the 4.2 ka BP event as a 300-year period characterized by a 30–50 percent reduction in precipitation and reduced temperatures with a sudden onset and equally punctuated termination (Bar-Matthews and Ayalon 2011; Frumkin 2009 as cited by Weiss 2015:36, 42, 2017:131). The economic and sociopolitical interactions between the Akkadian Empire and its provinces are poorly understood, but central to Weiss's synthesis is the notion that the megadrought dramatically lowered agricultural production in the Khabur, which played an important but ill-defined role in the collapse of the Akkadian Empire located in the irrigation agriculture zone of southern Mesopotamia. This line of causality is decidedly tenuous, but archaeological evidence from the Khabur from systematic surveys and excavations shows significant reductions in the number and sizes of settlements synchronous to the event that signal widespread settlement detachments and sociopolitical instability (Arrivabeni 2012; Ristvet 2012). Weiss summarizes the main dataset from the Tell Leilan subregion: "Region-wide, not only large cities but also their surrounding countrysides were deserted. In the Leilan Region Survey (1,650 sq. km), some 87 percent of dependent villages and towns were abandoned at the end of Leilan IIb1, 2254–2220 b.c. (68.2%), with the remainder disappearing completely less than 50 years later at the end of Leilan IIc, 2233–2196 b.c. (68.2%)" (Weiss 2017:139).

In the Khabur region, the refounding of settlements would not come quickly, "Following the brief post-Akkadian interval, sedentary settlement within the Leilan Survey Region, and most of the Khabur plains, abandoned the region for about 250 years, the Leilan IId Period, until the sudden return of pre-megadrought precipitation levels and Khabur-period resettlement at around 1950 b.c." (Weiss 2017:143). In Weiss's assessment, populations had few options, and the megadrought represented an inexorable destructive force. Whole communities detached from long-established settlements across the Mediterranean region and engaged in "habitat tracking" (migration to familiar environmental zones less effected by aridity, although this is not adequately explained) and mass migration to "refugia." According to Weiss, in Greater Mesopotamia, "These refugia included the close-to-sea-level irrigation agriculture of Tigris-Euphrates regions of southern Mesopotamia, soon filled with hypertrophic Ur III cities; the central Euphrates valley dotted with irrigation agriculture cities at Mari, Tuttul and Terqa, the Madekh, Ghab, Amuq, and Radd swamps; the cities of the karst-fed Orontes River; the riverside towns of coastal Syria and Lebanon; and the karst-spring towns of the southern Levant" (Weiss 2017:145).

THE TELL ES-SWEYHAT REGION, SYRIA:
AGROPASTORALISM VS. THE MEGADROUGHT

Tell es-Sweyhat lies in the Middle Euphrates region of northern Syria (figure 9.1) on the left bank of the river at the center of a crescent-shaped embayment, a mid-to-late Pleistocene terrace carved out of the high plateau by an arm of the river (deHeinzelin 1967; Wilkinson 2004:19 20). The three major environmental zones are the floodplain, the main terrace, and the high plateau. The settlement was occupied continuously from at least the early third until the early second millennium BC and consists of a high, central mound (H. 14.5 m) surrounded by an extensive low mound of 35–45 ha (figure 9.2). Following the site's abandonment in the early second millennium, it was not again occupied until the Seleucid and Late Roman periods (second century BC–AD third century), and then only as a small village on the main mound. The attested occupational periods at Sweyhat also represent peak periods of settlement in the embayment (Wilkinson 2004:136–43, 176–89) and to the east on the high plateau (Danti 2000:261–301) and overlap the megadrought, despite repeated attempts by diehard megadrought adherents to explain away this evidence, or occasionally simply ignore it, and similar contradictory datasets.

Tell es-Sweyhat and a few other neighboring ancient cities were conspicuous and unique in that they were situated far from the river, five kilometers in the case of Sweyhat, in a marginal agricultural environment on the

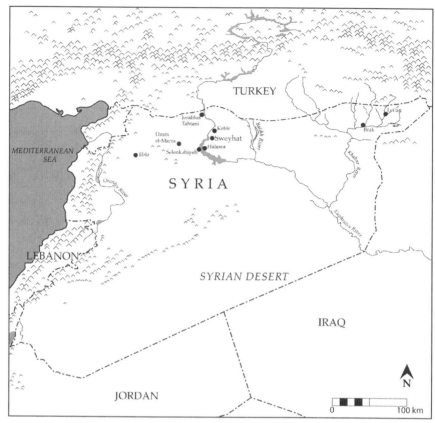

FIGURE 9.1. *Map of Syria showing the location of Tell es-Sweyhat and other sites mentioned in the text.*

unirrigable main terrace: the embayment steadily and markedly slopes up from the floodplain. Today the region averages 250 millimeters of precipitation per annum (figure 9.3) with an interannual variability of 25–35 percent (Wallén 1968:226–31). This is just enough rainfall to support the dry farming of drought-resistant varieties of barley with two successful crops every three years (Al-Ashram 1990:167), placing the region near the southern limit for rainfall agriculture today (Perrin de Brichambaut and Wallén 1963).

Middle and Late Holocene settlement patterns in the Sweyhat region are well documented through systematic archaeological surveys and excavations (Danti 2000; Danti and Zettler 1998; Holland 2006; Wilkinson 2004; Zettler et al. 1997). The Late Chalcolithic (LC) of the Middle Euphrates region

FIGURE 9.2. *Tell es-Sweyhat from the south in 2001. The slightly elevated area in the foreground represents the remains of the Outer City Fortifications, beyond which is the Low Mound / Outer City. The High Mound / Inner City is clearly visible in the distance, with the guard's tent at the mound's summit situated near the area of the Period 4 temple complex on the High Terrace.*

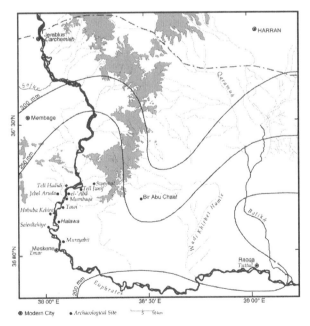

FIGURE 9.3. *Map of the Tell es-Sweyhat region showing annual rainfall isohyets. Shaded areas represent elevations over 500 meters (AMSL).*

witnessed a phase of urbanization and increased cultural complexity spurred by close connections with, and colonization by, southern Mesopotamian Uruk populations. This abortive urban revolution ended in the late fourth millennium BC with political decentralization and a return to regionalized cultural traditions (Akkermans and Schwartz 2003:209–11). Researchers have attributed this episode of settlement detachment and refounding to the 5.2 ka climate event (Staubwasser and Weiss 2006:379; Weiss and Bradley 2001). Concurrent with this event, that is, the terminal late Uruk period and LC-EBA transition (Hajji Ibrahim Period A in the Sweyhat area), the main terrace of the Sweyhat embayment was first settled (Danti 2000; Wilkinson 2004:179). The distance of this modest settlement system (sites on the order of 0.25 hectare) from the Euphrates suggests an emphasis on agropastoral production. This traditional economy of northern Mesopotamia, which predominated until the mid-nineteenth-century AD, couples the dry farming of barley (primarily as a fodder crop) with sheep-goat pastoralism.

Annually, pastoral production alternates from short-range transhumance following the availability of spring and early summer pastures to a high degree of sedentism and reliance on conserved fodder sources in late summer through winter. Detachment/attachment were regular parts of the annual cycle for a significant part of the region's population. The excavation of Tell Hajji Ibrahim (Danti 2000), a small archaeological mound situated 1 kilometer southeast of Sweyhat, revealed a small, fortified compound with a mud-brick fortification wall, plaster-lined mud-brick granaries, and a single house with domestic installations. Occupation at the site securely dates to the Terminal Uruk period and the first part of the Early Bronze Age (EB I–II). The reconstructed storage capacity of the mud-brick granaries exceeded the annual requirements of a single family, and so the storage of conserved fodder (straw and barley grain) for regional flocks and a largely nonsedentary population appear to be the compound's primary function. The identical, distinctive mound morphology and surface artifact assemblages of contemporary mounds in the Sweyhat embayment (Wilkinson 2004:136–38) indicate the presence of similar facilities.

Excavations at Tell es-Sweyhat, the preeminent regional center in later times, did not locate occupation levels contemporary with Hajji Ibrahim Period A. Elsewhere, we have argued against the interpretation that Tell Hajji Ibrahim and similar sites served as surplus-producing satellite settlements in a staple-finance redistributive network, and rather posited these sites were connected to a larger local population of transhumant agropastoralists (Danti 1997, 2000, 2010; Danti and Zettler 1998). Large-scale sheep-goat production in northern Mesopotamia requires conserved fodder (grain and straw) to sustain animals during the cold and wet winter and spring, when there is virtually no pasture of nutritive value and when the caloric and, especially, protein requirements of small ruminants are elevated due to the inclement weather. At this same time, the caloric and protein requirements of adult females in late gestation, lambing, and lactation (the birthing and milking seasons) are doubly elevated (Thompson and Bahhady 1995:7). This is a time of heightened risk for pastoralists and their flocks. Archaeologists often view grain production purely in terms of human diet, but conserved fodder (barley grain and straw) is a prerequisite of sustainable pastoral production. Another widely held misconception concerns the range of transhumance in the annual cycle of pastoralists in antiquity. Before the development of true nomadism in the later second millennium BC, dependent on domesticated camels and horses, pastoralists in northern Mesopotamia, like the so-called sheep-tribes of the modern era, almost certainly practiced short-distance transhumance unless severe stressors forced them out of their tribal territories (Charles 1939; d'Hont 1994:209–11; Oppenheim 1939:208–17). During the cold season, the scant desiccated pastures of northern Mesopotamia contain virtually no nutritional value and are virtually useless as a feed source. Moreover, long distance searches for feed in cold and rain would stress animals during the risky periods of late gestation in adult females and the following lambing season.

Pastoralism based on small ruminants has traditionally been the primary means for offsetting bad harvests and crop failures in the marginal zone of northern Mesopotamia. Syrian landrace sheep, varieties of fat-tailed sheep such as the Awassi (Epstein 1985), are famed for their fat storing capabilities and hardiness and were probably the main breed in antiquity (Ryder 1993; Steinkeller 1995). When mobilized by hunger, these fat reserves help the animal to survive in lean years (Ghosh and Abichandani 1981:24–25; Goodchild, El-Awad, and Gürsoy 1999). When crops fail due to drought, the unharvested remains serve as in-field fodder for animals rather than simply going to waste. Agropastoralists can slaughter more animals to offset food shortages and to reserve more grain for human consumption and as seed for the next planting season. Thus, small ruminants minimize risk due to interannual climatic fluctuations and provide valuable contributions to the subsistence economy in the form of meat and dairy products. Wool and textile production provided a form of storable wealth for regional and long-distance exchange, as did the production of surplus animals. This economy did not merely enable the inhabitants of the Middle Euphrates region to survive, but it would also eventually support prosperous city-states in the mid-to-late third millennium BC, even during the so-called megadrought. When we consider the stressors and enablers that influence detachment and refounding, the seasonal demands of people *and livestock* at the family/household level must be considered. Recurring stressors operating over millennia—unpredictable agricultural outputs, the fluctuating nutritional needs of small ruminants through annual life cycles, seasonal climate stressors, and the cyclical availability of suitable and economical feed sources—set the rhythm of seasonal pastoral movements and entangled small ruminant herding and dry-farming agriculture. Pastoralism also offered the region's inhabitants an option/enabler for detachment under extreme conditions: increased transhumance.

The succeeding periods, the EB I–III (Sweyhat Periods 1–3, Hajji Ibrahim Periods B–D), are best known from the lowest levels of Sweyhat and from the terminal phases of occupation at Hajji Ibrahim. In Hajji Ibrahim Periods B–C (EB I–II) the granaries were demolished, though the site continued to be occupied as a small fortified hamlet. Between circa 2900 and 2800 BC, we see detachments from long-occupied small sites. Hajji Ibrahim was abandoned, as were most of the other small sites on the main terrace like it (Danti 2000). This abandonment likely signals the consolidation of regional settlement at Sweyhat, which became a small village of about five hectares (Zettler et al. 1997:169). A large mud-brick fortress dominated the settlement by at least EBII, and likely as early as EBI, and was expanded throughout the EBII and EBIII periods, eventually measuring at least 75 meters east–west by 62 meters north–south and at least 3 meters high. At the time of excavation, the corbelled-arch roofs of the internal chambers were preserved in most exposures. Architectural remains at the outskirts of the settlement indicate that some of the inhabitants practiced, minimally, a biseasonal settlement pattern (Armstrong and Zettler 1997:16–17), and thus at least part of the population still engaged in seasonal transhumant pastoralism. In EBIII, the fortress was repeatedly enlarged, and the settlement slowly grew. Cemeteries of shaft-and-chamber tombs were located on the edges of the settlement in the EB III and EB IVa periods. Grave goods attest to a modicum of affluence and access to goods requiring long-distance exchange networks (Zettler et al. 1997:51–72). During EBIVa (Sweyhat Period 3), the equivalent of the later Early Dynastic III and Old Akkadian period in southern Mesopotamia, the town surrounding the fortress expanded until it covered an estimated fifteen hectares. This period is not well known, since building activities connected to the widespread redesign of the inner city at the beginning of Sweyhat Period 4 (see below) greatly disturbed Period 3 deposits. In late Period 2 and Period 3, houses were built against the sides of the fortress and, in Period 3, eventually over the top of it. The narrow chambers inside the massive brickwork of the fortress were first infilled to support the structures above, thus fully preserving the building to the level of its corbelled-arched roof.

In summary, as the Uruk State(s) collapsed, an unprecedented settlement pattern emerged in the Sweyhat region and along the Syrian Middle Euphrates supported by agropastoralism. The Sweyhat area was inhabited by a largely transhumant pastoralist population. Seasonal detachment from permanent settlements was the norm. Grain and fodder cultivated in the embayment was stored in fortified facilities and guarded and maintained by small year-round resident populations, as has been argued for the agriculturally marginal Middle Khabur region (McCorriston 1995; Hole 1991, 1999). Thus, we see a balanced subsistence economy utilizing several different resource zones (riparian Euphrates floodplain, main terrace, and undulating Steppic high plateau). The human diet was supplemented by hunting on the surrounding steppe and the exploitation of riverine resources such as fish and waterfowl, as in later periods (Weber 1997:141–42). Annual flooding of the Euphrates in April and May, just before grain ripened and could be harvested, prevented wheat and barley cultivation there. This riparian environment served as a source of wood and as a hunting ground, or it was developed for irrigated summer gardens. During these formative periods, there is no archaeological evidence for settlement in the high plateau (Danti 2000:279–80). The settlement surrounding the Sweyhat fortress gradually grew during Periods 2 and 3 to cover 10–15 hectares. There is no evidence from the later phases of the fortress town (Sweyhat Period 3) of serious disruptions associated with a major climate event or Akkadian military campaigns; however, as previously mentioned, deposits from this critical period are rare due to the substantial remodeling of the urban environment at the beginning of Sweyhat Period 4.

Around 2200 BC, Sweyhat's urban environment was suddenly and substantially altered, probably reflecting an equally abrupt sociopolitical reorganization of the city-state characterized by a higher degree of central authority. These changes mark the beginning of Period 4. These developments are securely dated by radiocarbon determinations, from both long- and short-lived samples, and through cross-sequence comparison of ceramic assemblages and other artifacts. The center of the Period 3 settlement—the area of the former fortress and its immediately adjacent town—was completely transformed into an Inner City surrounded by a 2.75-meter-thick mud-brick fortification wall—the Inner City Fortifications—with projecting, rectangular towers. The Inner City was concentrically divided into two levels. At the center lay the High Inner City, consisting of the High Terrace surmounted by a long-room temple with bent-axis approach and ancillary structures (figure 9.4). The

FIGURE 9.4. *The Period 4 temple showing the main phase of construction, looking east along the building's long axis toward the raised cult target and an aniconic stone stele. The temple was destroyed by fire at the end of Period 4.*

former Period 3 fortress had been completely abandoned, filled with debris to its roof level, and was now encased within the High Terrace.

The new Period 4 temple complex appears to have been the only structure on the High Terrace, and no evidence for palaces or for administrative facilities (including indigenous writing) has as yet been found at Sweyhat in any parts of the city. The pavement level of the High Inner City / High Terrace stood one full story above the surrounding Low Inner City. This lower area contained large production facilities, such as kitchens and bakeries, storage areas and granaries, ritual spaces, and residences. On the surrounding plain beyond the Inner City, an outer earthen rampart, fortification walls, and a ditch were built to protect a large Outer City, enclosing an area measuring roughly 700 by 600 meters (Holland 1976:36; Zettler et al. 1997:49–51). The Outer City Fortifications covered the entrances to many of the Sweyhat Period 3 tombs, representing a significant disjuncture in the use of space. The Outer City contained large houses, open spaces, and production facilities (Zettler et al. 1997:35–51). During Period 4, the settlement continued to grow, eventually expanding beyond the outer fortifications in at least the south, reaching a minimum size of 35–45 hectares. All this construction occurred during the onset of the hypothesized megadrought event. The growth and reorganization of Sweyhat at this time are all the more compelling given the city-state's agriculturally marginal territory.

While Sweyhat dominated the embayment in Period 4, other smaller cities were located on the main terrace and on the fringes of the floodplain (Wilkinson 2004:138–42). Sweyhat's growth in Period 4 was not the result of the detachment and relocation of populations from the surrounding countryside. Further afield, small settlements were situated amid the pockets of arable land in the high plateau, usually along seasonal streambeds (Danti 2000:261–65, 306–11). Modern climate records show that this area receives slightly more rainfall than the adjacent area of the Middle Euphrates; however, the water table is quite low, making it difficult to dig wells, and there are no perennial water sources. Traditionally, this area was used as seasonal pasture in spring and early summer. The Period 4 sites on the high plateau, which tend to be less than five hectares, were likely founded as part of a strategy of rangeland improvement. Small plots of barley could be cultivated there for use as fodder, and pastoral stations would have provided shelter, wells, and protection for herders and animals attached to the cities lining the Syrian Middle Euphrates and the Balikh River to the east. Place-making was highly influenced by the pastoral component of the economy. In sum, we see the extensive and intensive use of the Sweyhat region in the later third millennium BC, and this pattern holds for entire Middle Euphrates River and Balikh River catchment zones.

The Sweyhat Period 4 ends with at least three areas in the Inner City being destroyed by fire, including the temple on the High Terrace (Danti and Zettler 2002; Danti 2009, 2010), a storage facility in the western Low Inner City (Holland 2006:55–69), residential areas in the southwestern Inner City (Wallace 2014:59–73) built against the Inner Fortifications, and storage structures in the eastern Low Inner City. No evidence for a similar incident(s) was found in the Outer Town. It is not clear whether these burnings in the Inner City were simultaneous, but it seems likely. The buildings all contained large numbers of in situ finds of EBIVb date, indicating at least one violent disruption. Following the fire, some Low Inner City buildings were at least partially reconstructed along the same architectural lines. These phases of rebuilding constitute Periods 5 and 6.

Radiocarbon dates from the Sweyhat 4 burned level include three samples of charcoal from roof beams and one sample from cleaned grain from a storage jar (Danti 2010:table 1). The charcoal samples date the construction of the building—*and the beginning of Sweyhat 4*—to circa 2200–2100 BC or the onset of the 4.2–3.9 ka BP event. The grain tentatively places the destruction of the building toward the end of the third millennium BC. The residential structures located along the southwestern Inner Fortifications provide evidence of a similar sequence of events—however, with only limited evidence of burning. The structures were intentionally demolished with large numbers of in situ ceramic vessels and other in situ objects still in the rooms. These buildings were also at least in part reconstructed along the same architectural lines in Sweyhat Periods 5 and 6. The High Inner City Temple underwent several phases of rebuilding and modification before its destruction by fire. Three radiocarbon samples, likely the remains of poplar roof beams, were collected from its final floor (2010:table 1). These provide a date of circa 2200–2100 BC or later for the construction of the roof, and hence the destruction dates to sometime in the late third millennium BC (2010:table 1). There is evidence of building activity and occupation within the temple following the burning, but it does not appear to be more than a squatter occupation.

In the late third and early second millennium BC, Sweyhat Periods 5 and 6 or the EBA-MBA Transition, Sweyhat slowly faded away. Occupation was eventually confined to the High Mound, and the city's inner fortifications fell out of use. Houses were built atop the old foundations of the demolished city wall and towers. Sweyhat was completely abandoned in the early second millennium, and regional settlement was limited to the floodplain and the main terrace with the adjacent uplands apparently devoid of settlement. The former late Early Bronze Age scale and pattern of regional settlement in the steppe would not be matched for nearly four thousand years.

We see a process of gradual detachment from place at Sweyhat rather than a punctuated abandonment caused by a sudden catastrophe. The process began with disruptions at the end of Sweyhat Period 4, perhaps indicating the decline of the settlement's epicenter—in political terms, the state bureaucracy and a reversion to traditional powerbrokers—followed by a steady reduction in population and urban complexity in Sweyhat 5 and 6. Sedentary occupation in the region, albeit on a reduced scale, shifted to the vicinity of the floodplain with new and smaller walled towns attested in the Middle Bronze Age. This is the culmination of a gradual process of reorganization (detachment and refounding) started in the late third and early second millennia. Increased aridity at this time may have brought a gradual shift from intensive, urban-based agropastoralism to a more resilient strategy incorporating a higher degree of pastoral transhumance and increased socioeconomic separation between farmers and herders (selective economic detachment of one sector of the population). Thus, we see the development of a dimorphic form of agropastoralism characterized by greater socioeconomic separation between pastoral specialists and farmers. Unlike the Khabur, there is no Middle Bronze Age urban recovery on the main terrace and Steppic uplands in the Tell es-Sweyhat region.

Why did dense settlement not return to some areas as the aridification event abated? Climate-driven catastrophes alone do not account for such patterns. Instead, we should look at the effects of longer-term climate change, environmental degradation, and the interplay between sociopolitical organization and subsistence economies. The late EBA peak in settlement occurred during a time of strong regional polities promoting agropastoral production. Periods with more predatory political overlords see the destabilization of sedentary settlement and poor relations with transhumant and nomadic pastoralists. Late Bronze Age and early Iron Age settlement patterns resemble the MBA. In the sphere of agropastoral production, we see a "nomadic revolution" in northern Mesopotamia and western Syria. The period witnessed the rise of Aramaean states in the region and the emergence of true nomadism with the introduction of the domesticated camel and the realization of the capabilities of the horse. The camel made long-range seasonal migrations into the desert steppe possible, greatly altering patterns of seasonal transhumance, trade routes, regional politics, and settlement patterns. The settled populace was now confronted by a highly mobile, and potentially hostile, military power. The seasonal movements of transhumant "sheep tribes" were no longer dictated by the vagaries of rainfall and shifting tribal territories and alliances. Herders now had to contend with the seasonal arrival of waves of nomads. Climate seems to have trended toward increasing aridity in the Iron Age. In the early Iron Age, the Sweyhat region was almost exclusively used for nomadic and transhumant pastoralism with little to no settlement away from the river. The notable exception is the Seleucid to the Abbasid periods. Although we are in the process of refining our archaeological chronology of these periods in the Syrian Middle Euphrates, overall we see a settlement pattern similar to that of the Early Bronze Age. Once again sedentary occupation extended onto the main terrace and into the surrounding uplands (Danti 2000; Wilkinson 2004), though the sites are far more modest in comparison to those in the late third millennium BC. Interestingly, this spike in the number of sites and total occupied area was coterminous with a marked phase of aridity, evincing a trend seen previously with the 5.2 ka and 4.2 ka climate events. While developments in the Late Holocene, particularly the rise of nomadism and major shifts in settlement patterns, are especially interesting, much more archaeological research on this period is needed in the Middle Euphrates region. In particular, we must refine our archaeological chronology to match the resolution of paleoclimatology through the excavation of Iron Age sites, especially smaller sites in rural hinterlands.

CONCLUSIONS

What makes the Sweyhat Period 4 urbanization so compelling is that it occurred at the height of the 4.2–3.9 ka BP climatic event that brought centuries of aridification and abandonment to the Khabur region. Sweyhat was not abandoned until the early second millennium BC and provides a rare EB–MB transitional horizon. Weiss and his colleagues, in their reconstructions of the cultural response to the megadrought in western Syria, cite the widespread abandonment and decline of most sites (Staubwasser and Weiss 2006:381–82; Weiss 2000:88). Nevertheless, there are no widespread regional abandonments on the order of the Khabur collapse at 4.2 ka BP in other parts of northern Mesopotamia, though many settlements in the latter part of the third millennium experienced disruptions followed by rebuilding. For example, there is no major late third millennium BC break at Ebla, as evidenced by the remains of Period IIB2, until the disruption of around 2000 BC (Dolce 1999, 2001; Pinnock 2009; Schwartz 2017). Umm al-Marra has abundant evidence for occupation during the later third millennium (Schwartz et al. 2000:450) with a disruption in the EBA-MBA transition, though there is also evidence for continuity at sites in the Jabbul region from EBIVb to the MBA (Schwartz and Miller 2007). Jerablus Tahtani was abandoned around 2200 BC (Peltenburg 1999:103; Peltenburg et al. 1995:14–15), but the period from the late third millennium BC to the early second represents a peak period of settlement in the surrounding region (Algaze, Breuninger, and Knutstad 1994:14–17; Peltenburg 2007:17, fig. 6). Selenkahiye was at least partially destroyed at the end of EBIVa, followed by rebuilding and another destruction at the end of EBIVb (Van Loon 2001). In sum, in the northern Middle Euphrates region of Syria, the more pronounced break comes in the EBA-MBA transition of approximately 2000–1900 BC, two centuries or more after the onset of the 4.2 ka climate event, and even then there are important continuities between the EBA and the MBA (L. Cooper 2006:25–28; Schwartz and Miller 2007:199).

Many sites in the Syrian Middle Euphrates region decline in the late third millennium, including Halawa (Orthmann 1989), Tell Kebir (Porter 1995), and Hadidi (Dornemann 1985), and we see a similar pattern in the Sweyhat region around 2000–1900 BC. Nonetheless, Weiss and his colleagues have conflated the disruptions outside the Khabur and overstated their severity. In fact, the onset of the 4.2 ka BP event coincides with a peak period of settlement in the Balikh-Euphrates upland steppe (Danti 2000, 2010). Similarly, there is no evidence at Sweyhat for a decline until a *shift* in settlement patterns begins in the EBA-MBA transitional period, followed by the site's abandonment in the early second millennium BC in favor of a settlement pattern focused on or near the floodplain (Wilkinson 2004:143). This settlement pattern is, in effect, a return to the "norm" seen in previous periods and is, in general, the typical pattern of settlement until the second period of expansion onto the main terrace and into the high plateau in the Seleucid and Late Roman periods (145–47). Tony Wilkinson describes settlement patterns in later periods as a time of decreasing sedentism due to anthropogenic environmental degradation:

> There followed [after the Middle Bronze Age] a steady decline in settlement until the plain was virtually deserted by the 18th/19th century AD . . . Such a long-term decline suggests that after the 2nd Millennium BC settlement, although viable, could not occur on the scale that existed during the 4th, 3rd and early 2nd Millennium . . . If intensive cultivation was continued for sustained periods over such an area it is likely that soil deterioration would also have resulted. Periodic droughts or longer spells may have contributed a significant amount of dust to the atmosphere from the rain-fed zone, thereby exacerbating soil degradation and potentially influencing local climate. (1997:98–99)

The question is not whether there was a collapse in western Syria in the late third millennium concurrent with the 4.2 ka event, but rather why the Khabur region specifically experienced widespread urban devolution while other regions prospered until the EBA-MBA transition. Put another way, what factors made the Khabur region more susceptible to the 4.2 ka event and/or made other areas more resilient? Any investigation of the Khabur region must consider its putative ties with the Akkadian Empire at the time of the urban collapse.

The archaeological record of northern Mesopotamia lacks evidence that Middle and Late Holocene climate events exerted punctuated, monolithic cultural responses, and particularly widespread detachments outside the Khabur region. Mid- to Late Holocene shorter-term periods of pronounced aridity and a long-term trend toward increasing aridity profoundly shaped the region's subsistence economies, providing harsh tests of the resilience and stability of agropastoral systems. The fallback strategy during periods of stress was to emphasize the pastoral component of agropastoral economies by increasing mobility as environmental conditions deteriorated due to anthropogenic environmental degradation, climatic fluctuations, and climate change. The major stages in this process were, first, intensive agropastoralism, then dimorphic agropastoralism, and finally nomadism. This developmental trajectory was most apparent in the marginal zone of northern Mesopotamia, where climate was always a major challenge and the risks inherent in dry farming were offset by pastoral production.

As research on the cultural responses to climate events in northern Mesopotamia has continued, one of the more important developments has been a change in our understanding of the timing and uneven impact of these events, which do not necessarily correspond with widespread disruptions in settlement and detachments. In the case of the 4.2–3.9 ka BP climate event, there seems to have been no sudden impact in northern Mesopotamia outside of the collapse documented in the Khabur Plain. This is not the same as saying there was no cultural response, as we see only minor temporary disruptions in areas with smaller-scale states and balanced agropastoral economies. Increasingly, the archaeologist's attention has been shifting from the period of the Akkadian Empire to the EBA-MBA transition, which seems to correspond with the final part of the climate event. The EBA-MBA transition, as originally defined, marks a major cultural shift; change is manifest in the archaeological record, but there is also cultural continuity from the perspective of the Syrian Middle Euphrates and western Syria.

The Sweyhat embayment would not be substantially settled and intensively farmed until the modern era following the detachments of the EBA-MBA transitional period. Any theory advanced to explain these detachments must address this profound development. Wilkinson and other scholars have attributed this to anthropogenic environmental degradation linked to intensive dry farming. I would argue that more attention should be given to the impact of pastoral production. The overgrazing of Steppic pastures, particularly in regions prone to erosion such as the Balikh-Euphrates uplands, is linked to the decline of EBA intensive agropastoral production and the related settlement patterns. These marginal and delicate environmental zones were far more vulnerable, especially during punctuated climate events. In the case of the Syrian Middle Euphrates, during the mid-third millennium BC, a period of relatively moist climatic conditions, intensive agropastoral production flourished. This subsistence strategy provided a means for maximizing production by linking the pockets of arable land along the Euphrates to the adjacent upland Steppic pastures. It required minimal seasonal transhumance and thus could be fully integrated within individual sociopolitical and economic units. This strategy emphasized resilience, providing a means for coping with pronounced interannual variation in rainfall. In the late third millennium, we see the maximization of this system during a period of heightened aridity. The weak link in such a system would have been Steppic pastures and the destructive force of overgrazing. Declines in the quality of rangeland and the increasing aridity of the Late Holocene in the Middle Euphrates region would have resulted in lower potential stocking rates on Steppic pastures, and the attendant response would have been increased transhumance and the emergence of dimorphic agropastoral production in the region—the pattern documented in the MBA and later. In the Late Holocene, modest settlements lined the Euphrates floodplain, and the surrounding steppe was used almost exclusively as rangeland by transhumant and nomadic pastoralists. Further research is needed to test this in the Syrian Middle Euphrates region and in other areas, particularly in regions of the transitional zone of Syria that experienced similar long-term patterns.

10

*Entanglement and
Disentanglement at
the Medieval Capital
of Bagan, Myanmar*

GYLES IANNONE

Located on the east bank of the Ayeyarwady River, Bagan was the capital of the Burmese Empire during the "classical period" (ninth–fourteenth centuries CE; cf. Aung-Thwin 1995, 2011b). The urban center exhibits a complex developmental trajectory, beginning with its initial settlement in the ninth century CE, followed by its emergence as a state capital in the eleventh century, and culminating in its loss of "exemplary center" status in the fourteenth century, after which time Bagan was downgraded to a mere governorship. Regardless of this relegation, Bagan managed to maintain its status not only as one of history's great Buddhist capitals, but also as the fount of Burmese identity and tradition. To this day, "Old Bagan" continues to attract pilgrims and religious donations from across the country. Considering its history, the ancient Burmese capital makes for an interesting case study for thinking about how people detach from place. It is readily apparent that detachment at Bagan was a multiscalar process, in both spatial and temporal terms. On one hand, detachment at Bagan must be considered on a scale that includes not only the entire urban community, but also the broader geopolitical landscape—and one might argue even the wider sociospiritual universe. At the same time, it is also apparent that detachment from Bagan was both a complex and gradual process that was only partially achieved, in addition to being intrinsically recursive in character.

DOI: 10.5876/9781646420087.c010

THE CITY OF THE ENEMY CRUSHER AND
ITS BUDDHIST PLAIN OF MERIT

Also known as Arimadannapura—or the "City of the Enemy Crusher" (Higham 2001:133; Lieberman 2003:91; Luce 1969:5; Nyunt Nyunt Shwe 2011:25; Stadtner 2011:214, 2013:22; Strachan 1989:7)—classical Bagan had varying degrees of control over most of what is now the country of Myanmar (Lieberman 2003:112). Situated in the "dry-zone"—not unlike the vast majority of the country's successive capital cities—Bagan was strategically positioned to control trade up and down the Ayeyarwady River (figure 10.1). The city's agricultural productivity was constrained, however, by the limited rainfall it received during the annual monsoons, its comparatively poor soils, and the fact that the local topography did not facilitate extensive irrigation (Lieberman 1987:171, 2011:942–43). As such, agriculture in and around the capital focused on "dry weather crops" such as sesame, millet, legumes, palm trees, and dry rice (Aung-Thwin 1990:5–6; Kan Hla 1977:15; see also Spate 1945:524–26). This meant that the kingdom was forced to make significant investments in wet-rice production in areas more suitable for irrigation, such as the Mu, Kyaukse, and Minbu Valleys (Aung-Thwin 1987:94, Aung Thwin 1990:4, 8, 12–13; Aung-Thwin and Aung-Thwin 2012:38, 95; Hudson 2004:183–84; Lieberman 1987:171, 2003:91, 96, 2011:942–43; Luce 1969:31–33; Stadtner 2013:12). Surplus produce from these three "rice-bowls"—which were located some 50–200 kilometers away—was transported to the capital via the river systems (Fletcher 2012; Lieberman 2003:90–91; Lieberman and Buckley 2012:1061; Moore 2007:25).

Even with these challenges, Bagan's agrarian economy was able to support one of Southeast Asia's largest and most populous preindustrial urban centers. The capital city was focused on a walled and moated regal-ritual epicenter roughly 1.5 square kilometers (Aung-Thwin and Aung-Thwin 2012:78; see figure 10.2) that represented a "two-dimensional model" of Mount Meru—the home of the gods—a common practice in most of the early Buddhist kingdoms of Southeast Asia (Hudson 2004:222; Stuart-Fox and Reeve 2011:107–9). This "exemplary" center—imbued as it was with cosmological and regal-ritual significance (Aung-Thwin 2017:30; Errington 1989; Geertz 1980:13; Tambiah 1977; Wheatley 1971)—was also home to royals, nobles, military leaders, guards, servants, and elite craft workers, in addition to serving as the node from which economic control was initiated over the vast kingdom (Aung-Thwin 1985:50–51, 1987:88, 94–98, Aung Thwin and Aung-Thwin 2012:81, 100–101; Daw Thin Kyi 1966:187; Hudson 2004:221; Kan Hla 1977:21).

Retrospective chronicles and inscriptions suggest that the regal-ritual epicenter was surrounded by a roughly periurban settlement zone that was 80

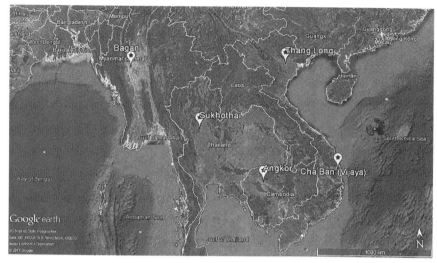

Figure 10.1. *Map of mainland Southeast Asia showing the location of Bagan and some of the other classical capitals of the region.*

square kilometers (Grave and Barbetti 2001:75; Hudson 2004:237; Hudson, Nyein, and Maung 2001:48; Moore, Win, and Kyaw 2016:294) containing as many as 4,000 temples (Aung-Thwin 1985:169; Kan Hla 1977:15; see figure 10.2). This dispersed, low-density urban matrix (Fletcher 2009, 2012; Hudson, Nyein, and Maung 2001:70; Stark et al. 2015:1442; cf. Aung-Thwin 1987:92; Kan Hla 1977:21–23) was inhabited by a population that is said to have been exceptionally diverse in terms of status, occupation, and ethnicity. Patron-client relationships appear to have been the norm, with most commoners being "bonded" by legal contract to wealthy nobles or, more often, to either the Crown or the Buddhist Church, or *Sangha* (Aung-Thwin 1985:71, 74, 78, 87, 1987:88; Aung-Thwin and Aung-Thwin 2012:97). The written records imply that Bagan's residential patterning developed a cellular character, with a combination of one's "socio-spiritual" status, clientage, occupation, and ethnicity serving to determine both where and with whom one lived (Aung-Thwin 1985:74, 91–96; Hudson 2004:212). We can therefore infer that greater Bagan was home to a myriad of villages and/or wards that exhibited an occupational, or "guild-like," character (Aung-Thwin 1985:91, 1987:92; Aung-Thwin and Aung-Thwin 2012:91; Kan Hla 1977:21). In other words, cellularity at Bagan did not lead to settlement redundancy, but rather specialized village clustering (Hudson 2004:219–20).

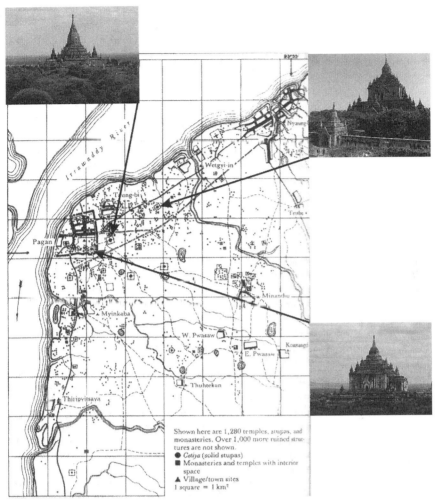

FIGURE 10.2. *Map of the Bagan epicenter and periurban zone, with examples of some of the larger temples (clockwise from the top): Ananda Phaya, Htilominlo, and Thatbyinnyu Pahto (modified from Kan Hla 1977:fig. 1 and Aung-Thwin 1985:map 4).*

Today, the remains of as many as 2,800 monuments exist within what were once Bagan's epicentral and periurban settlement zones (Pichard 1992–2003; see figure 10.2). These include temples with interior space, solid core stupas, ordination halls, libraries, monasteries, "preaching halls," and a palace (Aung-Thwin 1985:50–52, 1987:89–91; Aung-Thwin and Aung-Thwin 2012:81; Daw Thin Kyi

1966:179; Hudson 2004:220). Bagan's myriad temples and monasteries entangled the surrounding population by means of a shared belief in Buddhist merit-making, through which citizens secured social and spiritual benefits—including a higher-quality rebirth—by donating capital and both human and natural resources to the *Sangha* (Aung-Thwin 1985:26, 43–44, 169–71; Aung-Thwin and Aung-Thwin 2012:94; see also Luce 1969:89–90, 107, 109, 112, 115; Stadtner 2013:18). Another driving force behind such donations was that they were tax exempt, and even though the return on such investments was theoretically deferred to one's forthcoming rebirth, spending on merit for a future life was apparently favored over saving for the present or paying taxes to the Crown (Aung-Thwin 1985:170–71). Theoretically, individuals from across the social spectrum could make meritorious donations (Aung-Thwin 1985:26, 43–44, 169–71; Aung-Thwin and Aung-Thwin 2012:94), and the increasing prevalence of smaller monument constructions in the thirteenth century seems to corroborate the idea that "a broader range of individuals" were endowing monuments by this time (Hudson 20014:212; Hudson, Nyein, and Maung 2001:62; see also Aung-Thwin and Aung-Thwin 2012:84). That said, those with unfettered access to resources continued to make the largest, and hence the most spiritually valuable, donations. It is also true that those without means, even if they were small-scale donors, often found themselves being donated by their merit-seeking clients. Indeed, the inscriptions tell us that members of the royal family would sometimes donate entire villages to the Sangha (Aung-Thwin 1985:86). Equally important to the economic standing of Bagan's religious institutions was that they also received tax benefits to colonize and to improve unproductive lands, which in turn helped integrate an expanding population of cultivators (Aung-Thwin 1998:64; Aung-Thwin and Aung-Thwin 2012:103; Lieberman 2003:119–20, 228, 2011:940) and served to attract population to the capital itself (Lieberman 1987:171).

In summary, the significance of the Buddhist Church in Bagan society not only reflected the centrality of religion in the daily life of all of the citizens of the state (Aung-Thwin 1987:89; Aung-Thwin and Aung-Thwin 2012:83–85), but also the fact that it was the principal recipient of merit-driven donations of capital, produce and livestock, ritual items, building materials, goods and service, general labor, improved and unimproved land, and tax benefits (Aung-Thwin 1985:26, 43–44, 169–71, 1990:42, 89; Aung-Thwin and Aung-Thwin 2012:94; see also Luce 1969:89–90, 107, 109, 112, 115; Stadtner 2013:18). This resulted in the Sangha becoming an increasingly powerful patron with enhanced autonomy and economic influence over the population, especially given its expanding role in income redistribution (Aung-Thwin 1985:183–95, 1998:63; Aung-Thwin and Aung-Thwin 2012:85; Hudson 2004:245; Hudson,

Nyein, and Maung 2001:61–62; Lieberman 1987:170–71, 2003:95, 114, 120; cf. Lieberman 2011:942). It was through such meritorious donations and tax benefits that the plethora of Bagan's monuments was constructed and maintained (Hudson 2008:555), leading some to characterize Bagan's periurban zone as a "Buddhist Plain of Merit" (Stadtner 2013). In other words, daily engagement with, and support of, the various temples, stupas, and monasteries helped form relationships of "dependence" (Hodder 2011a:175, 2011b, 2012:17–18, 88, 2014, 2016b:235) that fostered the development and growth of an urban cityscape that was tightly integrated both economically and spiritually through what has been designated the "merit-path to salvation" (Aung-Thwin and Aung-Thwin 2012:84). As a result, the religious monuments that were scattered across Bagan's periurban zone emerged as nodal features (Hodder 2016b:247) within and around which relationships of environmental, economic, social, ideological, and spiritual significance were "bundled" (Pauketat 2013:34, 130) or "knotted" (Ingold 2015:13–16) together, creating a vast "meshwork" (3) of entanglements that imbued the cityscape with concentrated "agentic power" (Pauketat 2013:41) and enhanced "historical gravity" (Mrozowski 2016).

COLLAPSE AND DETACHMENT AT BAGAN

Both the Bagan polity and its capital city would flourish for three hundred years, but by the end of the thirteenth century it would enter into a period of declining resources, and its sociopolitical system would ultimately collapse (Aung-Thwin 2011b:37, 2017:43). This led to a period of reorganization that played itself out across the entire realm. The collapse was marked by a decrease in infrastructure investments (Lieberman 2011:943) and a loss of patronage, the latter leading to a marked decline in the donations required for temple-building activities (Aung-Thwin 1998:36, Aung-Thwin 2011b:47, 2017:29–30, 47; Kan Hla 1977:19; Stadtner 2011:215–16, 2013:15–18, 26). There is also textual evidence attesting to the erosion of state authority and internal discord (Lieberman 2009:17)—including conflicts within the royal court (Aung-Thwin 1998:94) and between the Crown and the Sangha (Kan Hla 1977:19)—as well as the out-migration of both noble families (19) and members of the general population, often along "cultural/ethnic" lines (Lieberman 2009:17; see also Fletcher 2012). The political and demographic downturns within the old capital were offset by increasing economic and political independence in the former hinterlands (Lieberman 2003:85).

By the early fourteenth century, Bagan the city no longer held exemplary center status (Aung-Thwin 2017:43)—principally because it was no longer the preeminent setting for regal-ritual, patronage, and merit-making activities—and Bagan the polity had clearly lost the capacity to "maintain its integrated character" (Aung-Thwin and Aung-Thwin 2012:102). Bagan's collapse is best characterized as having resulted in the demise of dynastic power specific to the center itself (105). This is because the fundamental aspects of Burmese life did not disappear; rather, they were simply more diffuse in their distribution. That is to say, although they were no longer concentrated to the degree they had been when the exemplary center of Bagan had served as the quintessential capital of an expansive kingdom, under a single authority and power structure, many of the characteristics of the Bagan polity continued virtually unchanged, including its conceptual, ideological, and patron-client systems; agrarian-based economy; population and settlement patterns; and religious and legal institutions (Aung-Thwin 2011b:37; Aung-Thwin and Aung-Thwin 2012:102).

Merit Making and Entrapment: The Ultimate Cause of Bagan's Collapse

The sociopolitical collapse at Bagan resulted from both internal, structural issues, and external, historical factors (Aung-Thwin and Aug-Thwin 2012:103–6). Michael Aung-Thwin's (1985) meticulous study of the inscriptional record suggests that although the Sangha and its religious complexes initially enabled the economic growth and integration of Bagan society (Aung-Thwin and Aung-Thwin 2012:85), as the number and size of tax-exempt donations to the Sangha grew they unwittingly served to undermine both the economic and ideological foundations of the Crown (see also Aung-Thwin 1995:90, 1998:64; Aung-Thwin and Aung-Thwin 2012:85). Indeed, it is estimated that by 1280 CE as much as two-thirds of all cultivable land in Upper Burma had been endowed to the Sangha (Aung-Thwin 1990:42, 89; Lieberman 2003:120, 126), and large portions of the state's hereditary labor and tangible wealth—in the form of gold and silver—was also controlled by the Church as a result of tax-exempt donations (Aung-Thwin and Aung-Thwin 2012:103). As labor was the key delimiting factor in state development and expansion across Southeast Asia (Andaya and Andaya 2015:4; Lieberman 2009:764–65, 2011:941), including at Bagan (Aung-Thwin 1985:95, 1987:88, Aung-Thwin and Aung-Thwin 2012:88), allocations of labor to the Sangha as part of tax-free donations was especially detrimental to the Crown's overall productive capacity (Aung-Thwin 1998:63). Equally significant, the polity's secular interests had a hard time challenging the "merit-making" intent of the donations that were increasingly made to the religious institutions. This is because kingly legitimacy was intricately entangled with both the health of these institutions and the donations that supported them, meaning that a certain path dependency developed from which the Crown could not easily extract itself (Aung-Thwin 1985; Aung-Thwin and Aung-Thwin 2012:103–5; cf. Lieberman 2011:941–42).

Considered in unison, it is clear that by the thirteenth century the various entanglements that were "bundled" together at the myriad temple complexes and stupas spread across Bagan's periurban settlement zone had begun to be the focus of countless societal "dependencies" that increasingly "entrapped" (Hodder 2016b:247–48) both the Crown and the Sangha in a situation where previously enabling relationships had become increasingly constraining over time. "What had been a blessing had become a curse" (Aung-Thwin and Aung-Thwin 2012:105). Because the legitimacy and economic standing of both the Crown and the Sangha were so fully entangled with merit-making donation activities, these two powerful institutions, by necessity, were predisposed to compete for the same finite resources (105). Seeing as the Sangha constituted a higher moral authority, and played a central role in the merit-making activities relating to *kamma* (intentional actions that have future consequences) and rebirth, it was an inherently more effective attractor of land, wealth, and labor when compared to the Crown, which itself was beholden to the Church (Aung-Thwin 1985:183–95; cf. Lieberman 2011:941–42). For this reason, it was principally the Crown's capacity to integrate its realm, in both political and economic terms, that was eroded over time due to the upsurge in merit-making activities (Aung-Thwin 1985:183–95; Aung-Thwin and Aung-Thwin 2012:85). Be that as it may, many of the existing religious complexes at Bagan would have also found themselves less able to maintain their temples, stupas, and monasteries as donations began to diminish in size and frequency because of the Crown's deteriorating resource base. This would have similarly reduced their capacity to consistently integrate the common folk and their precious labor. In other words, the Sangha —a religious institution with significant economic clout—had developed a comparable, albeit somewhat less debilitating, dependency on the merit system that coalesced within and around its myriad temples and stupas.

In summary, the alienation of natural and human resources to the Sangha appears to have been the "ultimate" cause of Bagan's sociopolitical collapse. That said, a number of proximate causes likely exacerbated the situation (Aung Thwin 1985:197; Aung-Thwin 1998:64, 94). The loss of material resources to the Sangha—including cultivable land, wealth, and labor—would have diminished the Crown's capacity to deal with these unexpected perturbations (Aung-Thwin and Aung-Thwin 2012:105).

By the thirteenth century, Bagan's economic development, agrarian expansion, and demographic growth had all started to decline (Lieberman 2011:945). Not only was new land suitable for irrigation increasingly scarce (942–43), but the "extensification" of agriculture, which resulted in large tracts of forest being converted to open fields—and often rice paddy—had also resulted in anthropogenic landscapes that were susceptible to erosion, loss of nutrients, and the effects of climate change (Fletcher 2012; Lieberman 2009:17). To make matters worse, although the warmer, wetter conditions of the Medieval Climate Anomaly (800/850–1250/1300 CE) had initially increased the productive capacity of Bagan's principal agricultural zones and promoted colonization of previously unproductive lands (Lieberman 2009:33, 2011:944–47; Lieberman and Buckley 2012; see also Hudson 2006), the subsequent shift into the more variable Little Ice Age (1300–1850 CE) climate regime would have ushered in an era of less-regular and generally weaker monsoons, stimulating an overall drying trend that would have led to a contraction in both yields and available land for cultivation (Fletcher 2012; Lieberman 2003, 2009:17, 33, 2011:939–44, 947; Lieberman and Buckley 2012). Ultimately, declining agricultural productivity—due to climate change and resource degradation—coupled with the diminishing availability of cultivatable land, appears to have driven taxable citizens and their labor away from the Crown, and toward both religious and private landholding estates (Lieberman 2011:943).

Equally problematic is the fact that even though the rate of polity growth and land reclamation had begun to decline in the thirteenth century, merit-driven, tax-free donations to the temples and monasteries continued to increase, further diminishing the capacity for the Crown not only to maintain itself economically, but also to sustain a strong military presence in the face of incursions by antagonistic groups (Lieberman 1987:171, 2003:120, 2009:56, 2011:942, 945). Of relevance here are invasions by Mongols and T'ai speakers from the north, which are traditionally thought to have played key roles in Bagan's demise (Coedès 1968:183, 189–94; Lieberman 1987:170, 2003:120–23, 2011:953–56; Luce 1969:10, 256; Pe Maung Tin and Luce 1923:176; Strachan 1989:11). Recent analyses have downplayed the role of these intrusions, implying that they were economically, sociopolitically, and ideologically disruptive but not entirely devastating (Aung-Thwin 1998:63–92, 121–43, 152, 2011b:34–35, 2017:2333–34; Aung-Thwin and Aung-Thwin 2012:105; Hudson, Nyein, and Maung 2001:53; Lieberman 2003:119; Stadtner 2013:26).

It is also significant that factional competition between members of the Bagan royal court also appears to have ensued after the death of King

Narathihapate in 1287 CE, mainly involving the dead king's legitimate heirs and those who controlled the military (Aung-Thwin 1998:94). This competition resulted in a period of economic and political decentralization (94–96, 132) that enhanced the autonomy and centrifugal pull of peripheral elites—and in some cases the state's own ministers—who continually struggled against the Crown to control more land and labor (Aung-Thwin 1985:186, 1998:96; Lieberman 2003:120, 2009:22, 2011:940–41). Such conflicts frequently resulted in rebellions in the hinterlands, especially when the central government was not able to meet the socioeconomic demands of its vassals (940). That power and resources were beginning to bleed into the hinterlands at this time is also suggested by the fact that Lower Myanmar began to exert its political and economic independence as a maritime-based polity (Aung-Thwin 1998:94, 102, 114–15, 121–43, 2011a:1, 2017:1; Lieberman 2003:85). Ultimately, the era between 1301 CE—corresponding with the retreat of the Mongols—and the consolidation that coincided with the establishment of the Ava polity in 1364 CE was a period of decentralization and comparative disunity, but not necessarily chaos (Aung-Thwin 1998:132, 135). That said, coinciding with the reign of King Kyawswa—between 1289 and 1298 CE—the principal economic and political focus of upper Myanmar clearly began to shift from Bagan to the Kyaukse region, and from the kingdom of Bagan to the diminutive statelets ruled by the infamous "Three Brothers" (Aung-Thwin 1998:94, 102, 114–15, 121–43, 2011a:1, 2017:1, 29).

RECURSIVE AND PARTIAL DETACHMENT AT BAGAN

The decline in monument construction and maintenance at Bagan has been attributed to the shift in patronage, and hence donations, away from the former capital, culminating in the deterioration and abandonment of many of its temples and monasteries (Stadtner 2013:17). This shift coincided with a decline in population across the periurban settlement zone (Fletcher 2012). Nevertheless, Bagan's royal court continued to hold some political clout in the Dry Zone until the reign of King Sawmunit (1325–68 CE), when it was downgraded to a governorship under the rule of the Three Brothers, a status it would continue to hold when the kingdom of Ava (1364–1527 CE) came to power (Aung-Thwin 1998:93, 2017:44, 58). With the establishment of the new capital at Ava, both patrons and their clients—the latter being intricately involved in the daily maintenance of the temples and monuments, and the former, namely, royals and/or wealthy elites, being key contributors of the funds required for their initial construction and ongoing upkeep costs—would have established similar sets of patronage relationships at the new exemplary center, much to the detriment of Bagan (Stadtner 2013:17). Indeed, Bagan's position as an exemplary center would die with King Sawmunit in 1368 CE (Aung-Thwin 2017:43).

The vacuum created by the decline of the Bagan polity was filled by the Buddhist Church, which continued to receive donations, construct new temples and monasteries, and maintain some of the existing complexes and institutional components (Lieberman 1987:171). In the fourteenth and fifteenth centuries, the Sangha was also able to sponsor new drainage and irrigation features, carry out land reclamation projects, purchase additional landholdings, and fund commercial initiatives, which may have hindered any state recentralization endeavors, thus perpetuating the comparatively fragmented sociopolitical landscape characteristic of the early Post-Classical era (171). Over this time, Bagan persisted as a center for religious studies and pilgrimages (Aung-Thwin 1985:197; Hudson 2004:234–45, 266, table 15, 2008:555; Hudson, Nyein, and Maung 2001:53; Stadtner 2011:216), but it was rarely a locus for significant patronage activities (Aung-Thwin 1998:96). For example, King Thadominbya (1364–67 CE) of Ava visited Bagan in 1366 CE, and although he did pay respects at some of the monuments in the old capital, he was there primarily to secure Sawmunit's loyalty and to acquire tribute (Aung-Thwin 2017:58).

That said, Bagan would remain, at least conceptually, the quintessential example of Burmese patronage and legitimacy for centuries to come (Aung-Thwin 1998:115). Bob Hudson (2004:238) notes that "during the fourteenth century, when Bagan is supposed to have gone into decline—it was no longer a polity capital—resource allocation to construction still exceeded 11th century levels." However, those who continued to patronize the old capital tended to channel their funds into the construction of new monuments, rather than existing ones, as this was believed to be a more effective way to acquire merit (Stadtner 2013:17). Although some architecturally elaborate monuments were constructed at Bagan in the fourteenth century (Strachan 1989:11), newer monuments tended to be smaller and less elaborate (Stadtner 2013:26). Donations of land to existing monasteries also persisted into the fourteenth century (Strachan 1989:11), and the most important temples and monasteries—meaning the largest and/or oldest—not only persevered across the transition, but they also continued to receive donations for their maintenance and refurbishments, though many others fell into disrepair (Strachan 1989:11; Stadtner 2011:216, 2013:26). Considered in combination, these data imply that those with means—often residing elsewhere in the former kingdom—continued to consider Bagan a place to build merit (Stadtner 2011:216).

To put this continued patronage in context, when compared to the over 2,000 monuments erected between the eleventh and fourteenth centuries, fewer than 200 were built between the fifteenth and twentieth centuries (Stadtner 2013:26). That said, references to ongoing temple and monastery repairs can be found in texts dating to the fifteenth, sixteenth, and seventeenth centuries (Hudson 2000). For example, during the Konbaung period (1752–1885 CE) many of Bagan's most important monuments—often the oldest and/or largest—were repaired and/or renovated, and new temples and monasteries continued to be built (Stadtner 2011:217, 2013:26). By the end of eighteenth century, however, European visitors were describing Bagan's monuments as "indistinguishable masses of rubbish, overgrown with weeds," and a century later we are told that many of the monuments were serving as cowsheds and homes for creatures of the night, such as bats and owls (Stadtner 2011:216, 2013:15). Be that as it may, it is documented that a king visited Bagan in 1806 to take possession of a royal white elephant arriving from Lower Myanmar, at which time he also raised a new metal finial above the Shwezigon pagoda, signs that the old capital's once exemplary standing still resonated in the minds of Myanmar's royals (Stadtner 2013:18). In the late nineteenth–early twentieth centuries the colonial authorities continued to fund repairs to the main temple and monastery complexes, and some new building projects were initiated (26–27). UNESCO assisted with a subsequent program of repairs following extensive damage to Bagan's monuments following an earthquake in 1975 (Stadtner 2011:217, 2013:27). Indeed, because it remains a "potent symbol" of past glories that is imbued with the residues of centuries of merit making, Bagan has witnessed successive rebuilding programs in the recent past, including a wide-ranging, government-led reconstruction and consolidation program beginning in the 1990s (Stadtner 2011:216–17, 2013:17–18). Another program of major repairs was initiated following an earthquake in 2016 (figure 10.3).

In truth, Bagan never fully lost its position as a focal point of religious life in Myanmar, and its deep history as an exemplary center has resulted in myriad new temples and stupas being constructed among the innumerable older monuments, as contemporary Myanma peoples continue to build their merit on the ancient plain that was once the quintessential locus for such activities (Stadtner 2011:22, 2013:18, 27, 72–73). Today, a steady stream of local devotees and Buddhist pilgrims continue to pray in and around the most famous temples and stupas on a daily basis. Thousands of tourists also visit Bagan annually to take in its majestic cultural landscape and engage with its various monuments, murals, and sculptures.

FIGURE 10.3. *Repairs being carried out to the So-Min Gyi stupa as a result of the earthquake that impacted Bagan on August 24, 2016.*

CONCLUSIONS

Detachment from Bagan continues to be both partial and recursive in character, even though its status as an exemplary center and state capital ended some seven centuries ago. Across a range of highly significant ecological, economic, and sociopolitical changes, Bagan has managed to maintain its sociospiritual status as both the fount of Burmese identity and nexus for Buddhist merit-making activities. Its various temples and stupas continue to serve as agentic nodes with the power to attract pilgrims and wealth, including merit-driven donations and tourist dollars. The historical gravity of the old capital also continues to entangle those seeking to legitimize their status, including Myanmar's military leaders, many of whom publicly patronize Bagan's monuments in a manner similar to the rulers and nobles of the Classical period. In broader terms, classical Bagan, and more specifically its state institutions and sociospiritual hierarchy, arguably provided the "charter" for all Myanma state formations to follow, including the present one (Aung-Thwin 1985:199; Lieberman 2003:23, 2009:15). Similarly, the complex relationship between the Crown and the Sangha that manifest at Old Bagan, and the importance given to traditional patron-client relationships, still resonate in contemporary Myanmar society (Aung-Thwin 1998:64, 158–59). In the end, the unmaking and remaking of Bagan appears to be a never-ending story. As such, physical and conceptual disentanglement and detachment from Bagan should be considered ongoing processes that will likely never be fully realized.

ACKNOWLEDGMENTS

I would like to thank the Social Sciences and Humanities Research Council of Canada and Trent University for their generous support of the field research that has informed this discussion. I also acknowledge the ongoing assistance of Myanmar's Department of Archaeology. My gratitude is also extended to all of the archaeologists and historians who have contributed to our understanding of the complex history of Bagan. Finally, I wish to express my thanks to all of the members of the Socio-ecological Entanglement in Tropical Societies (SETS) project and the IRAW@Bagan settlement archaeology project, who contributed to many insightful discussions on this topic, and many more, as we traveled across South and Southeast Asia, and traversed the fields surrounding Bagan's magnificent temple complexes.

11

New Approaches to Detaching from Place

CATHERINE M. CAMERON

Humans are a mobile species, though thirty years ago archaeologists (at least in North America) would have denied this. Given the renewed focus on migration since Anthony's (1990) "Baby and the Bathwater" paper, Americanist archaeologists have engaged in considerable productive study of various aspects of migration, including abandonment. One aspect that has received insufficient study is the making and unmaking—or remaking—of places that migration entails, a topic taken up by the authors of this volume. Abandonment as a fundamental aspect of site-formation processes has received considerable study, but it is far more difficult to assess how and why people made decisions to leave a place and how a sense of place might be transferred to a new location. The chapters in the volume consider detaching from place from the perspective of an impressive array of geographic regions and time periods: late third to early second millennia Mesopotamia, historic West Africa, eleventh- to fourteenth-century Southeast Asia, the Lower Southeast region of North America at about 3,000 years ago, and others. As they explore detaching from place the chapters emphasize the social and landscape entanglements in these places that make leaving so complex.

I begin with a consideration of how archaeologists have investigated abandonment processes over the past few decades. I then consider the contributions of these chapters to a new understanding of

DOI: 10.5876/9781646420087.c011

178

abandonment. Although some questions are the same—"why did people go?"—these authors take a much more nuanced approach to peoples' decisions to leave. They expose the meanings with which people endow their homes and surrounding landscapes, they explore the environmental conditions (drought, rising water) that force people to leave meaningful places, they examine the cultural practices that can make leaving imperative, as well as social dynamics (violence, growth, or decline of religious or political power) that can dictate leaving and the conditions under which it occurs.

In the following discussion, the chapters are divided by social scale: small-scale societies and state-level societies. For small scale I examine a series of increasing scales of movement. For state-level societies I consider the implications of the loss of power that central places must have experienced and then urge a rethinking of the abandonment behaviors of people of different social identities: men, women, children, captives, slaves, and others. Finally, I explore the meaning that abandoned places have for the people who left them and for later peoples. As I reflect on the contributions of the chapters, I offer some insights from my research area, the American Southwest, as well as some thoughts about aspects of abandonment that we may want to consider more deeply in future studies.

A LOOK BACK AT ABANDONMENT STUDIES

Abandonment is, of course, one end of the process of migration in most cases (except when residents die) and received heightened interest with renewed studies of migration in the early 1990s (Anthony 1990; Cameron and Tomka 1993; papers in the *Journal of Anthropological Archaeology*, Volume 14, no. 2, 1995). Archaeologists and the public have always been interested in catastrophic abandonment—exemplified by Pompeii and the empty cliff dwellings of Mesa Verde. But archaeologists also realized that such headline-grabbing events were not the norm and that abandonment was as much a part of the human process of living as settlement was.

Processual archaeology of the 1970s brought an interest in site-formation processes, and Michael Schiffer identified abandonment as an important process in the formation of the archaeological record (1972, 1976, 1985). Robert Ascher's "Time's Arrow: and the Archaeology of a Contemporary Community" (1968) provided an early example of how abandonment processes affect the sites we excavate. He showed the distribution of structures and artifacts across the landscape as the people of a Seri village created, abandoned, and rebuilt structures and activity areas through time. Studies during the next several decades explored the complex interaction between abandonment processes and archaeological patterns at regional and settlement scales, highlighting how different conditions of abandonment (speed of abandonment, completeness of abandonment, structure function [e.g., ritual vs domestic], status of structure's occupants, etc.) affect archaeological patterns of abandoned places (Cameron 1991, 1999; Cameron and Tomka 1993; Inomata and Webb 2003a; Stevenson 1982). In the Southwest, archaeologists studying Ancestral Pueblo people emphasized that the abandonment of a site did not necessarily imply regional depopulation (Nelson and Hegmon 2001; Upham 1984) and that social landscapes could be highly fluid (Bernardini 2011; Fowles 2011). In the past decade or so, studies of migration have increasingly focused on the interaction of migrants with hosts at their destination (Cabana and Clark 2011; Mills 2011; Ortman and Cameron 2011; Stone 2003), and archaeologists seem to have stepped back from studies of abandonment.

The present volume picks up the study of abandonment and moves it forward by looking at the process with different theoretical lenses. No longer are we interested simply in linking abandonment to site-formation processes. Instead, the authors of this volume seek to engage with ancient people's decision making regarding place-making and place-leaving. How were the imperatives of the natural and social environment entwined with cultural practices to condition the options available to those who detached from meaningful places? As these chapters have shown, this is an important new direction in our understanding of the beginning end of the process of migration, and it promises to encourage new directions of study.

THE SCALE OF DETACHMENT

Detaching from place has scalar and temporal aspects. One can leave (or move about) regions of variable size or, at a smaller spatial scale, one can leave a settlement. Leaving can be rapid or gradual, take a day, or years, be voluntary or forced. Each of these dimensions affect decision making regarding leaving, the ways in which migrants leave, and postabandonment interaction with the place. The places considered in this volume are of two broad types, which adds another level of complexity to assessing how people detached from place. Several chapters focus on small-scale societies (Birch and Lesage [chapter 4], Sassaman and Randall [chapter 5], Glowacki). Two (Danti [chapter 9] and de Barros [chapter 8]) explore small-scale societies that are embedded in or adjacent to larger social entities. Three focus on state-level societies (Lamoureux-St. Hilaire et al. [chapter 7], Iannone, Macrae et al. [chapter 6]), two of which examine a single large settlement (Lamoureux-St. Hilaire et al. [chapter 7] and Iannone [chapter 10]).

State-level societies have far more investment in settlement architecture than small-scale societies; they also have larger supporting populations, often longer-term occupation of a single place, and a concentration of power in that place. Small-scale societies such as the ones profiled here often use mobility as a long-term subsistence and social strategy, even the supposedly "sedentary" Pueblo people of the Southwest. This means that for small-scale societies, abandonment of places was almost certainly more frequent and more familiar, and involved less disruption of power relationships. Whether small scale or state level, the societies profiled in these chapters have different types and levels of entanglement with the natural and man-made environments that make decisions to leave and the process of leaving different in each case. Still, patterns are evident, and the chapters are asking similar questions. On the broadest level, they ask, "why did people leave" and more specifically "how were decisions to leave made." In one case, they ask "did people actually leave at all?" Each of the cases discusses patterns in the abandonment process, including termination rituals, and most make the point that even when a place is abandoned, it often still has meaning to the people who once lived there or to their descendants.

I use social scale to organize the comments that follow. For small-scale societies I examine first the movement of individuals and households between settlements, then movements around a region, and then movements between regions. For state-level societies I examine the ways in which large powerful settlements were abandoned. I highlight the contributions of these chapters to a new understanding of the causes of abandonment, the ways in which people detached from place or power, the creation of new meaningful places, and the meaning that still resides in the places that were left.

LEAVING PLACES AND REGIONS IN SMALL-SCALE SOCIETIES

Archaeologists who study small-scale horticultural societies have often considered detaching from places to be an economic behavior, sometimes the result of soil degradation, environmental downturn (a drought), or other problems of food production. The chapters in this volume move beyond this narrow perspective. Instead, they consider social issues such as population size, factionalism, social conflict, religious practices (a rethinking of the cosmos), and historical contingencies. This shift allows them to consider a far broader set of causes for abandonment and achieve a better understanding of how the process of detaching takes place.

This broader set of causes requires a reconsideration of the speed of departure. We often imagine that leave taking was the result of careful consideration of when and where to go. This certainly must have been true much of the time, as in the generational village relocation practiced by the ancestral Wendat that involved considerable preparation of a new homesite. We know that leaving is not unusual or unexpected. As Charles Cobb noted more than a decade ago with regard to small-scale premodern societies, "there is abundant evidence to suggest that significant population movement and the creation of place were part of everyday life, rather than unusual or periodic occurrences in the life of stable communities" (2005:565). Cobb's study focused on the North American Southeast (as do Sassaman and Randall, chapter 5 in this volume), but among the Pueblo people of the Southwest a similar commitment to movement was also part of their worldview (Fowles 2011). In a now famous quote, Tessie Naranjo, a scholar from Santa Clara Pueblo, said, "Movement is part of us." The same ethos may have imbued the Huron/Wendat movements described by Birch and Lesage in chapter 4.

These chapters also emphasize that not all leaving was slow and carefully considered. Social conflict and violence within or between settlements could cause small numbers or large groups of people to flee, abandoning homes, gardens, and places of spiritual meaning. Calculating where they might go, with sometimes limited options, could be fraught and involve complex negotiation with other settlements. Although these sorts of rapid detachment may be evident in the archaeological record (burned buildings, abandoned tools, and domestic goods), understanding where people went, why, and how is much more difficult. Still, we should recognize that rapid abandonment must often have resulted from the fissioning of settlements and the reforming of others with a scrambled set of actors (see Glowacki, chapter 3 in this volume).

Detaching at the Smallest Scale

At the smallest scale, individuals and households moved, leaving homes in established communities and finding new ones elsewhere. This is a process Birch and Lesage call "population circulation" (after Schachner 2012) and Glowacki refers to as "serial migration" (after Bernardini 2005). Birch and Lesage (chapter 4) provide evidence that not all longhouses in a Wendat settlement were coterminously constructed when the settlement was established and suggest that intersettlement movement was an option for Wendat families. Glowacki (chapter 3) sees similar processes in the Southwest. Although the reasons for such moves are difficult to retrieve, ethnographic and ethnohistoric data suggest that there must have been multiple factors, including intermarriage, trade, efforts to maximize social positioning, and social conflict. Glowacki identifies social conflict as a factor in social fission and fusion in the Southwest, yet she also notes that intraregional movement of individuals and households can foster social connections across regions that may facilitate later movements of larger groups. In the Southwest, settlements may have been abandoned because of perceived immorality by residents, unexpected or ominous deaths, or other events that make the location an uncomfortable place to live (Snead 2004:256–57). We are unlikely to be able to retrieve such causes archaeologically, but should acknowledge them as factors.

In chapter 8, De Barros's longitudinal data from the Bassar gives us some sense of the effect of violence on these small-scale societies as state-level groups formed on their margins and conducted slave raids into their territory. Although the distance in time prevents us from seeing exactly how and how quickly Bassar people left their homes, we know that because of marauding cavalry "most populations fled the Bassar peneplain, leaving it deserted of any major village or hamlet." It seems that those families who may have wished to stay did not have that option. Their choices were to abandon their home and flee to the mountains or face death or a life of servitude. Although Africa during the eighteenth and nineteenth centuries was experiencing unprecedented upheaval from warfare and slave raiding, we should not discount that these activities operated at some level at other times and places, as the chapters by Glowacki and Birch and Lesage (chapter 4) show.

Social conflict within small-scale communities must often have been resolved by forcing troublesome families out or causing them to choose to leave. In chapter 3, Glowacki highlights processes of fission and fusion in the Southwest that resulted from small groups detaching from settlements and seeking entry at others (also Bernardini 2005). Ethnographic accounts suggest that village fission might be sudden, the result of a fight, murder, sexual infidelity, or simply growing social tension (Cameron 2013:222–23). We should acknowledge that for those leaving, options about where to move may have been seriously constrained. For example, in the Amazon, Napoleon Chagnon (1992) points out that fleeing families seeking refuge in another settlement may be vulnerable to the whims of their hosts who may have seen them as an encumbrance on community resources. Less perilously, among the Hopi of the Southwest, unmoored "sub-clans" had to offer ceremonial knowledge or a similar contribution in order to be admitted to a new settlement (Bernardini 2005:35).

Recent studies of warfare and captive taking in small-scale societies reveal that conflict results in significant movement of individuals, generally women and children, between settlements at distances that extend across regional and even interregional landscapes (Brooks 2002; Cameron 2011, 2013, 2016; DeBoer 2008, 2011; Donald 1997; Snyder 2010). Thus, we might expect that most small-scale settlements included some proportion of people with different social and cultural backgrounds. Although captives may have been incorporated into the lowest social strata of the settlements they unwillingly joined, they could create opportunities for cultural exchange and even trade and other sorts of interaction between donor and captor groups (Albers 1993; Cameron 2016; DeBoer 2008). The implications for the present volume are that abandonment may often have been violent, that decisions to abandon may have been coerced, and the unit of abandonment may have been smaller than the household.

Where can we locate the decision-making process when focused on this small scale? Individuals can be forcibly moved, households can be expelled from communities, and villages can fission, sending resulting segments in different directions. Such moves cannot be seen as the result of decision making at the household level, even when there was time for careful consideration. As many of the chapters make clear, households are so enmeshed in their communities that their ability to go against the flow of the rest of the group would have been seriously constrained. Even when social conflict was not directly involved, individuals and households were responding to the social milieu that surrounded them. In an important analysis, Gregson Schachner (2012) urges archaeologists to readjust the focus of their studies to recognize multiple spatial and social scales of population movement that continually reshuffle the membership of even small groups. His example (Schachner 2012:18) from Highland New Guinea is an apt illustration: "Tairora individuals and groups constantly readjust their settlement and mobility decisions to subtle shifts in the social field brought about by factionalism, changing alliances, and open conflict."

Detaching within Regions

How can communities abandon their settlements frequently and still retain a sense of place? The answer is that their sense of place is crafted at a larger scale than a single settlement, a point made clearly here by Birch and Lesage (chapter 4), by Sassaman and Randall (chapter 5), by Glowacki (chapter 3), and by de Barros. Birch and Lesage use the concept of emplacement to describe the creation of a landscape-scale connection to place through processes of moving through a landscape, modifying it, and visiting the dead in abandoned villages. Here the placement of ossuaries "created ancestral landscapes inhabited by communities of the dead." In the Southeast, Sassaman and Randall recover an ancient cosmology of earth and water where places and regions were never really abandoned, merely repositioned as part of well-understood and long-remembered patterns of change; detaching from place was part of societal renewal. In the Southwest, traditional accounts of indigenous people's origins describe their movement through and pauses at various places in the landscape, retelling of events that happened at various locations (Bernardini 2005; Fowles 2011; Ortman 2008). As Glowacki emphasizes in chapter 3, oral traditions and ethnographic accounts can provide some of the human dimension that is missing from the archaeological record (but see Chilton [2005:153–54] for how the lack of fixed settlement among northeastern groups in the past has affected efforts of these groups to achieve federal recognition today).

In the sense presented by these three groups of scholars, detaching from a specific place may not have been as wrenching as we might imagine. Instead, it was relocating to another part of a well-known homeland. Leaving was an anticipated and expected part of every individual's experience. The wide sense of ownership in the landscape was reinforced in each case by continued interaction with "abandoned" places, places where the ancestors now dwelt, places that brought forth memories and embodied the narratives that constituted a group's history. As revealed by Sassaman and Randall in chapter 5, we might also consider the sense of renewal that leaving created. At a smaller scale, Birch and Lesage in chapter 4 show that village relocation contributed to the maintenance of equality among members of Iroquoian communities. In other words, establishing a new village likely offered opportunities to shuffle social relations, repositioning houses to separate feuding neighbors, allowing ambitious families to claim advantageous locations near plazas or other public spaces. The sadness of leaving may have been far outweighed by the sense of a "fresh start" for all community members.

Regardless of the regularity of movement, conflict almost certainly entered the decision-making process at the scale of settlement movement. Birch and Lesage (chapter 4) describe settlement aggregation and a decrease in population circulation that came with evidence of violence among Wendat communities during the late fifteenth and the sixteenth centuries. The result was large, fortified settlements that reveal evidence of traumatic death and trophy taking. In Togo, the Bassar moved to rugged mountainous regions where they could better defend themselves from raiders. In the Southwest, Glowacki finds evidence of intense violence in the Mesa Verde region during the Pueblo III time period, including dismembering of bodies and postmortem processing (see chapter 3 in this volume). The graceful cliff dwellings of the Mesa Verde region are now much-visited tourist destinations, but in the past were likely places of refuge from enemy attacks. In both instances, the periodicity of settlement abandonment seems to have increased as the social landscape outside villages became more hostile. As Glowacki shows, the trauma of the Pueblo III period seems to have transformed the demography of the entire Southwest.

Detaching from Regions

Regular movement across a familiar landscape is, of course, only one aspect of detaching from place. Growing populations may expand into new territories, and sometimes entire regions are abandoned. Chapters in this volume explore the causes and implications of these sorts of detachment, providing insight into the lived experiences of moving communities and the implications for the ways formerly occupied landscapes were incorporated into regional worldviews. The causes of such large-scale moves may be different than those just discussed and involve larger-scale social processes. The chapters in this volume provide much food for thought concerning these more extensive movements.

Birch and Lesage (chapter 4) describe movement into new territory for ancestral Wendat communities that expanded into Simcoe County and the Trent Valley, a process apparently facilitated by "signaling" between groups already in place with those in areas providing migrants. These interactions created long-lasting social networks that linked large parts of south-central Ontario. Seventeenth-century historic accounts report that families preserved the names and memories of their founders, the original immigrant stressors, even as they integrated into their new homelands. For these sorts of moves, we should be alert to processes of ethnogenesis in which new social formations emerge and, in the process, create new memories and attachments to the landscape they now inhabit (Anschuetz and Wilshusen 2011; Bernardini and Fowles 2011).

In chapter 3, Glowacki makes the important point that if we want to understand detachment from place at the regional scale (or any scale), we must consider the social context within which decisions to leave are made. At the end of the thirteenth century, Pueblo people left the northern San Juan region and relocated more than 200 miles to the southeast in the northern Rio Grande. While drought and warfare certainly must have been stressors, it was the social and historical context within which people operated that determined how they responded to the stress. They could and had survived droughts, but after a century of population decline, coalescence, and frequent violence, the decision was not strictly an economic one.

Like Glowacki, in chapter 8 de Barros takes an admirably broad view of the social landscape within which the Bassar people of Togo moved during the seventeenth–nineteenth centuries. Through extensive ethnographic interviews, he was able to tease out the causes of migration and the processes that allowed migrants to select a new home. People moved in response to violence (warfare, slave raiding, cattle raiding, and demands for tribute), but they were also influenced by opportunities at the other end of the journey—useful resources, the ability to continue the blacksmithing trade, good farmland, and professional and kin connections. De Barros's exploration of how migrants interact with hosts in new areas gives us much to ponder in our studies of detaching from place. He provides a valuable view of how people negotiate a new home and then make it their own. Ceremonies of "capturing the earth" provide important insights that we may be able to apply to the creation of a sense of place elsewhere in the world.

Danti's interesting chapter 9 brings up the problem of correctly interpreting what might seem archaeologically to be regional abandonment. He shows that by assuming that climatic change during the Near Eastern Bronze Age caused abandonment, we may be overlooking land use patterns that don't leave strong archaeological signatures, such as pastoralism. This is an issue we have also dealt with in the Southwest, contrasting "power" stages—when social groups concentrate in specific areas, centralize production, and so on—with "efficient" stages—when social groups are broadly distributed across the landscape (Stuart and Gauthier 1981; Upham 1984; see also Nelson and Hegmon 2001). Efficient stages are much less archaeologically visible. Danti's points deserve far more attention from archaeologists when we are looking at regional-level abandonment.

In chapter 5, Sassaman and Randall provide a wonderful space-shuttle-eye view of the southeastern part of the continent. It is a carefully crafted reconstruction of the geographic cosmology, or *cosmunity*, of the Archaic peoples of the Lower Southeast, and they make the parameters of this world so clear. Their idea of a *futurescape* is intriguing—the idea that indigenous understanding of the universe creates places on the landscape for people fleeing flooding or who detach from landscapes for other reasons. However, I wondered about the social landscape. Perhaps indigenous cosmology dictated where people could go or would go, but what about their interactions with people who were already there? Did people at Poverty Point welcome additional hands to build the monuments being created there? How might cosmology have blocked normal tendencies to see intruders as "others?" Sassaman and Randall have created a stunning reconstruction of Archaic Southeastern cosmology that offers new ways to think about small-scale societies and detaching from place at a very large scale.

DETACHING IN STATE-LEVEL SOCIETIES

Chapters by Lamoureux-St-Hilaire and his colleagues (chapter 7), Macrae et al. (chapter 6), and Iannone (chapter 10) explore detaching from place at a significantly different social scale from the small-scale societies discussed above. In each case, detaching is from a strong and centuries-old polity with multiple social classes, elaborate economies, and complex and extensive religious practices. Unlike the settlements of the Wendat, the Pueblo, or the people of Togo, the places described in these three chapters were significant features on the landscape for hundreds of years. Yet the power of these places eventually dissipated, and their residential population dispersed. Lamoureux-St-Hilaire and his colleagues aptly describe the process as a "detachment from power": as people left, much of the power of the place did, too. Although I do not study state-level societies, I found a great deal in these chapters that should help us understand detachment from place in other times and places and for societies of different social scales.

Bagan, La Corona, and Minanha were places of power in large part because they were sacred places. At the other end of the settlement continuum, it is interesting to consider what aspects of these places made them a focus of sacred activity, though that is not our mandate here. It is interesting to consider the historical memories that invested the abandoned settlements of the Wendat, the Pueblo, and the Archaic peoples of the Southeast with sacred significance and wonder if some similar process created the Burmese temples or Maya palaces. Almost certainly the larger populations, the more intensive agricultural practices, and the development of state-level political developments allowed these places to maintain their regional prominence over many centuries. How did these same factors combine in their eventual demise? And when power left these places, how was leaving accomplished?

The authors of these three chapters make the very valuable point that by watching how long-standing central places fall apart, we can learn a great deal about the institutions that comprised the polity. In chapter 7, Lamoureux-St-Hilaire et al. show how the slow diminution of power at La Corona was linked to the downfall of their Kaanul benefactors and to the gradual end of the institution of divine kingship. In chapter 10, Iannone recounts the slow fade from power of the great economic and ritual center of Bagan, observing changes in how and where ritual donations were made that weakened the

Crown, movement of taxable populations away from areas where they could be controlled, factional competition among members of the royal court, and anthropogenic and natural environmental problems that exacerbated social ones. In chapter 6, Macrae and his colleagues work from the outside of the Minanha polity, showing the importance of the support populations in the Waybil area and the Contreras Valley to the maintenance of the polity.

Equally important, Macrae and his colleagues illuminates how the support populations of Minanha invested in landscape development in the form of agricultural terraces and eventually developed a strong sense of place that was in some ways detached from that of the center. When Minanha's power came to an end, the Waybil area was abandoned, but in the Contreras Valley some of the larger settlements continued to be occupied. Macrae and his colleagues logically link these differences to the stronger sense of place developed in the Contreras Valley because of its longer tenure as a meaningful spot on the landscape.

Rulers vest their power in large, long-lived places: cities and ceremonial centers. Decisions to leave and establish power centers elsewhere must usually be a highly risky venture. Certainly, at times moving a center of power may have been a strategy to extend or consolidate power, but more often abandonment may have been the result of desperation or even violent attack. Regardless, we can be fairly certain that the power of the place diminished significantly, and its meaning to anyone who stayed or encountered the place later had changed. Maya urban centers such as La Corona were part of an extensive monumental landscape with authority concentrated in palaces. Lamoureux-St-Hilaire et al. emphasize that the Maya collapse sometimes resulted in the immediate extinction of kings and their courts, while in other cases rulers simply faded away. La Corona seems to have experienced that later sort of abandonment, with rulers first visually severing their ties with the Kaanul polity through rituals of termination and then gradually losing influence and ceasing construction on the monumental core. Similarly, the ritual and economic power that once resided in the great center of Bagan ebbed slowly after the thirteenth century, but it never completely ceased to be an important place to many people in Myanmar.

Here I'd like to consider social landscape in a slightly different way. Members of the small-scale societies discussed above certainly were strongly constrained by the social context in which they existed. The societies discussed by Birch and Lesage (chapter 4), Glowacki (chapter 3), and Sassaman and Randall (chapter 5) were, at least historically, matrilineal, and women certainly must have had a role in decision making, though perhaps not as strong a role as men did. The level of violence we know existed among the ancestral Wendat and Huron means that low-status captives also likely resided among the residents, and these people likely had little voice in how and when they left a place. In the complex societies represented by Bagan, La Corona, and Minanha, we should consider the different decision-making abilities of the elite residents versus support populations. How did leaders implement power regarding their servants and their followers? Did these support personnel have any real decision-making power? In the Contreras Valley, what aspects of the social environment allowed some people stay? Might they have attached themselves to another polity nearby?

At some Maya sites, scholars have found that social status has significant effects on how people abandon a place. For example, Takeshi Inomata (2003) found that when Aguateca was attacked, nonelite people were able to gather their belongings and leave in an unhurried way, while nobles apparently ran for their lives. In Myanmar, Iannone reports, "patron-client relationships appear to have been the norm." Yet, Anthony Reid (1983), a historian who studies Southeast Asia, has clarified that the "clients" in such relationships meet many of the definitions of slaves (Reid and Brewster 1983). How did the abandonment of Bagan affect these many, many servants or slaves who must have had very limited abilities to make decisions about their own movements as the power of this center dissolved? Among the Maya, how much latitude did the support populations of these centers have to leave and perhaps join a different center? While difficult to address archaeologically, we should consider how the gender and status of those leaving affected the process (see, e.g., McAnany et al. 2016).

THE CONTINUED IMPORTANCE OF PLACE

Chapters in this volume are concerned with the concept of a "sense of place." In chapter 6, it is defined by Macrae and his colleagues as the interaction between humans and their environment, which "includes histories, memories, and symbolic meanings" that make places meaningful. Most of them argue that places often continued to be meaningful even after they were abandoned. All human groups have meaningful places from their past, regardless of social scale, and it would be wrong to suggest that the abandoned villages visited by the Wendat or Pueblo peoples were any less profoundly important to them than was Bagan to the people who continued to visit it long after its power had ebbed. We might usefully consider this process.

We find evidence of termination rituals at some of the places discussed in this book suggesting active engagement with the transformation of living spaces to places of memory. Such rituals may be more common that we imagine but are not accessible to archaeologists. Sassaman and Randall (chapter 5) found the emplacement of caches of soapstone vessels at wide spots on the Southeastern landscape and a cache of broken vessels played a role in ending active use of the Poverty Point ceremonial center. At La Corona, termination rituals marked the end of Kaanul dominance at the site. In the Mimbres region of the Southwest, archaeologists have found that when rooms in a settlement were abandoned, they frequently were given ceremonies of termination, including demolition or burning of the room, burial within the room, or the deposit of ritual objects (Russell, Nelson, and Harkness 2013). Archaeologists are becoming more alert to such activities, and they may improve our understanding of detaching from place.

Regardless of the scale of a society, the construction of settlements, ceremonial centers, or shrines changes the landscape, creating focal points for human reference, even when they are no longer used for their original purpose. The ossuaries of the Wendat, the abandoned settlements of the Pueblo, the earthen crescents and mounds of Poverty Point, the great palaces of the Maya and the temples Bagan—all left profound marks on the landscape. These places were used to claim land even if the original occupants were no longer nearby. Even in our modern world, indigenous people use "abandoned" places to mark their ancestral territory. In chapter 4, Birch and Lesage note, "their ancestral places and lands are also Wendat through their inclusion in Wendat history, society, and identity." In the Southwest, the current dispute between Pueblo and Navajo people over the material heritage of the past is centered on ancient places. We might imagine that people who had once been part of La Corona or Minanha and who remained nearby continued to reference these places as part of their past.

Nothing lasts forever, even memories. Abandoned places may remain on the landscape, but with each succeeding generation, their meaning might change either slightly or completely. In a study of ethnogenesis in the San Juan region of the American Southwest, Kurt Anschuetz and Richard Wilshusen (2011:336) make an apt observation on landscapes: "The San Juan drainage is almost like an M. C. Escher drawing in which landscape shifts to either foreground or background depending on which cultural eyes look upon it." Our perception of places and their meaning is highly determined by our cultural and historic perspective. The significance of this was emphasized to me by a recent *Nature* article that described a large-scale European DNA study. The findings showed that the Neolithic people who built Stonehenge in southern England had been completely replaced by people from continental Europe about 4,500 years ago (Callaway 2018). Local understanding of the extensive monumental landscape of Stonehenge must have changed profoundly, though the structures were still there and still the same. We should keep this in mind.

CONCLUSIONS

The chapters in this volume take a fresh look at the process of abandonment, reframing it as "detaching from place" and exploring the myriad processes leaving involved. The chapters focus on both small-scale and state-level societies that, in the cases presented, exhibited different ways of detaching from place. Causes for movement varied from the environmental to the social, and conflict was a common motivator. Among the Wendat and the Pueblo, individuals and households moved between settlements, and this same process seemed to be evident among the Bassar. Settlements were relocated within regions, and abandoned settlements served as memory pieces within a landscape pervaded with history. Moving within such a landscape did not require people to truly abandon their home; they simply moved to a different part of it, continuing to visit and respect the memories and people who had occupied previous living spaces. Detaching from regions, as expressed in these chapters, was the result of perhaps the most varied set of causes, ranging from changes in Archaic cosmological systems to nineteenth-century slave raiding. In such moves, processes of ethnogenesis may have been in play. In chapter 9, Danti, however, cautions us not to assume abandonment in situations where changes in subsistence systems make human settlements less visible.

In state-level societies, the process of abandonment involved the detachment of power from places. Large centers with monumental cores consisting of palaces and temples slowly "collapsed" as rulers and their retinue left and eventually support populations left, too. The slower processes involved make determining causes of detachment difficult, except where historical records are available, as with Bagan. For La Corona and Minanha, violence may have been involved, but is apparently not archaeologically evident. In any case, these places had existed for centuries, and detachment likely was initiated long before any final push of residents to leave. I suggest that scholars studying such populous places compare, where possible, the experiences of individuals of different genders and social classes. Especially in complex societies with multiple social tiers, the decision-making process and the experience of detaching from place must have been strikingly different for different social strata.

Abandoned places can be evident on the landscape for variable amounts of time depending on their original size and construction. Most of the societies discussed in this volume emphasize that places continued to have meaning, even if they were no longer places where people lived. Many of them have meaning to this day, though a meaning different from what the people who originally occupied them must have had. By exploring detachment from the many places described in this volume, we can recover some of that original meaning.

12

Focus and Resolution

Challenges in Archaeology and Contemporary Migration Studies

JEFFREY H. COHEN

In chapter 2, Patricia McAnany and Maxime Lamoureux-St-Hilaire describe the archaeological investigations of detachment and abandonment as characterized by a "long-focus with low-resolution." That a long-focus, low-resolution approach to mobility brings unique challenges, particularly details that are of a short duration in time, is critical as we grow theory, revise methods, and improve our ability to describe migratory events, and in particular migratory events surrounding abandonments. Furthermore, the belief that archaeology (and for that matter, cultural anthropology) can make a contribution to understanding the processes of abandonment and mobility is critical. Bjørnar Olsen et al. clearly make this point as they note that the field of archaeology "encompasses the mundane and the material; its work is the tangible mediation of past and present, of people and their cultural fabric, of the tacit, indeed, the ineffable" (2012:2).

The reconceptualization of archaeological investigations by the authors of this collection captures the value of the field to mobility research. The challenges that confront archaeologists are not limited to those associated with a long-focus, low-resolution approach. Rather, for archaeologists (and others) the challenges of theory, method, and practice do not diminish. In fact, as I will argue below, they define a set of challenges that must be addressed by social scientists as we endeavor to understand migration, detachment, and abandonment.

DOI: 10.5876/9781646420087.c012

A long-focus, low-resolution frame captures one way that archaeologists define mobility and it is not incompatible with the analysis of migration, detachment, and abandonment. Nevertheless, its use does raise critical concerns. The chapters in this collection are part of the response to those concerns and the organization of an alternative that recognizes and embraces the complexities associated with human mobility. The authors show that by using a variety of evidence from a diversity of places and times, and by changing our frame of references to look beyond the common explanations we anticipate, we can better capture the breadth of human mobility. What is critical to the responses included here are the ways in which the authors reject common explanations. Rather than turning a blind eye to the mess that can be human life, they face it directly, search for solutions, offer working alternatives, and perhaps, most important, define options that welcome the muddle and embrace confounding evidence. In other words, instead of maintaining an orthodoxy that would blame errors on low-resolution research they respond to ecological and sociocultural processes and how those processes change, develop, appear, and are replaced (see, e.g., Hodder 2012; Ingold 2000).

It is easy to assume that the challenges associated with a long focus, low-resolution approach to migration are unique to archaeology and that they set archaeologists apart from other social science researchers (particularly cultural anthropologists). Arguing against long-focus, low-resolution research, the search for new options might focus on ethnographic alternatives. In fact, that is what sometimes happens as researchers celebrate ethnographies of migration as an apt and realistic response to the errors of the long-focus, low-resolution (see the discussion in Xiang 2013). Yet, to assume that the challenges confronting archaeology are somehow more fundamental, more "real" and more "confounding" than those that challenge ethnography, history, or demography suggests that we are maybe just avoiding how messy the alternatives can become.

To move beyond the criticisms and place archaeology into a world of research that includes other social scientists—and in particular, cultural anthropologists—I use this chapter to focus on the challenges that confront cultural anthropologists as they work on contemporary mobilities. Cultural anthropologists share theory and methods with others, including archaeologists, in their investigations of migration, detachment, and abandonment. Yet, to assume that cultural anthropology is problem free is quite a fantasy. In fact, K. Malterud (2001) points out how many of the challenges that confront cultural anthropologists in the conduct of ethnography are shared by other investigators across the social sciences. Many issues challenge cultural models of migration. The challenges include theoretical frameworks that can limit what we see; methodological shortcomings that may depend too heavily on the ethnographic moment; and explaining practices that make assumptions about mobility that may have little to do with real-world choices and outcomes.

While theory can limit what we see, methods limit what we hear and, when applied to practice theory and methods, combine to limit our interpretations. There is one additional challenge that brings the cultural analysis of migration and mobility to the table set by Maxime Lamoureux-St-Hilaire, Scott Macrae, and Patricia McAnany and embraced by the authors of this volume. Grounded in the belief that archaeological analysis of migration, detachment, and abandonment are often plagued by long-focused, low resolution, I propose that ethnographic work on migration is challenged by the short-focus, high-resolution nature of our investigations. I begin with a few thoughts on the challenges we share regardless of our approach—long or short focus, low or high resolution that the contemporary investigation of mobility must acknowledge. From this foundation, I argue that ethnographic work and the biased, short-focus, high-resolution analysis of mobility that is common to ethnography create a unique set of challenges around theory, method, and practice that undermines an ability to talk about what humans are doing on the landscape. Finally, in my conclusion, I explore the commonalities that connect archaeological and cultural/ethnographic investigations of migration, detachment, and abandonment, and argue that we share great strengths.

CHALLENGING FOCUS AND RESOLUTION

Characterized as a long-focus, low-resolution approach, archaeology's approach to place, mobility, detachment, and abandonment carries challenges that can fundamentally undermine analyses. The challenges are not isolated or reserved for archaeologists. Cultural anthropology and the discussion of contemporary examples of abandonment, detachment, and mobility are equally at risk. In other words, a focus on the contemporary world does not come with immunity. We can miss local details, misinterpret events, and mislabel processes and outcomes as easily in the present. Technical failures and methodological errors can overwhelm our ability to capture the passage of events, whether they are long term or short, temporary or permanent, and whether they occur on the ground, in the margins, or on the page. A second challenge follows as the researcher of the past and present "misread" the people and events taking place due to bias and prejudice. It is unfortunately very easy for bias and prejudice to interfere in research. Bias manifests itself as we miss events or their broader outcomes in response to poorly organized theory or common assumption that, while strong, may have little to do with the world we study. The outcomes are misrepresented mobilities, mischaracterized abandonments, and detachments that may have little to do with the events we study (see Bryce and Carnegie 2013).

The challenge of misrepresentations does not end with their effect upon our work; rather they are often repeated, and as they are repeated they become the very biases that build and lead to a third concern as the misrepresentation of events become theoretically powerful and, as Moro Abadía notes, inhibit dialogue, and close debate (2017). While these shifts are sometimes associated with a lack of technology—or limits on the tools necessary to make an interpretation (see Dunning et al. 2015)—biases can emerge as the way to fill the empty spaces in the record. Trouble grows when the stories that we use as placeholders become real and part of the framework. From framework, they become a foundation upon which new theories are built and through which new assumptions gain their status as correct and potentially "truthful." One example of this process, of the way the present and past mix together in unanticipated ways, is captured in Rhonda Brulotte's discussion of archaeological replicas sold by local folks living around Monte Alban, an important archaeological site in Oaxaca, Mexico (Brulotte 2012; Brulotte and Starkman 2014). Brulotte notes that carefully crafted archaeological replicas are often disparaged, as are their makers. The artisan's status is thrown in doubt based largely on the statements of outsiders who condemn the makers for misrepresenting the past. Artisans who make "fake" pre-Colombian figurines to sell are important not because archaeologists, historians, or cultural anthropologists might misrepresent the past (though they do); it is that, as the makers of the figures, they are described as posers abusing the past instead of individuals building opportunities around available resources.

Too often the misrepresentation of the native mover follows a similar path. Movers are presented and described as troublemakers who will undermine traditions and challenge anthropological knowledge. In other words, their stories of movement are filled with assumptions that are grounded in invented and imagined outcomes. These invented and imagined possibilities become the givens or the common beliefs that limit our opportunities to listen and learn why certain decisions are made and why certain outcomes (including migration across international borders) may occur. Processes that are explained away as an outcome of bad choices, putting the personal before the communal or simply part of the "natural world" of the group under investigation, become real barriers to understanding complexity. Research fails, books are closed, and new authenticities are organized that can take hold and are not easily altered.

This is not a new problem. In fact, it is the sort of problem that reaches back centuries as stories are told and retold, as fictions become facts, and as the reasons behind a particular text or argument are lost (Desmond 2004; Kirk 2014). For example, consider the writings of Herodotus. His work tells in a historiographic fashion the story of the Greco-Persian wars. While we can describe his inquiry as organized around fact, it is clear that much of what he wrote was based in retelling fictions. Nevertheless, his interpretations are repeated and build toward models of the past and the other that have little grounding in historical processes.

Misrepresentations that become fact (or at least land as alternative explanations) are difficult to correct. Challenges to misrepresentations are often measured against impossibly high standards. In many cases, the responses to misrepresentations are defined as just one of many available interpretations. This is perhaps most obvious in the strong objections that doubters make to arguments concerning evolution, climate change, and the like. Social scientists who capture the dynamics of human mobility are similarly challenged by critics who assume migration is unidirectional and founded in the economically rational choices of individual movers. Mobility is not unidirectional; humans move, move again, and return to whence they came throughout history. Defining humans as rational and progressive makes for a well-argued story, but it ignores the complex and dynamic drivers that underlie how and why people move. The point of identifying and moving beyond misrepresentations is not to reject the stories and histories that we've recorded; rather, it is to advance the field, revise understanding, correct errors, and remember that the original interpretation cannot stand.

The challenges that confront us as we put together long-focused, low-resolution or short-focused, high-resolution models of human detachment, abandonment, and mobility are complex and, as McAnany and Lamoureux-St-Hilaire note, scalar in nature. Past or present, we stand to lose the details that surround mobility outcomes (the forces driving migration). We also must rethink how we measure and demarcate detachment and abandonment.

The entanglements that define human life in the moment include a range of forces that can supersede our abilities to explain them. Yet, the alternative—to seek safety in imagined and invented past—can also confront us with worlds that do not exist. Unless we confront the challenges (whether real or imagined), we lose the ability to talk about community and the lives of individuals we hope to understand, except as they are representations of the fictional accounts; a point I will return to below.

Before turning to short-focused, high-resolution approaches to human mobility, it is important to understand how we use terms such as *abandonment* and *detachment*. Abandonment is a process as is detachment, and both play out over space and time unwinding through history. Ignoring the temporal process of abandonment and the complex relationships that motivate and frame detachment risks creating lacunae that disrupt our analyses.

The evidence of abandonment is typically founded in the assumed exit of a population—no surprise. But what constitutes exit? There are times when abandonment does not include exit, and, to paraphrase McAnany and Lamoureux-St-Hilaire, how should we discuss stressors, enablers, and actors? To further capture the complexities that are associated with mobility and abandonment, we can add a few more questions and ask: Is it abandonment if a group continues to live in a place? Is there a point where, regardless of who is in a space, abandonment has happened? Perhaps this moment is better defined as detachment? Timing is difficult to capture, but as Pétursdóttir and Olsen point out, "fragmentation, decay, inconsistency, detachment and entanglement are not so much the 'problems' archaeology deals with on daily basis, as the nuances that actually constitute our craft" (2018:114).

Abandonment, then, does not signify emptiness but instead defines an action. And while abandonment is associated with the action of leaving and moving on, it should be clear that the places that are abandoned are likely not empty; rather, they are in transition. We should approach detachment in a similar fashion: like abandonment, it defines an action. The challenge is not to figure out how detached something or someone might be; instead, it is to understand how detachment figures into the transitions we want to explain (and see the discussion in McAnany and Rowe 2015). Capturing the dynamics of abandonment and complexities of detachment can confound the long-focus and low-resolution approach, but it also challenges short-focus, high-resolution models.

Short Focus, High Resolution

Cultural anthropology and allied social sciences that study mobility carry their own unique set of concerns. While a "short-focus, high-resolution" approach is key to understanding some of the contrasts separating ethnography and archaeology, it does not absolve cultural anthropology of challenges. Short-focus, high-resolution research can excel at understanding the structure, nature, and scope of contemporary mobility, abandonment and more; nevertheless, it also carries serious challenges and is potentially as vexing as any archaeological alternative. References to contemporary patterns of abandonment, detachment, and mobility can include their own spurious narratives.

Theory. Perhaps most vexing is when the narratives of present-day mobility overestimate the unique, special quality of the moment and create exceptional examples. This might best be thought of as mobility's "Washington slept here" phenomenon. In this example, the process and outcomes of abandonment and migration lose their status among the many possibilities that confound mobility. The limited and myopic view of events and outcomes that a short-focus, high-resolution approach captures creates examples that are special because they are assumed to be unique. With no connections to other outcomes or other people, the events are unlike anything that has come before or that will exist in the future. Placing a community and its movers in such a rarified framework, such as a short or long focus, carries several risks. First, it disregards history and misrepresents events and outcomes that have meaning and importance to the moment. It ignores lived experiences beyond the small window of interest—leaving the examples as exceptions and free of association. It also discounts connections. An emphasis on the exceptional tends to miss patterns, and patterns are, at least for some anthropologists, at the core of what we search for and explain (Amato 2014).

An example captures some of the challenges that a short focus, high resolution can bring to research. Using research on migration in Oaxaca, Mexico, we can follow how short-focus, high-resolution models disregard history, ignore lived experience, and miss patterns.

Oaxaca has become a central sending region for migrants traveling to other parts of Mexico and, perhaps for many anthropologists, migrants crossing the border and moving into the United States. Since the late 1980s, it has been tempting to find migration and abandonment throughout rural communities in the state. The short-focus, high-resolution ethnographies that document Oaxacan movement can emphasize costs, benefits, patterns, and possibilities (Massey and Espinosa 1997; Kanaiaupuni 2000; Rose and Shaw 2008); nevertheless, these reports can also avoid history and are overly concerned with functional, positivistic frameworks.

Beginning in the 1980s, migration in Oaxaca grew increasingly important as a way to make a living, to escape the demands of managing a milpa, and to find opportunity. Yet, while migration was building quickly as an important strategy for individuals, their households, and their communities, it was nothing new. Rather, migration was part of a set of strategies that individuals had at their disposal as they managed their lives.

Research into migration in Oaxaca shows that internal migration was more typical in the past, and in particular in the central valleys of the state, through about 1980. People traveled for work, for education, to escape trouble and abuse at home, and to find acceptance and security that was lacking (Humphrey 2013). Nevertheless, by the 1980s, internal migration was outpaced by international-border crossing. The argument for the shift in migration from internal to cross-border destinations typically described Mexico's ongoing economic crises as a critical driving force behind the change. But there were other forces at work as well. First, there was a decline in governmental funding in the region, meaning that statement investments were dropping for the region. Second, a long-term drought that included not only a decline in rainfall, but also a change in the timing of rainfall, meant that many families could no longer meet even a part of their needs through farming. Finally, a lack of opportunity for advancement contributed to the increase in US-bound migration (Cohen 2004).

Walking into a rural Oaxacan community during those years—the 1980s, 1990s, and first decade of this century often felt like walking into the quintessential Mexican-migrant community. Towns seemed empty, people, particularly working-aged adults, were missing, and those who remained were the very old or the very young.

Ask a local to talk about migration, and very often the stories and experiences fit expectations. People left looking for jobs, seeking wages that paid in a day what might be earned in a week, with the hope that they could leave behind the ever-more-difficult life of a rural, self-sufficient farmer. The anthropologists, while seeking response to lots of questions, were often predisposed to listen to the stories of migration and talk about "the migration problem," particularly as it referenced rural villages that were "empty" and abandoned. Yet, with a little more time in the field and a slightly more programmatic organization of fieldwork as well as selection of informants, the empty villages grew harder to find, while concepts including abandonment were harder to define. While many rural villages were home to the elder and the very young, they were never empty. Using the concept of abandonment in writing brings a dramatic value to the report, but it does not capture what was.

Walk into a village, set up interviews, and begin to question those locals who were defined as "stay-at-homes," nonmigrants, and returnees, it became clear that most able-bodied, working-age adults had not turned their backs upon their villages. In fact, as Lynn Stephen (2007) and others have pointed out, they developed strong, transnational ties that reached across borders, ignored physical space, and established communities that were emergent, growing, and real.

Many anthropologists listened, and the stories of transnational communities and the growing interest in transnational migration, transnational social formations, and more helped us reject the assumption that abandonment was inevitable, unidirectional, and irreversible (see critique in G. Rumbaut Ruben 1997). Archaeologists working in the region made parallel arguments about mobility and abandonment in the past (Blanton et al. 1999). From their work, we realized that human populations had likely been mobile for centuries and communities were not simply defined by their geography; they were socially constructed. Through time the changes that played out in and around the community did not happen against a backdrop of abandonment (as perhaps was thought in the past) but in relation to social and ecological transformations (Kirby 1973). Oaxacans did not abandon sites in response to a single force or due to a one-time event—they shifted their practices as they responded to ongoing climatic change, regional politics; and later things such as colonialism and more recently market expansion and globalization (see Cook and Diskin 1976; O'Connor 2016).

Methods. While there are many parts to ethnographic research, perhaps most central is the interview. And much of the work on migration is founded in the interviews that take place between researchers and the community members (movers and nonmovers among others). There is nothing wrong with a focus that highlights migration and the experience of movers and nonmovers. The narratives and stories anthropologists collect from movers, returnees, and those who simply never left can be defined by the single events they cover. Following movers and nonmovers through a specific moment (in this case a migration) can have the effect of overrepresenting the importance and meaning of the moment; in other words, the migration event becomes the focus and is no longer a part of a series of ongoing decisions, outcomes, and processes. In some cases, a focus on the migration event makes understanding other outcomes, including abandonment, problematic. In fact, there are likely moments when the migration event becomes so critical and central to our discussion that we do not recognize additional outcomes. This does not have to be a problem, and a focus on a migration event does not mean we ignore other factors. There is much to be learned from following a decision and a specific event; nevertheless, it is critically important to remember that migration is more than a short-term event or the movement from place A to place B. There are decisions to be made before a migration takes place, there are the people involved (some of whom do not move), the moves, and the various components the moves may include. Following a migration there are questions surrounding settlement; and once people are settled, there are new decisions to make. There are also those folks who were left behind, returnees who may have done well, and others who failed in their new homes. Finally, there are those villagers who are removed entirely from migration. Looking beyond the migration event itself (i.e., the movement from place of origin to destination) transforms our discussion of the moment (mobility) and brings us back to the complexities of daily social life. This is important; the question is not about abandonment or detachment—these are outcomes of decisions and take place over a very long haul. In most of the contemporary examples we can find (including the examples from Oaxaca), no one migrates to abandon their home or to detach themselves from community. This is true even if the migrant in question establishes a new home. The transnational ties that link movers to their sending communities and homes mean that attachment is far more important than detachment. The village scenes and the narratives we collect define the costs of migration, highlight the complex processes that surround decision making, and emphasize how movement plays out against the desires for continuity, continued engagement, and transnational connections (Cohen 2001).

Practice. While the realities of mobility, abandonment, and detachment are complex, an expectation exists that defines mobility as migration and the critical moments we must pay attention to as a sojourn plays out over time and space. There is no doubt that Oaxacans, like so many others in similar positions around the world, migrate. In a physical sense, they also abandoned their natal, rural homes, and detach from space as they search for opportunities elsewhere. Judith Hellman (2008) captures these qualities in her discussion of Mexican migration that aptly describes how Mexican movers are caught between a rock and a hard place as they cross from limited opportunities at home to discrimination abroad. Yet, migration is more than the sojourn, and while there is physical evidence of abandonment, the reality is that people typically remain engaged in both their sending and destination communities regardless of where they may be in the process of moving. Furthermore, these engagements are not simply positive and there to ease transitions. Engagements, like detachments, can create tense and difficult moments as movers manage and negotiate their relationships with others (including nonmovers) as well as the stressors and enablers that surround them.

Outcomes of migration are never clear, and success is not guaranteed. And while migrants are celebrated by the state as critical to local development and entrepreneurial growth (Cohen 2005), failures can happen. Movers and nonmovers face stressors that range from the real to the imagined and forced decisions that may not always be beneficial. Balancing stressors and seeking opportunities can also place movers and nonmovers at odds as they sort through competing needs, wants, and demands, through household and community resources and experiences. In the end, the resources that define opportunity and support mobility enable and support certain outcomes (Sirkeci 2009), but they can also become stressors that limit opportunity and contribute to failure (Brown and James 2000; Huschke 2014; Toselli and Gualdi-Russo 2008).

Approaching migration as something that is part of a household's response to the world and the reality of a changing landscape contrasts with a focus on abandonment and the choices of the individual. The narrative is much different when migration is a response, not a problem, and when the focus is on the process as well as the outcome of movement, not simply the sojourn. In practice, migrants are not exceptional, solitary figures; rather, they are members of households, and, with their friends and families—including nonmigrants—they are defining a new kind of rural lifestyle. In other words, rather than focusing on "abandoners" and their decisions to move, we should define the decision to migrate as part of a broader set of concerns. These concerns revolve around movers and nonmovers at points of origin and destination working together to manage life and to define the best response to limited opportunities.

Here is how the rural Oaxacan village appears if we reject the limits associated with theory, method, and practice in the past. In this version of the story, we do not arrive at an empty or abandoned community; rather, we arrive in a rural village that is vibrant and includes a range of people, from the very young to the very old and from those who are present to those living abroad. Migrants are preparing to leave, or perhaps they have just returned. Children born in the United States are visiting families, and there is a flow of goods, food, information, and more between rural town and new destinations in the United States (and elsewhere) that reveal the dynamic nature of transnational life (see the discussions in Alvarez 1994; Fletcher 1999; Grigolini 2005; Heymann et al. 2009; Oliveira 2017).

In these communities, everyone knows a migrant, and migration is just one option open to adults looking for new opportunities. Rather than migration, they might choose to train in a local tech school or, particularly following 9/11 and the increasingly militarized Mexican/US border, find work in nearby Oaxaca City (Cohen and Ramirez Rios 2016). We would find that many of the local folks who left the village as migrants in the past have returned and do so regularly. They are investing in the life of their community, and they seek to build upon the local traditions and practices that defined their childhoods even as they reinvent those practices across the border (Cohen 2002).

We have moved through two different versions of the migrant community. The first version is based on classic migration theory and the assumption that abandonment is inevitable. We assume that almost everyone has left the village and joined the ranks of the ever-expanding urban proletariat in places such as Los Angeles, California. While the migrants hope for different lives elsewhere, the very old and very young remain behind—living in a shell of their traditional past. The second version of our village also includes movers and migrants, but now we are focused on more than their sojourns, and we place the decision to migrate within a framework that emphasizes the importance of household decision-making and recognizes how a mover's strengths and weaknesses can influence outcomes. In this example, individuals engaged in migration just as they did in the first example. The difference is that, now, the migrants are embedded within households; they are rooted in community life, and they are engaged at points of origin and destination with the invention and reinvention of who they are.

In truth, it is likely that many of the migrant communities we hope to understand in the present (as well as the past) include a combination of both examples. The communities and their households are divided into unique parts. While some migrants have left their homes and turned their backs on friends and relatives, other migrants work closely with others and straddle several distinct locations. Their decisions reflect both their needs and wants, as well as those of others (including nonmovers). There are also households with members who have never migrated. These are the folks who do not think about migration and do not worry about its effects. It is important to remember that these people are not simply the elderly but come from a variety of backgrounds. Their decisions likely reflect specific strengths or weaknesses that limit the viability and usefulness of migration.

These patterns remind us that in reality, the percentage of a community's members who elect to migrate varies greatly. In some towns, it can be quite high and in others, low. There are likely different factors that influence outcomes, sometimes climatic and other times political, and in any case, the job falls to the researcher to figure out what is happening.

DISCUSSION

Understanding the differences that confound migration includes understanding short- and long-term trends and patterns. In other words, focus matters, but limiting our discussion to short or long term is actually a problem as there are historical as well as immediate concerns. Furthermore, the processes at work influence outcomes and may need to be measured against events that occur quite far away. In the case of Oaxacan migration, diachronic events in the United States and in Mexico City have consequences.

Just as focus matters, so too does resolution. Understanding abandonment and mobility, as well as the meaning of detachment, demands more than one kind of resolution. Maybe we miss local events if our resolution is low, but when resolution is high we also risk exaggerating what we see. In the example of rural Oaxacan migration, too high a resolution could lead us to embellish what migration means and to focus on the details, including those of the sojourn, rather than more general processes. If we vary our approach and use a range of lenses in our analysis—the ability to triangulate a realistic model of migration is much more likely within our grasp.

Even when we approach a problem and its effects from a variety of angles and combine long and short foci with both high and low resolutions, we may still face problems. Not the least of these are the ways in which our theory fails to capture the breadth of the data we have collected. It is important to remember that our dedication to a specific theoretical model can, in the end, limit our ability to identify the diverse possibilities of the moment.

Modeling abandonment captures just how difficult it is to connect theory to outcomes on the ground. The challenge of abandonment can seem central to any migration. Yet, as the various possibilities we encounter become clearer, it becomes difficult to maintain a story of abandonment. The challenge is even greater when it comes to detachment. The reality of circular migration and of the technology that facilitates remittances—as well as the constant movement of goods, services, and information—reminds us that people do not need to be physically present to be engaged.[1]

Modeling migration, abandonment, and detachment demands careful methodology. Methodological demands and critiques are nothing new for archaeologists and cultural anthropologists. Our approaches to the past, whether framed by middle-range theory in archaeology (see Raab and Goodyear 1984) or defining the "crucial meso-level" in cultural models (Cohen and Sirkeci 2011; Faist 1997), are focused on understanding and explaining events on the ground as they are produced and are part of ongoing events. In addition, if our theory is based largely (or solely) in a set of assumptions based in short-focus, high resolution research, we jeopardize the place of history, process, and overall patterns in movement and mobility (including abandonment). The history of migration cannot be ignored—otherwise we are apt to mistake our theory as legitimate and tied to the unique and special present.

Embracing history can take on many forms as the example of Oaxacan migration reveals. There are the origin stories for many communities that are founded in the pre-Colombian history of the region (Thieme 2009). More important, for many of rural Oaxacan communities, the arrival of the Spanish and the growth of New Spain signified a second kind of birth as new models for living took hold, people were relocated (sometimes forcibly), and socioeconomic systems, religious life, and other institutions were challenged (Romero Frizzi 1996).

The interactions of communities, and the movements of individuals and families, as well as the waxing and waning of state control played out over hundreds of years (e.g. Taylor 1976). More recently, changes continue to influence mobility as federal funding has declined, dropping by nearly 75 percent since the 1970s (Smith 2003; Tyburski 2012), climate is shifting (Dilley 1993), and economic well-being is under pressure (Cohen 1999).

While theory can limit how we model outcomes, our methods limit what we hear, and practice limits our interpretations. There is a broad range of methods we can bring to our studies of abandonment, detachment, and mobility. Beyond defining what we mean by each term, it is critical to define how our tools support our work. It is perhaps even more important to consider how our methods or tool kit limit that work. In other words, we should always consider how our theories and methods create blind spots and how those blind spots become something more.

Doing work around mobility, abandonment, and detachment is particularly hard; the narratives people share about each of these can be quite contradictory. Nevertheless, the careful deployment of well-thought-out questions and the consistent use of those can create understanding that reaches well beyond the high-resolution work we do in the field. More to the point, the careful conduct of inquiry allows us to let our informants speak (or in the case of the archaeologist, the past speak) in a way that we can understand. The words may not fit our assumptions, but they will reveal the reasons people leave, the goals they have as movers, and the politics that characterize detachment (Baláz, Williams, and Fifeková 2016).

CONCLUSIONS

There isn't a simple corrective that will bring studies of contemporary migration and archaeological studies of mobility together. If we were to define a hybrid that was long focused and high resolution it would create new challenges, not the least of which would revolve around how to fund such projects (and see De León 2015 for an example of what is possible). The challenge that we can respond to and effectively reverse is how best to confront spurious narratives regardless of their origins in long-focus, low-resolution, or short-focus, high-resolution work.

The point here is not to reject the focus and resolution of our approach, but rather to embrace the possibility of multiple foci in our research. The chapters in this collection are clear indications of how to accomplish this goal. We can begin by understanding and confronting the limitations of our methods and perhaps, just as important, defining just what we hope to accomplish. We can recognize that there are different kinds of abandonments and different kinds of detachments and that these abandonments and detachments are not only spatial but intellectual, social, biological, and, in an important way, transnational. There are also different periods that we must take into account, and we need to be ready when events occur that interrupt what we originally were focused on.[2]

While it can seem like archaeology and cultural anthropology diverge around the study of migration, we have a great deal in common. First, there are the basic concerns over the structure of human mobility, including its motivations. Second, there are shared concerns to understand the history behind mobility and migration. Third, the consequences and effects of mobility are critical and not simply for movers. Archaeologists, like cultural anthropologists, are asking hard questions concerning those people who do not move and those who do, as well as those who must adjust as migrants arrive.

Human mobility is not always easy to explain, and defining why a group would leave its homeland is not intuitive. In fact, for a great deal of migration research, the argument went that mobility was an opportunity. This bias is evident in the discussion of contemporary migration that emphasizes economic gain. Yet, it is clear that there is no one "enabler" that can explain migrations, and perhaps, more important, there are many times when the drivers are not opportunities but rather quite problematic challenges that threaten security. In fact, insecurities—whether they are cultural fears, assumed dangers, or real violence—range from the environmental to the social and may be as important, or perhaps even more important than other processes and events. The role of insecurity in migration outcomes is perhaps most obvious when we think of a group fleeing a natural disaster or social upheaval and war, but it can be much more nuanced as well as when a mover takes his or her leave to escape abuse.

The history behind mobility and migration is also critical to understand, representing a common goal for archaeologists and cultural anthropologists. For all of us a concern with history is associated not only with ecological process (though those can sometimes dominate discussions), but also with cultural, ecological, and social processes that influence movement (Heyman 2007; Jokisch 2002; Verner 2010). Sometimes these drivers are clear in specific ecological and climatological events or moments, or in the contacts between cultures and social groups. And contemporary parallels exist as movers negotiate ecology, social rules, cultural beliefs, and more as they move. Nevertheless, the underlying goal is to gain perspective on mobility. Migration does not simply appear out of thin air. A group does not decide to move on a whim. History is critical. Regardless of the example, it is growing clearer that history informs mobility, and attention must be paid to both immediate and long-term processes.

There is a lot of common ground to consider as archaeologists and cultural anthropologists approach mobility—the difference concerning issues such as detachment and abandonment, connections, and settlement are not very different. We are all focused on developing the tools for investigation and theory building that will help us best understand human mobility, its drivers and outcomes, and its history and future, as well as what might keep someone "home." This common drive returns me to our starting point. Archaeological studies of mobility may often be "long-focus, low-resolution" in structure and design, but this does not mean that cultural anthropology doesn't also face challenges.

Can our discussions of migration and mobility produce a richness that captures a migrant and shares a community's story? What if instead of asking why a group migrated and abandoned its home, we instead ask "why now?" I have argued the challenge is to place mobility, abandonment, and detachment into a cultural framework that captures the complexity of the process—not only the sojourn. Asking why a group left at a specific moment moves us away from the discussion of the sojourn to its cause and to understanding the complexities of mobility. While archaeologists and cultural anthropologists have different methods in their tool kits, the questions we ask link us in important ways. Understanding abandonment and detachment are part of that discussion. The volume's chapters suggest a continuum that is linked not to the sojourn but rather to complexities that come before and after the sojourn and that are captured in the ways we rethink outcomes, including abandonment.

NOTES

1. In a sense, this is the point that George Marcus (1995) make as he argues for multisited ethnographies. Lives and culture transcend space and place to create flexible, adaptive systems that keep them engaged.

2. For example, the central valleys of Oaxaca have suffered from a drought for decades, yet in 2014, there were flooding rains and at least one report suggested the drought was over. It was not and the rains came at such an inopportune moment as to destroy crops rather than support farming. It can be easy to mistake or misrepresent time in our research.

Achebe, Chinua. 1958. *Things Fall Apart*. Heinemann Publishers, Johannesburg, South Africa.

Adams, E. Charles, and Andrew Ian Duff, eds. 2004. *The Protohistoric Pueblo World, AD 1275–1600*. University of Arizona Press, Tucson.

Adams, Karen R., and Kenneth L. Petersen. 1999. "Environment." In *Colorado Prehistory: A Context for the Southern Colorado River Basin*, edited by W. D. Lipe, M. D. Varien, and R. H. Wilshusen, 14–50. Council of Professional Archaeologists, Denver.

Adams, Ron L., and Stacie M. King, eds. 2011. *Residential Burial: A Multiregional Perspective*. Archaeological Papers of the American Anthropological Association, Number 20. Wiley Subscription Services, Hoboken, NJ.

Aimers, James. 2007. "What Maya Collapse? Terminal Classic Variation in the Maya Lowlands." *Journal of Archaeological Research* 15(4):329–77.

Akers, Pete D. 2011. "Climate and Maya Culture Change: Detecting Connections Using Belizean Stalagmites." MA thesis, Department of Geography, University of Georgia, Athens.

Akers, Pete, D. George A. Brook, L. B. Railsback, Liang Fuyuan, Gyles Iannone, James W. Webster, Philip P. Reeder, Cheng Hai, and Edward R. Lawrence. 2016. "Extended and Higher-Resolution Record of Climate and Land Use from Stalagmite MC01 from Macal Chasm, Belize: Connections between Major Dry Events, Overall Climate Variability, and Maya Sociopolitical Change." *Palaeogeography, Palaeoclimatology, Palaeoecology* 459:268–88.

DOI: 10.5876/9781646420087.c013

Akkermans, Peter M. M. G., and Glenn M. Schwartz. 2003. *The Archaeology of Syria: From Complex Hunter-Gatherers to Early Urban Societies (c. 16,000–300 BC)*. Cambridge University Press, Cambridge.

Al-Ashram, M. 1990. "Agricultural Labor and Technological Change in the Syrian Arab Republic." In *Labor and Rainfed Agriculture in West Asia and North Africa*, edited by Dennis Tully, 163–84. Kluwer Academic Publishers, Dordrecht, Netherlands.

Albers, Patricia. 1993. "Symbiosis, Merger, and War: Contrasting Forms of Intertribal Relationship among Historic Plains Indians." In *The Political Economy of North American Indians*, edited by John H. Moore, 94–132. University of Oklahoma Press, Norman.

Algaze, Guillermo, Ray Breuninger, and James Knutstad. 1994. "The Tigris-Euphrates Archaeological Reconnaissance Project: Final Report of the Birecik and Carchemish Dam Survey Areas." *Anatolica* 20:1–96.

Alvarez, Robert R. 1994. "Changing Ideology in a Transnational Market: Chile and Chileros in Mexico and the US." *Human Organization* 53(3):255–62.

Amato, Paul R. 2014. "Approaches to Measuring Families." In *Emerging Methods in Family Research*, edited by Susan M. McHale, Paul R. Amato, and Alan Booth, 179–262. Springer, New York.

Andaya, Barbara Watson, and Leonard Y. Andaya. 2015. *The History of Early Modern Southeast Asia, 1400–1830*. Cambridge University Press, Cambridge.

Anschuetz, Kurt F., and Richard H. Wilshusen. 2011. "Ensouled Places: Ethnogenesis and the Making of the Dinétah and Tewa Basin Landscapes." In *Movement, Connectivity, and Landscape Change in the Ancient Southwest*, edited by Margaret C. Nelson and Colleen Strawhacker, 321–44. University Press of Colorado, Boulder.

Anschuetz, Kurt F., Richard H. Wilshusen, and Cherie L. Scheick. 2001. "An Archaeology of Landscapes: Perspectives and Directions." *Journal of Archaeological Research* 9(2):157–211.

Anthony, David W. 1990. "Migration in Archeology: The Baby and the Bathwater." *American Anthropologist* 92(4):895–914.

Arakawa, Fumiyasu. 2012. "Cyclical Cultural Trajectories: A Case Study from the Mesa Verde Region." *Journal of Anthropological Research* 68(1):35–69.

Armstrong, James A., and Richard L. Zettler. 1997. "Excavations on the High Mound (Inner Town)." In *Subsistence and Settlement in a Marginal Environment: Tell es-Sweyhat, 1989–1995 Preliminary Report*, edited by Richard L. Zettler, 11–34. MASCA Research Papers in Science and Archaeology 14. University of Pennsylvania Museum of Archaeology and Anthropology, Philadelphia.

Arrivabeni, Monica. 2012. "Post-Akkadian Settlement Distribution in the Leilan Region Survey." In *Seven Generations Since the Fall of Akkad*, edited by Harvey Weiss, 261–78. Studia Chaburiensia 3. Harrassowitz, Wiesbaden, Germany.

Arz, Helge W., Frank Lamy, and Jürgen Pätzold. 2006. "A Pronounced Dry Event Recorded around 4.2 kyr in Brine Sediments from the Northern Red Sea." *Quaternary Research* 66(3):432–41.

Ascher, Robert. 1968. "Time's Arrow and the Archaeology of a Contemporary Community." In *Settlement Archaeology*, edited by K. C. Chang, 43–52. National Press Books, Palo Alto, CA.

Ashmore, Wendy. 2002. "Decisions and Dispositions": Socializing Spatial Archaeology. *American Anthropologist* 104(4):1172–83.

Ashmore, Wendy, Samuel V. Connell, Jennifer J. Ehret, C. H. Gifford, L. T. Neff, and J. C. Vandenbosh. 1994. "The Xunantunich Settlement Survey." In *Xunantunich Archaeological Project: 1994 Field Season*, edited by Richard M. Leventhal and Wendy Ashmore, 248–90. Institute of Archaeology, Belmopan, Belize.

ASI (Archaeological Services Inc.). 2008. "Report on the Stage 3–4 Salvage Excavation of the Alexandra Site (AkGt-53) Draft Plan of Subdivision SC-T2000u001 (55T-00601) Geographic Township of Scarborough Now in the City of Toronto, Ontario." Report on file. Ontario Ministry of Culture, Toronto.

ASI (Archaeological Services Inc.). 2009. "The Stage 4 Excavation of the Holly Site (BcGw-58). Dykstra Subdivision, Holly Secondary Planning Area (43T-92026), Part of the Northeast Half of Lot 2, Concession 12, City of Barrie, Simcoe County, Ontario." Report on File. Ontario Ministry of Culture, Toronto.

ASI (Archaeological Services Inc.). 2010. "Report on the Salvage Excavation of the Antrex site (AjGv-38) City of Mississauga, Regional Municipality of Peel, Ontario." Report on file, Ontario Ministry of Culture, Toronto.

ASI (Archaeological Services Inc.). 2017. "Stage 4 Archaeological Salvage Excavation and Ossuary Potential Monitoring of the Otsistoret site (BaGv-75). Bathurst Street Reconstruction, Lot 10, Concession 2, Township of King and Lots 103–4, Concession 1, Town of East Gwillimbury, Regional Municipality of York." Report on File. Ontario Ministry of Recreation, Tourism, and Sport.

Aung-Thwin, Michael. 1985. *Pagan: The Origins of Modern Burma*. University of Hawaii Press, Honolulu.

Aung-Thwin, Michael. 1987. "Heaven, Earth, and the Supernatural World: Dimensions of the Exemplary Center in Burmese History." In *The City as Sacred Center: Essays on Six Asian Contexts*, edited by Bardwell Smith and Holly Baker Reynolds, 88–102. E. J. Brill, New York.

Aung-Thwin, Michael. 1990. *Irrigation in the Heartland of Burma: Foundations of the Pre-Colonial Burmese State*. Center for Southeast Asian Studies, Occasional Paper No. 15. Northern Illinois University, DeKalb.

Aung-Thwin, Michael. 1995. "The 'Classical' in Southeast Asia: The Present in the Past." *Journal of Southeast Asian Studies* 26(1):75–91.

Aung-Thwin, Michael. 1998. *Myth and History in the Historiography of Early Burma*. Ohio University Center for International Studies, Athens.

Aung-Thwin, Michael. 2011a. "A Tale of Two Kingdoms: Ava and Pegu in the Fifteenth Century." *Journal of Southeast Asian Studies* 42(1):1–16.

Aung-Thwin, Michael. 2011b. A "New/Old Look at 'Classical' and 'Post-Classical' Southeast Asia/Burma." In *New Perspectives on the History and Historiography of Southeast Asia: Continuing Explorations*, edited by Michael A. Aung-Thwin and Kenneth R. Hall, 25–55. Routledge, New York.

Aung-Thwin, Michael. 2017. *Myanmar in the Fifteenth Century: A Tale of Two Kingdoms*. University of Hawai'i Press, Honolulu.

Aung-Thwin, Michael, and Maitrii Aung-Thwin. 2012. *A History of Myanmar since Ancient Times: Traditions and Transformations*. Reaktion Books, London.

Austin, Shawn J. 1994. "The Wilcox Lake Site (AgGu-17): Middle Iroquoian Exploitation of the Oak Ridges Moraine." *Ontario Archaeology* 58:49–84.

Aveni, Anthony. 2008. *People and the Sky: Our Ancestors and the Cosmos*. Thames and Hudson, New York.

Baillie, Ian C., A. C. S. Wright, M. A. Holder, and E. A. FitzPatrick. 1993. *Revised Classification of Soils of Belize*. Natural Resources Institute, Kent, UK.

Baláz, Vladimir, Allan M. Williams, and Elena Fifeková. 2016. "Migration Decision Making as Complex Choice: Eliciting Decision Weights Under Conditions of Imperfect and Complex Information Through Experimental Methods." *Population, Space and Place* 22(1):36–53.

Balée, William L. 1998. "Historical Ecology: Premises and Postulates." In *Advances in Historical Ecology*, edited by William L. Balée, 13–29. Columbia University Press, New York.

Balée, William L., and Clark L. Erickson. 2006. "Time and Complexity in Historical Ecology." In *Time and Complexity in Historical Ecology: Studies in the Neotropical Lowland*, edited by William L. Balée and Clark L. Erickson, 1–20. Columbia University Press, New York.

Barbier, Jean-Claude. 1982. *L'Histoire présente, Exemple du Royaume Kotokoli du Togo*. Centre d'Etudes d'Afrique Noire, Bordeaux.

Bar-Matthews, Miryam, and Avner Ayalon. 2011. "Mid-Holocene Climate Variations Revealed by High-Resolution Speleothem Records from Soreq Cave, Israel and Their Correlation with Cultural Changes." *Holocene* 21(1):163–71.

Barrientos, Tomás, Marcello Canuto, David Stuart, Luke Auld-Thomas, and Maxime Lamoureux-St-Hilaire. 2016. "Memoria social escrita en piedra: Cambios y reconfiguraciones del discurso político en las Tierras Bajas durante el periodo Clásico." In *XXIX Simposio de Investigaciones Arqueológicas en Guatemala*, edited by Bárbara Arroyo, Luis Méndez Salinas, and Gloria Ajú Álvarez, 103–20. Asociación Tikal, Guatemala City.

Basso, Keith H. 1996. "Wisdom Sits in Places: Notes on Western Apache Landscape." In *Senses of Place*, edited by Steven Feld and Keith H. Basso, 53–90. School of American Research Press, Santa Fe, New Mexico.

Batun Alpuche, Adolfo Ivan, Patricia A. McAnany, and Maia Dedrick. 2017. "Tiempo y paisaje en Tahcabo, Yucatán." *Arqueología Mexicana* 145:66–71.

Benson, Larry V. 2010. "Factors Controlling Pre-Columbian and Early Historic Maize Productivity in the American Southwest, Part 2: The Chaco Halo, Mesa Verde, Pajarito Plateau/Bandelier, and Zuni Archaeological Regions." *Journal of Archaeological Method and Theory* 18(1):61–109.

Benson, Larry V. 2011. "Factors Controlling Pre-Columbian and Early Historic Maize Productivity in the American Southwest, Part 2: The Chaco Halo, Mesa Verde, Pajarito Plateau/Bandelier, and Zuni Archaeological Regions." *Journal of Archaeological Method and Theory* 18:61–109.

Bernardini, Wesley. 2005. *Hopi Oral Tradition and the Archaeology of Identity*. University of Arizona Press, Tucson.

Bernardini, Wesley. 2011. "Migration in Fluid Social Landscapes: Units and Processes." In *Rethinking Anthropological Perspectives on Migration*, edited by Graciela S. Cabana and Jeffery J. Clark, 31–44. University of Florida Press, Gainesville.

Bernardini, Wesley, and Severin Fowles. 2011. "Becoming Hopi, Becoming Tewa: Two Pueblo Histories of Movement." In *Movement, Connectivity, and Landscape Change in the Ancient Southwest*, edited by Margaret C. Nelson and Colleen Strawhacker, 253–74. University Press of Colorado, Boulder.

Berry, Michael S., and Larry V. Benson. 2010. "Tree-Ring Dates and Demographic Change in the Southern Colorado Plateau and Rio Grande Regions." In *Leaving Mesa Verde: Peril and Change in the Thirteenth-Century Southwest*, edited by T. A. Kohler, M. D. Varien, and A. M. Wright, 53–74. University of Arizona Press, Tucson.

Billman, Brian R., Patricia M. Lambert, and Banks L. Leonard. 2000. "Cannibalism, Warfare, and Drought in the Mesa Verde Region During the Twelfth Century AD." *American Antiquity* 65(1):145–78.

Binford, Lewis R. 1981. "Behavioral Archaeology and the 'Pompeii Premise.'" *Journal of Anthropological Research* 37(3):195–208.

Birch, Jennifer. 2012. "Coalescent Communities: Settlement Aggregation and Social Integration in Iroquoian Ontario." *American Antiquity* 77(4):646–70.

Birch, Jennifer. 2015. "Current Research on the Historical Development of Northern Iroquoian Societies." *Journal of Archaeological Research* 23(3):263–23.

Birch, Jennifer, and Sturt Manning. 2016. "Bayesian Modelling and Refinement of Iroquoian Settlement Histories." Paper presented at the 81st Annual Meeting of the Society for American Archaeology, Orlando.

Birch, Jennifer, and Ronald F. Williamson. 2013. *The Mantle Site: An Archaeological History of an Ancestral Wendat Community*. AltaMira Press, Lanham, MD.

Birch, Jennifer, and Ronald F. Williamson. 2015. "Navigating Ancestral Landscapes in the Northern Iroquoian World." *Journal of Anthropological Archaeology* 39:139–50.

Blanton, Richard E., Gary Fineman, Stephen Kowalewski, and Linda Nicholas. 1999. *Ancient Oaxaca: The Monte Albán State*. Cambridge University Press, Cambridge.

Bocinsky, Ronald K., and Timothy A. Kohler. 2014. "A 2,000-Year Reconstruction of the Rain-Fed Maize Agricultural Niche in the US Southwest." *Nature Communications* 5:5618–29.

Borck, Lewis. 2012. "Patterns of Resistance: Violence, Migration, and Trade in the Gallina Heartland." Master's thesis, School of Anthropology, University of Arizona, Tucson.

Bourdieu, Pierre. 1977. *Outline of a Theory of Practice*. Cambridge University Press, Cambridge.

Bove, Frederick J. 1981. "Trend Surface Analysis and the Lowland Classic Maya Collapse." *American Antiquity* 46(1):93–112.

Boyer, J. L., J. L. Moore, S. A. Lakatos, NJ Akins, C. D. Wilson, and E. Blinman. 2010. "Remodeling Immigration: A Northern Rio Grande Perspective on Depopulation, Migration, and Donation-Side Models." In *Leaving Mesa Verde: Peril and Change in the Thirteenth-Century Southwest*, edited by T. A. Kohler, M. D. Varien, and A. M. Wright, 285–323. University of Arizona Press, Tucson.

Brandt, Elizabeth. 1994. "Egalitarianism, Hierarchy, and Centralization in the Pueblos." In *The Ancient Southwestern Community: Models and Methods for the Study of Prehistoric Social Organization*, edited by W. H. Wills and R. D. Leonard, 9–24. University of New Mexico Press, Albuquerque.

Brecher, Kenneth, and William G. Haag. 1980. "The Poverty Point Octagon: World's Largest Prehistoric Solstice Marker?" *Bulletin of the American Astronomical Society* 12:886–87.

Brook, George A., and Pete Akers. 2010. "Report on Stalagmite Work Completed in 2010." In *Archaeological Investigations in the North Vaca Plateau, Belize: Progress Report of the Twelfth (2010) Field Season*, edited by Gyles Iannone, Jaime J. Awe, Maxime Lamoureux St-Hilaire and Matthew Longstaffe, 186–90. Social Archaeology Research Program, Trent University, Peterborough, ON.

Brookfield, Harold C. 1984. "Intensification Revisited." *Pacific Viewpoint* 25(1):15–44.

Brookfield, Harold C., and Michael Stocking. 1999. "Agrodiversity: Definition, Description and Design." *Global Environmental Change* 9(2):77–80.

Brooks, James F. 2002. *Captives and Cousins: Slavery, Kinship, and Community in the Southwest Borderlands.* University of North Carolina Press, Chapel Hill.

Brooks, Nick. 2006. "Cultural Responses to Aridity in the Middle Holocene and Increased Social Complexity." *Quaternary International* 151(1):29–49.

Brown, Bill. 2001. "Thing Theory." *Critical Inquiry* 28(1):1–22.

Brown, Daniel E., and Gary D. James. 2000. "Physiological Stress Responses in Filipino-American Immigrant Nurses: The Effects of Residence Time, Life-Style, and Job Strain." *Psychosomatic medicine* 62(3):394–400.

Brulotte, Ronda L. 2012. *Between Art and Artifact: Archaeological Replicas and Cultural Production in Oaxaca, Mexico.* University of Texas Press, Austin.

Brulotte, Ronda L., and Alvin Starkman. 2014. "Caldo de Piedra and Claiming Pre-Hispanic Cuisine as Cultural Heritage." In *Edible Identities: Food as Cultural Heritage,* edited by Rhonda L. Brulotte and Michael A. Di Giovine, 109–24. Ashgate, Farnham, UK.

Bruseth, James E. 1991. "Poverty Point Development as Seen at the Cedarland and Claiborne Sites, Southern Mississippi." In *The Poverty Point Culture: Local Manifestations, Subsistence Practices, and Trade Networks,* edited by Kathleen M. Byrd, 7–25. *Geoscience and Man.* Vol. 29. Louisiana State University, Baton Rouge.

Bryce, Derek, and Elizabeth Carnegie. 2013. "Exhibiting the Orient: Historicising Theory and Curatorial Practice in UK Museums and Galleries." *Environment and Planning A* 45(7):1734–52.

Bullard, William R. 1960. "Maya Settlement Pattern in Northeastern Peten, Guatemala." *American Antiquity* 25(3):355–72.

Bustamante, Eduardo. 2016. "Operación CR21O y CR20O, sección oeste del palacio." In *Proyecto Arqueológico La Corona: Informe Final, Temporada 2015,* edited by Marcello Canuto, Tomás Barrientos, and Eduardo Bustamante, 31–52. PRALC, Guatemala City.

Bustamante, Eduardo. 2017. "Operaciones CR20E, CR20D, y CR20O: Excavaciones en las secciones Sur y Suroeste del Palacio de La Corona." In *Proyecto Arqueológico La Corona: Informe Final, Temporada 2016,* edited by Marcello Canuto, Tomás Barrientos, and Eduardo Bustamante, 75–101. PRALC, Guatemala City.

Butzer, Karl W. 2012. "Collapse, Environment, and Society." *Proceedings of the National Academy of Sciences,* 109(10):3632–39.

Cabana, Graciela S., and Jeffery J. Clark, eds. 2011. *Rethinking Anthropological Perspectives on Migration.* University of Florida Press, Gainesville.

Callaway, Ewen. 2018. "Ancient-Genome Study Finds Bronze Age 'Beaker Culture' Invaded Britain: Famous Bell-Shaped Pots Associated with Group of Immigrants Who May Have Displaced Neolithic Farmers." *Nature* 545:276–77.

Cameron, Catherine M. 1991. "Structure Abandonment in Villages." In *Archaeological Method and Theory*, vol. 3, edited by Michael B. Schiffer, 155–94. University of Arizona Press, Tucson.

Cameron, Catherine M. 1993. "Abandonment and Archaeological Interpretation." In *Abandonment of Settlements and Regions: Ethnoarchaeological and Archaeological Approaches*, edited by Catherine M. Cameron and Steve A. Tomka, 3–7. Cambridge University Press, Cambridge.

Cameron, Catherine M. 1995. "Migration and the Movement of Southwestern Peoples." *Journal of Anthropological Archaeology* 14(2):104–24.

Cameron, Catherine M. 1999. *Hopi Dwellings: Architecture at Orayvi*. University of Arizona Press, Tucson.

Cameron, Catherine M. 2003. "A Consideration of Abandonment from Beyond Middle America." In *The Archaeology of Settlement Abandonment in Middle America*, edited by T. Inomata and R. W. Webb, 203–10. University of Utah Press, Salt Lake City.

Cameron, Catherine M., ed. 2008. *Invisible Citizens: Captives and Their Consequences*. University of Utah Press, Salt Lake City.

Cameron, Catherine M. 2011. "Captives and Culture Change: Implications for Archaeologists." *Current Anthropology* 52(2):169–209.

Cameron, Catherine M. 2013. "How People Moved among Ancient Societies: Broadening the View." *American Anthropologist* 115(2):218–31.

Cameron, Catherine M. 2016. *Captives: How Stolen People Changed the World*. University of Nebraska Press, Lincoln.

Cameron, Catherine M., and Steve A. Tomka, eds. 1993. *Abandonment of Settlements and Regions: Ethnoarchaeological and Archaeological Approaches*. Cambridge University Press, Cambridge.

Canuto, Marcello A., and Anthony P. Andrews. 2008. "Memories, Meanings, and Historical Awareness: Post-Abandonment Behaviors among the Lowland Maya." In *Ruins of the Past: The Use and Perception of Abandoned Structures in the Maya Lowlands*, edited by T. W. Stanton and A. Magnoni, 257–73. University Press of Colorado, Boulder.

Canuto, Marcello A., and Tomás Barrientos Q. 2011. "La Corona: Un acercamiento a las políticas del reino Kaan desde un centro secundario del noroeste del Petén." *Estudios de Cultura Maya* 37:11–43.

Canuto, Marcello A., and Tomás Barrientos Q. 2013a. The Importance of La Corona. *La Corona Notes* 1(1), Mesoweb. http://www.mesoweb.com/LaCorona/LaCorona Notes01.html.

Canuto, Marcello A., and Tomás Barrientos Q. 2013b. "Proyecto Regional Arqueológico La Corona: Resultados generales y conclusiones de la temporada 2012." In *Proyecto Arqueológico La Corona: Informe Final, Temporada 2012*, edited by Marcello Canuto, Tomás Barrientos, and Jocelyne Ponce, 367–92. PRALC, Guatemala City.

Canuto, Marcello A., Tomás Barrientos, Maxime Lamoureux-St-Hilaire, and Eduardo Bustamante. 2017. "La Casa de los Tronos: El Palacio de La Corona y la gobernación hegemónica de Kaanal." In *XXX Simposio de Investigaciones Arqueológicas en Guatemala*, edited by Bárbara Arroyo and Lorena Paiz. Asociación Tikal, Guatemala City.

Carleton, Chris W., Gyles Iannone, and James Conolly. 2010. "Dating Minanha Using a Bayesian Chronological Framework." In *Archaeological Investigations in the North Vaca Plateau, Belize: Progress Report of the Twelfth (2010) Field Season*, edited by Gyles Iannone, Jaime J. Awe, Maxime Lamoureux-St-Hilaire, and Matthew Longstaffe, 109–31. Social Archaeology Research Program. Trent University, Peterborough, ON.

Chagnon, Napoleon. 1992. *Yanomamö: The Last Days of Eden*. San Diego: Harcourt Brace Jovanovich.

Charles, Henri. 1939. *Tribus moutonnières du Moyen Euphrate*. Documents d'Études Orientales VIII. Institut Français de Damas, Beirut.

Child, Mark B., and Charles W. Golden. 2008. "The Transformation of Abandoned Structures at Piedras Negras." In *Ruins of the Past: The Use and Perception of Abandoned Structures in the Maya Lowlands*, edited by Travis W. Stanton and Aline Magnoni, 65–89. University Press of Colorado, Boulder.

Chilton, Elizabeth. 2005. "Farming and Social Complexity in the Northeast." In *North American Archaeology*, edited by Timothy R. Pauketat and Diana DiPaolo Loren, 138–60. Blackwell, Malden.

Chouin, Gerard. 2009. *Forests and Power and Memory: An Archaeology of Sacred Groves in the Eguafo Polity, Southern Ghana (c. 500–1900 AD)*. PhD diss., University of Syracuse, Syracuse, New York.

Clapperton, Hugh. 1829. *Journal of a Second Expedition into the Interior of Africa*. John Murray, London.

Clark, Jeffrey J., Deborah L. Huntley, J. Brett Hill, and Patrick D. Lyons. 2013. "The Kayenta Diaspora and Salado Meta-identity in the Late Precontact US Southwest." In *The Archaeology of Hybrid Material Culture*, edited by Jeffrey J. Card, 399–424. Southern Illinois University Carbondale, Center for Archaeological Investigations, Occasional Paper No. 39. Southern Illinois University Press, Carbondale.

Clark, Jeffrey J., and Karl W. Laumbach. 2011. "Ancestral Pueblo Migrations in the Southern Southwest: Perspectives from Arizona and New Mexico." In *Movement, Connectivity, and Landscape Change in the Ancient Southwest*, edited by M. C. Nelson and C. Strawhacker, 297–320. University Press of Colorado, Boulder.

Clark, John E. 2004. "Surrounding the Sacred: Geometry and Design of Early Mound Groups as Meaning and Function." In *Signs of Power: The Rise of Complexity in the Southeast*, edited by J. L. Gibson and P. J. Carr, 162–213. University of Alabama Press, Tuscaloosa.

Clark, J. J., J. A. Birch, M. Hegmon, B. J. Mills, D. M. Glowacki, S. G. Ortman, J. S. Dean, R. Gauthier, P. D. Lyons, M. A. Peeples, L. Borck, and J. A. Ware. 2019. "Resolving the Migrant Paradox: Two Pathways to Coalescence in the Late Precontact U.S. Southwest." *Journal of Anthropological Archaeology* 53:262–87.

Cobb, Charles R. 2003. "Mississippian Chiefdoms: How Complex?" *Annual Review of Anthropology* 32:63–84.

Cobb, Charles R. 2005. "Archaeology and the 'Savage Slot': Displacement and Emplacement in the Premodern World." *American Anthropologist* 107(4):563–74.

Cobb, Charles R., and Brian M. Butler. 2006. "Mississippian Migration and Emplacement in the Lower Ohio Valley." In *Leader and Polity in Mississippian Society*, edited by Brian M. Butler and Paul D. Welch, 328–50. Southern Illinois University Carbondale, Center for Archaeological Investigations, Occasional Paper No. 33. Southern Illinois University Press, Carbondale.

Coedès, George. 1968. *The Indianized States of Southeast Asia*. University of Hawaii Press, Honolulu.

Cohen, Jeffrey H. 1999. *Cooperation and Community: Economy and Society in Oaxaca*. University of Texas Press, Austin.

Cohen, Jeffrey H. 2001. "Transnational Migration in Rural Oaxaca, Mexico: Dependency, Development and the Household." *American Anthropologist* 103(4):954–67.

Cohen, Jeffrey H. 2002. "Migration and 'Stay at Homes' in Rural Oaxaca, Mexico: Local Expression of Global Outcomes." *Urban Anthropology* 31(2):231–59.

Cohen, Jeffrey H. 2004. *The Culture of Migration in Southern Mexico*. University of Texas Press, Austin.

Cohen, Jeffrey H. 2005. "Remittance Outcomes and Migration: Theoretical Contests, Real Opportunities." *Studies in International Comparative Development* 40(1):88–112.

Cohen, Jeffrey H., and Bernardo Ramirez Rios. 2016. "Internal Migration in Oaxaca: Its Role and Value to Rural Movers." *International Journal of Sociology* 46(3):223–35.

Cohen, Jeffrey H., and Ibrahim Sirkeci. 2011. *Cultures of Migration: The Global Nature of Contemporary Mobility*. University of Texas Press, Austin.

Colwell-Chanthaphonh, Chip, and T. J. Ferguson. 2006. "Rethinking Abandonment in Archaeological Contexts." *SAA Archaeological Record* 6(1):137–41.

Conway, Verona M. 1948. "Von Post's Work on Climatic Rhythms." *New Phytologist* 47(2):220–37.

Cook, Edward R., Connie A. Woodhouse, C. Mark Eakin, David M. Meko, and David W. Stahle. 2004. "Long-Term Aridity Changes in the Western United States." *Science* 306:1015–18.

Cook, Scott, and M. Diskin. 1976. *Markets in Oaxaca*. University of Texas Press, Austin.

Cooper, Jago, and Payson Sheets, eds. 2012. *Surviving Sudden Environmental Change: Understanding Hazards, Mitigating Impacts, and Avoiding Disasters*. University Press of Colorado, Boulder.

Cooper, Lisa. 2006. "The Demise and Regeneration of Bronze Age Urban Centers in the Euphrates Valley of Syria." In *After Collapse: The Regeneration of Complex Societies*, edited by Glenn M. Schwartz and John J. Nichols, 18–37. University of Arizona Press, Tucson.

Cornevin, Richard. 1957. "Le Centre urbain de Bassari." *Bulletin de l'I.F.A.N.*, Série B, No. 11(1–2):72–110.

Cornevin, Richard. 1962. *Les Bassari du Nord-Togo*. Berger-Levrault (Mondes d'Outre-Mer), Paris.

Creese, John L. 2012. "The Domestication of Personhood: A View from the Northern Iroquoian Longhouse." *Cambridge Archaeological Journal* 22(3):365–86.

Creese, John L. 2013. "Rethinking Early Village Development in Southern Ontario: Toward a History of Place-Making." *Canadian Journal of Archaeology* 37(2):185–218.

Crumley, Carole L. 1993. "Analyzing Historic Ecotonal Shifts." *Ecological Applications* 3(3):377–84.

Crumley, Carole L. 1994. *Historical Ecology: Cultural Knowledge and Changing Landscapes*. 1st ed. School of American Research Press; Distributed by the University of Washington Press, Santa Fe.

Crumley, Carole L. 2006. "Archaeology in the New World Order: What We Can Offer the Planet." In *Space and Spatial Analysis in Archaeology*, edited by Elizabeth C. Robertson, 383–96. University of New Mexico, Albuquerque.

Crumley, Carole L., and William H. Marquardt, eds. 1987. *Regional Dynamics: Burgundian Landscapes in Historical Perspective*. Academic Press, London.

Cullen, Heidi M., Peter B. deMenocal, Sidney Hemming, Gary Hemming, Francis H. Brown, Thomas Guilderson, and Frank Sirocko. 2000. "Climate Change and the Collapse of the Akkadian Empire: Evidence from the Deep Sea." *Geology* 28(4):379–82.

Cushing, Frank Hamilton. 1896. *Outlines of Zuni Creation Myths*. Thirteenth Annual Report of the Bureau of American Ethnology. Government Printing Office, Washington, DC.

Danti, Michael D. 1997. "Regional Surveys and Excavations." In *Subsistence and Settlement in a Marginal Environment: Tell es-Sweyhat, 1989–1995 Preliminary Report*, edited by Richard L. Zettler, 85–94. MASCA Research Papers in Science and Archaeology 14. University of Pennsylvania Museum of Archaeology and Anthropology, Philadelphia.

Danti, Michael D. 2000. "Early Bronze Age Settlement and Land Use in the Tell es-Sweyhat region, Syria." PhD diss., Department of Anthropology, University of Pennsylvania, Philadelphia.

Danti, Michael D. 2009. "The Tell es-Sweyhat Archaeological Project 2008." *Context* 20 (1):1–5.

Danti, Michael D. 2010. "Late Middle Holocene Climate and Northern Mesopotamia: Varying Cultural Responses to the 5.2 and 4.2 ka Aridification Events." In *Climate Crises in Human History*, edited by A. Bruce Mainwaring, Robert Giegengack, and Claudio Vita-Finzi, 139–72. Transactions of the American Philosophical Society. American Philosophical Society, Philadelphia.

Danti, Michael D., and Richard L. Zettler. 1998. "The Evolution of the Tell es-Sweyhat (Syria) Settlement System in the 3rd millennium BC." In *Espace naturel, espace habité in Syrie du Nord (10e–2e millénaires av. J.-C.)*, edited by Michel Fortin and Olivier Aurenche, 209–28. Bulletin of the Canadian Society for Mesopotamian Studies 33. Maison de l'Orient, Lyons.

Danti, Michael D., and Richard L. Zettler. 2002. "Excavating an Enigma: The Latest Discoveries from Tell es-Sweyhat." *Expedition* 44 (1):36–45.

Darling, Andrew J. 1998. "Mass Inhumation and the Execution of Witches in the American Southwest." *American Anthropologist* 100(3):732–52.

Davis, Emma Lou. 1964. "Anasazi Mobility and Mesa Verde Migrations." PhD diss., Department of Anthropology, University of California, Los Angeles.

Daw Thin Kyi. 1966. "The Old City of Pagan." *Artibus Asiae. Supplementum* 23:179–88.

de Barros, Philip L. 1985. *The Bassar: Large-Scale Iron Producers of the West African Savanna*. PhD diss., University of California, Los Angeles.

de Barros, Philip L. 1986. "Bassar: A Quantified, Chronologically Controlled, Regional Approach to a Traditional Iron Production Centre in West Africa." *Africa* 56(2):148–73.

de Barros, Philip L. 1988. "Societal Repercussions of the Rise of Large-Scale Traditional Iron Production: A West African Example." *African Archaeological Review* 6(1):91–113.

de Barros, Philip L. 2000. "Iron Metallurgy: Sociocultural Context of Ironworking." In *Ancient African Metallurgy*, edited by Joseph O. Vogel, 147–98. AltaMira, Walnut Creek, CA.

de Barros, Philip L. 2001. "The Effect of the Slave Trade on the Bassar Ironworking Society." In *West Africa during the Atlantic Slave Trade: Archaeological Perspectives*, edited by Chris DeCorse, 59–80. Leicester University Press, London.

de Barros, Philip L. 2012. "The Bassar Chiefdom in the Context of Theories of Political Economy." In *Métallurgie du fer et Sociétés africaines. Bilans et nouveaux paradigmes dans la Recherche anthropologique et archéologique*, edited by Caroline Robion-Brunner and Bruno Martinelli, 73–95. BAR International Series 2395. Cambridge Monographs in African Archaeology 81, Oxford.

de Barros, Philip L. 2013a. "A Comparison of Early and Later Iron Age Societies in the Bassar Region of Togo." In *The World of Iron*, edited by Jane Humphris and Thilo Rehren, 10–21. Archetype, London.

de Barros, Philip L. 2013b. "The Rise of the Bassar Chiefdom in the Context of Africa's Internal Frontier." In *Power and Landscape in Atlantic West Africa: Archaeological Perspectives*, edited by J. Cameron Monroe and Akinwumi Ogundiran, 255–77. Cambridge University Press, Cambridge.

de Barros, Philip L. 2016. "Project SIDERENT, Jan–Feb 2016. Bandjeli Area of the Bassar Region of Togo. Report on Excavations at BAS-296 (Titur)." Manuscript on file with Caroline Robion-Brunner, Co-Director of Pôle Afrique, TRAcES (Travaux et Recherches Archéologiques sur les Cultures, les Espaces et les Sociétés), Université Jean-Jaurès, Toulouse.

de Barros, Philip L., and Lantame T. Assouman. 2017. "Field notes on file with Philip de Barros." Behavioral Sciences Department, Palomar College, San Marcos, CA.

de Barros, Philip L., and Gabriella Lucidi. 2017. "Is This an Anvil? The Multi-Functionality of Iron Bloom Crushing (Likumanjool) Sites in the Bassar Region of Northern Togo." In *African Archaeology without Frontiers: Papers from the 2014 PanAfrican Archaeological Association Congress, Johannesburg*, edited by Karim Sadr, Amanda Esterhuysen, and Chrissie Sievers, 60–84. Wits University Press, Johannesburg.

Dean, Jeffery S. 2010. "The Environmental, Demographic, and Behavioral Context of the Thirteenth-Century Depopulation of the Northern Southwest." In *Leaving Mesa Verde: Peril and Change in the Thirteenth-Century Southwest*, edited by Timothy A. Kohler, Mark D. Varien, and Aaron M. Wright, 324–45. University of Arizona Press, Tuscon.

DeBoer, Warren. 2008. "Wrenched Bodies." In *Invisible Citizens: Captives and Their Consequences*, edited by Catherine M. Cameron, 233–61. University of Utah Press, Salt Lake City.

DeBoer, Warren. 2011. "Deep Time, Big Space: An Archaeologist Skirts the Topic at Hand." In *Ethnicity in Ancient Amazonia: Reconstructing Past Identities from Archaeology, Linguistics, and Ethnohistory*, edited by Alf Hornborg and Jonathan D. Hill, 75–98. University Press of Colorado, Boulder.

Deevey, E. S. 1964. "General and Historical Ecology." *BioScience* 14(7):33–35.

Deevey, E. S., Don S. Rice, Prudence M. Rice, H. H. Vaughan, Mark Brenner, and M. S. Flannery. 1979. "Mayan Urbanism: Impact on a Tropical Karst Environment." *Science* 206(4416):298–306.

deHeinzelin, J. 1967. "Investigations on the Terraces of the Middle Euphrates." In *The Tabqa Dam Reservoir Survey*, edited by Maurits van Loon, 22–27. Direction Générale des Antiquités et des Musées, Damascus.

De León, Jason. 2015. *The Land of Open Graves: Living and Dying on the Migrant Trail.* Berkeley: University of California Press.

Demarte, Pete, Sonja A. Schwake, Kendall B. Hills, Megan Clarke, Sarah Duignan, Steven L. Kawell, Emma Schlegl, and Gyles Iannone. 2013. "Ancient Lowland Maya Middle-Level Settlement Investigations: Results of the 2013 Settlement Excavations at the Site of Waybil." In *Archaeological Investigations in the North Vaca Plateau, Belize: Progress Report of the Fifteenth (2013) Field Season*, edited by Gyles Iannone, Jaime J. Awe, Sonja A. Schwake, and Kendall B. Hills, 56–108. Social Archaeology Research Program, Trent University. Peterborough, ON.

D'Hont, Olivier. 1994. *Vie Quotidienne des 'Agedat.* L'Institut Français D'Études Arabes de Damas, Damascus.

deMenocal, Peter B. 2001. "Cultural Responses to Climate Change during the Late Holocene." *Science* 292(5517):667–73.

Desmond, William. 2004. "Punishments and the Conclusion of Herodotus' Histories." *Greek, Roman and Byzantine Studies* 44:19–40.

Diedrich, Martin. 2019. "Late Classic Maya Period Ending Costumes of Western Petén, Guatemala." Paper presented at the 2019 Mesoamerica Meetings. Mesoamerica Center, Austin.

Dillehay, Tom D. 2007. *Monuments, Empires, and Resistance: The Araucanian Polity and Ritual Narratives.* Cambridge University Press, Cambridge.

Dilley, F. Brian. 1993. *Climate Change and Agricultural Transformation in the Oaxaca Valley, Mexico.* PhD diss., Pennsylvania State University, Anthropology.

Dolce, Rita. 1999. "The 'Second Ebla': A View on the EB IVB City." *ISIMU* 2:293–304.

Dolce, Rita. 2001. "Ebla after the 'Fall'—Some Preliminary Considerations on the EB IVB city." *Damaszner Mitteilungen* 13:11–28.

Donald, Leland. 1997. *Aboriginal Slavery on the Northwest Coast of North America.* University of California Press, Berkeley.

Donoghue, Joseph F. 2011. "Sea Level History of the Northern Gulf of Mexico Coast and Sea Level Rise Scenarios for the Near Future." *Climatic Change* 107(17):17–34.

Dorigo, Guido, and Waldo Tobler. 1983. "Push-Pull Migration Laws." *Annals of the Association of American Geographers* 73(1):1–17.

Dornemann, Rudolph. 1985. "Salvage Excavations at Tell Hadidi in the Euphrates River Valley." *Biblical Archaeologist* 48(1):49–59.

Drysdale, Russell, Giovanna Zanchetta, John Hellstrom, Roland Maas, Anthony Fallick, Matthew Pickett, Ian Cartwright, and Leonardo Piccini. 2006. "Late Holocene Drought Responsible for the Collapse of Old World Civilizations Is Recorded in an Italian Cave Flowstone." *Geology* 34(2):101–4.

Dugast, Stéphan. 1986. "La pince et le soufflet: Deux techniques de forge tradition-nelle au Nord-Togo." *Journal des Africanistes* 56(2):29–53.

Dugast, Stéphan. 1987. "L'Agglomération de Bassar." Manuscript on file at l'Office de la Recherche Scientifique et Technique d'Outre-Mer (ORSTOM, now IRD [l'Institut de Recherche pour le Développement]), Paris.

Dugast, Stéphan. 1992. "Rites et organisation sociale: L'Agglomération de Bassar au Nord-Togo." PhD diss., École des Hautes Études en Sciences Sociales, Paris.

Dugast, Stéphan. 2004. "Une agglomération très rurale: Lien clanique et Lien territo-rial dans la Ville de Bassar (Nord-Togo)." *Journal des Africanistes* 74(1–2):203–48.

Dugast, Stéphan. 2008. "Incendies rituels et bois sacrés en Afrique de l'Ouest: Une Complémentarité méconnue." *Bois et Forêts des Tropiques* 296(2):17–26.

Dugast, Stéphan. 2013. "Des pierres pour travailler le fer: Les outils lithiques des Forgerons Bassar du Nord-Togo. I: Techniques, Nomenclatures et Répartition des Tâches." *Journal des Africanistes* 83(2):23–57.

Dugast, Stéphan. 2016. "Rapport de Mission 2016. SIDERENT Project." Manuscript on file at IRD (Institut de Recherche pour le Développement), Paris.

Dunning, Nicholas P., Carmen McCane, Tyler Swinney, Matthew Purtill, Jani Sparks, Ashley Mann, Jon-Paul McCool, and Chantal Ivenso. 2015. "Geoarchaeo-logical Investigations in Mesoamerica Move into the 21st Century: A Review." *Geoarchaeology* 30(3):167–99.

Ebert, Claire E., Keith M. Prufer, and Douglas L. Kennett. 2012. "Maya Monuments and Spatial Statistics: A GIS-based Examination of the Terminal Classic Period Maya Collapse." *Research Reports in Belizean Archaeology* 9:91–105.

Engelbrecht, William. 2003. *Iroquoia: The Development of a Native World*. Syracuse University Press, Syracuse, NY.

Epstein, Hellmut. 1985. *The Awassi Sheep with Special Reference to the Improved Dairy Type*. FAO Animal Production and Health Paper 57. Food and Agriculture Orga-nization of the United Nations, Rome.

Erickson, Clark. L. 2006a. "The Domesticated Landscapes of the Bolivian Amazon." In *Time and Complexity in Historical Ecology: Studies in the Neotropical Lowlands*, edited by William L. Balée and Clark L. Erickson, 235–78. Columbia University Press, New York.

Erickson, Clark. L. 2006b. "Intensification, Political Economy, and the Farming Community: Defense of a Bottom-Up Perspective of the Past." In *Agricultural Strategies*, edited by Joyce Marcus and Charles Stanish, 233–65. Cotsen Institute, Los Angeles.

Erickson, Clark. L. 2008. "Amazonia: The Historical Ecology of a Domesticated Landscape." In *The Handbook of South American Archaeology*, edited by Helaine Silverman and William H. Isbell, 157–83. Springer Science and Business Media, New York.

Errington, Shelly. 1989. *Meaning and Power in a Southeast Asian Realm*. Princeton University Press, Princeton, NJ.

Faist, Thomas. 1997. "The Crucial Meso-Level." In *International Migration, Immobility and Development: Multidisciplinary Perspectives*, edited by T. Hammar, G. Brochmann, K. Tamas, and T. Faist, 187–218. Berg, New York.

Faught, Michael K. 2004. "Submerged Paleoindian and Archaic Sites of the Big Bend, Florida." *Journal of Field Archaeology* 29(3/4):273–89.

Faulseit, Ronald K. 2015. "Collapse, Resilience, and Transformation in Complex Societies: Modeling Trends and Understanding Diversity." In *Beyond Collapse: Archaeological Perspectives on Resilience, Revitalization, and Transformation in Complex Societies*, edited by Ronald K. Faulseit, 3–26. Southern Illinois University Carbondale, Center for Archaeological Investigations, Occasional Paper No. 41. Southern Illinois University Press. Carbondale.

Fedick, Scott L. 1995. "Land Evaluation and Ancient Maya Land Use in the Upper Belize River Area, Belize, Central America." *Latin American Antiquity* 6(1):16–34.

Feld, Steven, and Keith H. Basso, eds. 1996. *Sense of Place*. School of American Research Press, Santa Fe.

Finlayson, William D. 1985. *The 1975 and 1978 Rescue Excavations at the Draper Site: Introduction and Settlement Patterns*. Mercury Series Archaeological Survey of Canada Paper 130. National Museum of Man, Ottawa.

Finlayson, William D. 1998. *Iroquoian Peoples of the Land of Rocks and Water AD 1000–1650: A Study in Settlement Archaeology*. London Museum of Archaeology, London.

Fitzgerald, William R. 1995. "A Late Sixteenth-Century European Trade Assemblage from Northeastern North America." In *Trade and Discovery: The Scientific Study of Artefacts from Post-Medieval Europe and Beyond*, edited by Duncan R. Hook and David R.M. Gaimster, 29–44. Occasional Paper 109. British Museum Press, London.

Fletcher, Peri L. 1999. *Las Casa de Mis Sueños: Dreams of Home in a Transnational Mexican Community*. Westview Press, Boulder, CO.

Fletcher, Roland. 2009. "Low-Density, Agrarian-Based Urbanism: A Comparative View." *Insights* 2(4):2–19.

Fletcher, Roland. 2012. "The Dynamics of Angkor and Its Landscape: Issues of Scale, Non-Correspondence and Outcome." In *Old Myths and New Approaches: Interpreting Ancient Southeast Asia*, edited by Alexandra Haendal, 42–62. Monash University, Clayton, Australia.

Fowler, P. J. 1995. "Writing on the Countryside." In *Interpretive Archaeology: Finding Meaning in the Past*, edited by Ian Hodder, Michael Shanks, A. Alexandri, V. Buchli, J. Carman, J. Lase, and G. Lucas, 100–109. Routledge, London.

Fowles, Severin M. 2005. "Historical Contingency and the Prehistoric Foundations of Moiety Organization among the Eastern Pueblos." *Journal of Anthropological Research* 61(1): 25–52.

Fowles, Severin M. 2009. "The Enshrined Pueblo: Villagescape and Cosmos in the Northern Rio Grande." *American Antiquity* 74(3): 448–66.

Fowles, Severin M. 2011. "Movement and the Unsettling of the Pueblos." In *Rethinking Anthropological Perspectives on Migration*, edited by Graciela S. Cabana and Jeffrey J. Clark, 45–67. University of Florida Press, Gainesville.

Fox, William A. 1986. "The Elliott Villages (AfHc-2)—An Introduction." *Kewa* 86(1):11–17.

Freidel, David A. 2008. "Maya Divine Kingship." In *Religion and Power: Divine Kingship in the Ancient World and Beyond*, edited by Nicole Brisch, 191–206. Oriental Institute of the University of Chicago, Chicago.

Freidel, David A., Marilyn A. Masson, and Michelle Rich. 2016. "Imagining a Complex Maya Political Economy: Counting Tokens and Currencies in Image, Text and the Archaeological Record." *Cambridge Archaeological Journal* 27(1):29–54.

Froelich, Jean-Claude, and Pierre Alexandre. 1960. "Histoire traditionnelle des Koto-koli et des Bi-Tchambi du Nord-Togo." *Bulletin de l'I.F.A.N.*, Série B, No. 12(1-2):247–60.

Frumkin, Amos. 2009. "Stable Isotopes of a Subfossil Tamarix Tree from the Dead Sea Region, Israel, and Their Implications for the Intermediate Bronze Age Environmental Crisis." *Quaternary Research* 71 (3):319–28.

Gagliano, Sherwood M., and Clarence H. Webb. 1970. "Archaic-Poverty Point Transition at the Pearl River Mouth." In *The Poverty Point Culture*, edited by Bettye J. Broyles, 47–72. Southeastern Archaeological Conference Bulletin 12. Morgantown, WV.

Gates St-Pierre, Christian. 2004. "The Middle Woodland Ancestors of the St. Lawrence Iroquoians." In *A Passion for the Past: Papers in Honor of James F. Pendergast*, edited by Jean-Luc Pilon and James V. Wright, 395–417. Mercury Series, No. 164. Archaeological Survey of Canada, Canadian Museum of Civilization, Gatineau.

Gates St-Pierre, Christian. 2016. "Iroquoians in the St. Lawrence River Valley before European Contact." *Ontario Archaeology* 96:47–64.

Gaudreau, Mariane, and Louis Lesage. 2016. "Understanding Ethnicity and Cultural Affiliation: Huron-Wendat and Anthropological Perspectives." *Ontario Archaeology* 96:6–16.

Geertz, Clifford. 1980. *Negara: The Theatre State in Nineteenth-Century Bali.* Princeton University Press, Princeton, NJ.

Gell, Alfred. 1998. *Art and Agency: An Anthropological Theory.* Clarendon Press, Oxford.

Ghosh, P. K., and R. K. Abichandani. 1981. *Water and the Eco-Physiology of Desert Sheep.* Central Arid Zone Research Institute, Jodhpur, India.

Gibson, Jon L. 2000. *The Ancient Mounds of Poverty Point: Place of Rings.* University of Alabama Press, Tuscaloosa.

Glowacki, Donna M. 2011. "The Role of Religion in the Depopulation of the Central Mesa Verde Region." In *Religious Transformation in the Late Pre-Hispanic Pueblo World,* edited by D. M. Glowacki and S. Van Keuren, 66–83. Amerind Foundation Seminar Series. University of Arizona Press, Tucson.

Glowacki, Donna M. 2015. *Living and Leaving: A Social History of Regional Depopulation in Thirteenth-Century Mesa Verde.* University of Arizona Press, Tucson.

Glowacki, Donna M., and Scott G. Ortman. 2012. "Characterizing Community Center (Village) Formation in the VEP Study Area, . . . AD 600–1280." In *Emergence and Collapse of Early Villages: Models of Central Mesa Verde Archaeology,* edited by T. A. Kohler and M. D. Varien, 219–46. University of California Press, Berkeley.

Gnon, A. 1967. *L'aménagement de l'espace en pays Bassari—Kabou et sa région.* DES Géographie, l'Université de Caen.

Goodbred, S. L., A. C. Hine, and E. E. Wright. 1998. "Sea-Level Change and Storm Surge Deposition in a Late Holocene Florida Salt Marsh." *Journal of Sedimentary Research* 68(2):240–52.

Goodchild, A. V., A. I. El-Awad, and O. Gürsoy. 1999. "Effect of Feeding Level in Late Pregnancy and Early Lactation and Fibre Level in Mid Lactation on Body Mass, Milk Production and Quality in Awassi Ewes." *Animal Science* 68(1):231–41.

Graham, Helen, Rhiannon Mason, and Andrew Newman. 2009. *Literature Review: Historic Environment, Sense of Place, and Social Capital.* International Centre for Cultural and Heritage Studies (ICCHS), Newcastle, UK.

Grainger, John. 1946. "Ecology of the Larger Fungi." *Transactions of the British Mycological Society* 29(1–2):52–63.

Grantham, Bill. 2002. *Creation Myths and Legends of the Creek Indians.* University Press of Florida, Gainesville.

Grave, Peter, and Mike Barbetti. 2001. "Dating the City Wall, Fortifications, and the Palace Site at Pagan." *Asian Perspectives* 40(1):75–87.

Greenlee, Diana M. 2009. "Annual Report of the Station Archaeology Program at Poverty Point State Historic Site." Report on file, Division of Archaeology, Louisiana Department of Culture, Recreation and Tourism, Baton Rouge.

Greenlee, Diana M. 2010. "Annual Report of the Station Archaeology Program at Poverty Point State Historic Site." Report on file, Division of Archaeology, Louisiana Department of Culture, Recreation and Tourism, Baton Rouge.

Greenlee, Diana M. 2013. "Annual Report of the Station Archaeology Program at Poverty Point State Historic Site." Report on file, Division of Archaeology, Louisiana Department of Culture, Recreation and Tourism, Baton Rouge.

Greenlee, Diana M. 2015. "Annual Report of the Station Archaeology Program at Poverty Point State Historic Site." Report on file, Division of Archaeology, Louisiana Department of Culture, Recreation and Tourism, Baton Rouge.

Grigolini, Silvia. 2005. "When Houses Provide More than Shelter: Analyzing the Uses of Remittances within their Social Context." In *Migration and Economy: Global and Local Dynamics*, Vol. 22, Monograph of the Society for Economic Anthropology, edited by Lilian Trager, 193–224. AltaMira Press, Walnut Creek, CA.

Habicht-Mauche, Judith A. 1993. *The Pottery from Arroyo Hondo Pueblo, New Mexico: Tribalization and Trade in the northern Rio Grande*. School of American Research (SAR) Press, Santa Fe, NM.

Håkansson, Thomas N., and Mats Widgren, eds. 2016. *Landesque Capital: The Historical Ecology of Enduring Landscape Modifications*. Routledge, New York.

Hall, Robert L. 1976. "Ghosts, Water Barriers, Corn, and Sacred Enclosures in the Eastern Woodlands." *American Antiquity* 41(3): 360–64.

Halstead, P., and J. O'Shea, eds. 2004. *Bad Year Economics: Cultural Responses to Risk and Uncertainty*. Cambridge University Press, Cambridge.

Harrison-Buck, Eleanor, Patricia A. McAnany, and Rebecca Storey. 2007. "Empowered and Disempowered during the Late to Terminal Classic Transition: Maya Burial and Termination Rituals in the Sibun Valley, Belize." In *New Perspectives on Human Sacrifice and Ritual Body Treatments in Ancient Maya Society*, edited by V. Tiesler and A. Cucina, 74–101. Springer Science+Business Media, LLC, New York.

Hart, John P., and William Engelbrecht. 2012. "Northern Iroquoian Ethnic Evolution: A Social Network Analysis." *Journal of Archaeological Method and Theory* 19(2):322–49.

Hart, John P., Termeh Shafie, Jennifer A. Birch, Susan Dermarkar, and Ronald F. Williamson. 2016. "Nation Building and Social Signaling in Southern Ontario: AD 1350–1650." *PLoS ONE* 11(5):e0156178

Hays, Christopher T., Richard A. Weinstein, and James B. Stoltman. 2016. "Poverty Point Objects Reconsidered." *Southeastern Archaeology* 35(3):213–36.

Hegmon, M. 2017. "Path Dependence." In *The Oxford Handbook of Southwest Archaeology*, edited by B. J. Mills and S. M. Fowles, 155–66. Oxford University Press, Oxford.

Heidegger, Martin. 1977. *Poetry, Language, Thought*. Harper and Row, New York.

Hellman, Judith Adler. 2008. *The World of Mexican Migrants: The Rock and the Hard Place*. New Press.

Heyman, Josiah. 2007. "Environmental Issues at the U.S.-Mexican Border and the Unequal Territorialization of Value." In *Rethinking Environmental History: World-system History and Global Environmental Change*, edited by Alf Hornborg, J. R. McNeill, and Joan Martinez-Alier, 327–44. AltaMira Press, Lanham, MD.

Heymann, Jody, Francisco Flores-Macias, Jeffrey A. Hayes, Malinda Kennedy, Claudia Lahale, and Alison Earle. 2009. "The Impact of Migration on the Well-Being of Transnational Families: New Data from Sending Communities in Mexico." *Community, Work and Family* 12(1):91–103.

Higham, Charles F. W. 2001. "Commentary: Archaeology in Myanmar: Past, Present, and Future." *Asian Perspectives* 40(1):127–38.

Hill, Erica, and Jon B. Hageman, eds. 2016. *The Archaeology of Ancestors: Death, Memory, and Veneration*. University Press of Florida, Gainesville.

Hills, Kendall B. 2012. *A Contextual Analysis of the Artifact Assemblage from the Epicenter of the Ancient Maya site of Minanha, Belize*. MA thesis, Trent University, Peterborough, ON.

Hills, Kendall B., Morgan Moodie, Gyles Iannone, and Jack Barry. 2012. "Investigations in the Waybil Epicenter: Results from the 2012 Excavations of Group A." In *Archaeological Investigations in the North Vaca Plateau, Belize: Progress Report of the Fourteenth (2012) Field Season*, edited by Gyles Iannone, Jaime J. Awe, Sonja A. Schwake, and Kendall B. Hills, 33–60. Social Archaeology Research Program, Trent University. Peterborough, ON.

Hirsch, E. 1995. "Landscape: Between Place and Space." In *The Anthropology of Landscape: Perspective on Place and Space*, edited by Eric Hirsch and Michael O'Hanlon, 1–30. Clarendon Press, Oxford.

Hodder, Ian. 1990. *The Domestication of Europe*. Blackwell, Oxford.

Hodder, Ian. 2011a. Wheels of Time: Some Aspects of Entanglement Theory and the Secondary Products Revolution. *Journal of World Prehistory* 24:175–87.

Hodder, Ian. 2011b. Human-Thing Entanglement: Towards an Integrated Archaeological Perspective. *Journal of the Royal Anthropological Institute* 17:154–77.

Hodder, Ian. 2012. *Entangled: An Archaeology of the Relationships between Humans and Things*. John Wiley and Sons Ltd., Chichester, UK.

Hodder, Ian. 2014. "The Entanglements of Humans and Things: A Long-Term View." *New Literary History* 45(1):19–36.

Hodder, Ian. 2016a. *Studies in Human-Thing Entanglement*. Open Access Book.

Hodder, Ian. 2016b. "Degrees of Dependence: The Example of the Introduction of Pottery in the Middle East and at Çatalhöyük." In *Archaeology of Entanglement*, edited by Lindsay Der and Francesca Fernandini, 235–50. Left Coast Press, Walnut Grove, CA.

Hodge, Fredrick Webb. [1913] 1971. *Handbook of the Indians of Canada*. Coles Publishing, Toronto.

Hole, Frank. 1991. "Middle Khabur Settlement and Agriculture in the Ninevite V Period." *Canadian Society for Mesopotamian Studies Bulletin* 21:17–30.

Hole, Frank. 1994. "Environmental Instabilities and Urban Origins." In *Chiefdoms and Early States in the Near East: The Organizational Dynamics of Complexity*, edited by Gil J. Stein and Mitchell Rothman, 121–51. Monographs in World Archaeology 18. Prehistory Press, Madison.

Hole, Frank. 1999. "Storage Structures at Tell Ziyadeh, Syria." *Journal of Field Archaeology* 26:269–83.

Holland, Thomas A. 1976. "Preliminary Report on Excavations at Tell es-Sweyhat, Syria, 1973–74." *Levant* 8:36–70.

Holland, Thomas A. 2006. *Excavations at Tell es-Sweyhat, Syria 2. Archaeology of the Bronze Age, Hellenistic, and Roman Remains at an Ancient town on the Euphrates River*. 2 vols. Oriental Institute Publication 125. Oriental Institute of the University of Chicago, Chicago.

Hudson, Bob. 2000. "The Merits of Rebuilding Bagan." *Orientations* 31(5):85–86.

Hudson, Bob. 2004. "The Origins of Bagan: The Archaeological Landscape of Upper Burma to AD 1300." PhD diss., University of Sydney, Sydney.

Hudson, Bob. 2006. "Climate Change in Prehistory, and Some Climatic Implications for Early Urban Myanmar." *Bulletin of the Field School of Archaeology* 1:15–21.

Hudson, Bob. 2008. "Restoration and Reconstruction of Monuments at Bagan (Pagan), Myanmar (Burma), 1995–2008." *World Archaeology* 40(4):553–71.

Hudson, Bob, Lwin Nyein, and Win Maung (Tanpawady). 2001. "The Origins of Bagan: New Dates and Old Inhabitants." *Asian Perspectives* 40(1):48–74.

Humphrey, Michael. 2013. "Migration, Security and Insecurity." *Journal of Intercultural Studies* 34(2):178–95.

Huschke, Susann. 2014. "Fragile Fabric: Illegality Knowledge, Social Capital and Health-Seeking of Undocumented Latin American Migrants in Berlin." *Journal of Ethnic and Migration Studies* 40(12):2010–29.

Iannone, Gyles. 2005. "The Rise and Fall of an Ancient Maya Petty Royal Court." *Latin American Antiquity* 16(1):26–44.

Iannone, Gyles. 2014. *The Great Maya Droughts in Cultural Context: Case Studies in Resilience and Vulnerability*. University Press of Colorado, Boulder.

Iannone, Gyles. 2017. "Architecture, Activities, and Authority in the Ancient Maya World: Some Insights from the Middle Level of the Settlement Continuum." Paper presented at the 14th Annual Belize Archaeology Symposium, San Ignacio, Belize.

Iannone, Gyles, Arlen F. Chase, Diane Z. Chase, Jaime J. Awe, Holley Moyes, George A. Brook, Jason Polk, James W. Webster, and James Conolly. 2014. "An Archaeological Consideration of Long-Term Socioecological Dynamics on the Vaca Plateau, Belize." In *The Great Maya Droughts in Cultural Context: Case Studies in Resilience and Vulnerability*, edited by Gyles Iannone, 271–300. University Press of Colorado, Boulder.

Iannone, Gyles, and Samuel V. Connell. 2003. "Perspectives on Ancient Maya Rural Complexity: An Introduction." In *Perspectives on Ancient Maya Rural Complexity*, edited by Gyles Iannone and Samuel V. Connell, 1–6. Cotsen Institute of Archaeology at UCLA, Los Angeles.

Iannone, Gyles, Brett A. Houk, and Sonja A. Schwake. 2016. "Introduction." In *Ritual, Violence, and the Fall of the Classic Maya Kings*, edited by Gyles Iannone, Brett A. Houk, and Sonja A. Schwake, 1–22. University Press of Florida, Gainesville.

Iannone, Gyles, and Matthew Longstaffe. 2010. "The 2010 Excavations in the Stairway Leading to Minanha's Royal Residential Compound (Group J)." In *Archaeological Investigations in the North Vaca Plateau, Belize: Progress report of the Twelfth (2010) Field Season*, edited by Gyles Iannone, Jaime Awe, Maxime Lamoureux St-Hilaire, and Matthew Mosher, 63–75. Social Archaeology Research Program, Trent University, Peterborough, ON.

Iannone, Gyles, Scott Macrae, Maxime Lamoureux St-Hilaire, Jack Berry, Pete Demarte, and James Conlon. 2011. "Preliminary Investigations at the Minor Center of Waybil: Results of the 2011 Field Season." In *Archaeological Investigations in the North Vaca Plateau, Belize: Progress Report of the Thirteenth (2011) Field Season*, edited by Gyles Iannone, Sonja A. Schwake, Jaime J. Awe, and Phillip P. Reader, 97–114. Social Archaeology Research Program, Trent University, Peterborough, ON.

Iannone, Gyles, Carmen McCormick, and James Conolly. 2008. "Community Archaeology at Minanha: Some Preliminary Insights from the Phase II Settlement Study." *Research Reports in Belizean Archaeology* 5:149–58.

Iannone, Gyles, Jesse Phillips, and Carmen McCormick. 2006. "Community Archaeology at Minanha: Some Preliminary Musings on the 2006 Field Season." In *Archaeological Investigations in the North Vaca Plateau, Belize: Progress Report of the Eighth (2006) Field Season*, edited by Gyles Iannone, Jeffery Seibert, Jason Seguin, and Laura McRae, 115–27. Trent University, Peterborough, ON.

Iannone, Gyles, and Claudia Zehrt. 2005. "The 2005 Excavations in Minanha's Royal Residential Courtyard (Group J)." In *Archaeological Investigations in the North Vaca Plateau, Belize: Progress Report of the Seventh (2005) Field Season*, edited by Gyles Iannone, 12–23. Social Archaeology Research Program, Trent University, Peterborough, ON.

Iannone, Gyles, Claudia Zehrt, Carmen McCormick, Jeffery Seibert, Matthew Mosher, Scott Macrae, and James Conolly. 2007. "The Phase II Settlement Study at Minanha: New Data, New Insights." In *Archaeological Investigations in the North Vaca Plateau, Belize: Progress Report of the Ninth (2007) Field Season*, edited by Gyles Iannone and Scott Macrae, 150–62. Trent University, Peterborough, ON.

Ingerson, Alice E. 1994. "Tracking and Testing the Nature-Culture Dichotomy." In *Historical Ecology: Cultural Knowledge and Changing Landscapes*, edited by Carole L. Crumley, 43–66. School of American Research Press, Distributed by the University of Washington Press, Santa Fe, NM.

Ingold, Tim. 2000. *The Perception of The Environment: Essays on Livelihood, Dwelling and Skill*. Routledge, New York.

Ingold, Tim. 2007. *Lines: A Brief History*. Routledge, New York.

Ingold, Tim. 2015. *The Life of Lines*. Routledge, New York.

Inomata, Takeshi. 2003. "War, Destruction, and Abandonment: The Fall of the Classic Maya Center of Aguateca, Guatemala." In *Archaeology of Settlement Abandonment in Middle America*, edited by T. Inomata and Ronald W. Webb, 43–60. University of Utah Press, Salt Lake City.

Inomata, Takeshi. 2016. "Concepts of Legitimacy and Social Dynamics. Termination Ritual and the last King of Aguateca, Guatemala." In *Ritual, Violence, and the Fall of the Classic Maya Kings*, edited by Gyles Iannone, Brett A. Houk, and Sonja A. Schwake, 89–107. University Press of Florida, Gainesville.

Inomata, Takeshi, and Ronald W. Webb, eds. 2003a. *The Archaeology of Settlement Abandonment in Middle America*. University of Utah Press, Salt Lake City.

Inomata, Takeshi, and Ronald W. Webb. 2003b. "Archaeological Studies of Abandonment in Middle America." In *The Archaeology of Settlement Abandonment in Middle America*, edited by Takeshi Inomata and Ronald W. Webb, 1–12. University of Utah Press, Salt Lake City.

Issar, Arie S., and Mattanyah Zohar. 2004. *Climate Change: Environment and Civilization in the Middle East*. Springer, New York.

Jackson, H. Edwin. 1991. "The Trade Fair in Hunter-Gatherer Interaction: The Role of Intersocietal Trade in the Evolution of Poverty Point." In *Between Bands and States*, edited by Susan A. Gregg, 265–86. Occasional Papers 9, Center for Archaeological Investigations, Southern Illinois University, Carbondale.

Jameson, Fredric. 2005. *Archaeologies of the Future: The Desire Called Utopia and Other Science Fictions.* Verso, London.

Johnson, Robert E. 1998. "Phase II Archaeological Investigation of Sites 8DU5544 and 8DU5545 Queen's Harbour Yacht and Country Club, Duvall County, Florida." Florida Archaeological Services, Inc., Jacksonville.

Jojola, Ted. 2006. "Notes on Identity, Time, Space, and Place." In *American Indian Thought: Philosophical Essays*, edited by Anne Waters, 87–96. Blackwell Publishing, Malden, MA.

Jokisch, Brad D. 2002. "Migration and Agricultural Change: The Case of Small-holder Agriculture in Highland Ecuador." *Human Ecology* 30(4):523–51.

Jones, Eric E., and James W. Wood. 2012. "Using Event-History Analysis to Examine the Causes of Semi-Sedentism among Shifting cultivators: A Case Study of the Haudenosaunee, AD 1500–1700." *Journal of Archaeological Science* 39(8):2593–2603.

Joyce, Rosemary A., and Julia A. Hendon. 2000. "Heterarchy, History, and Material Reality: 'Communities' in Late Classic Honduras." In *The Archaeology of Communities: A New World Perspective*, edited by Marcello A. Canuto and Jason Yaeger, 143–60. Routledge, New York.

Kanaiaupuni, Shawn Malia. 2000. *Sustaining Families and Communities: Nonmigrant Women and Mexico-U.S. Migration Processes.* CDE Working Paper #83, Center for Demography and Ecology, University of Wisconsin, Madison.

Kan Hla, U. 1977. "Pagan: Development and Town Planning." *Journal of the Society of Architectural Historians* 36(1):15–29.

Katzenberg, M. Anne, Henry Schwarcz, M. Knyf, and F. Jerry Melbye. 1995. "Stable Isotope Evidence for Maize Horticulture and Paleodiet in Southern Ontario, Canada." *American Antiquity* 60(2):335–50.

Kenyon, Walter A. 1968. *The Miller Site.* Occasional Paper 14, Art and Archaeology, Royal Ontario Museum and University of Toronto, Toronto.

Kidder, Tristram R. 2006. "Climate Change and the Archaic to Woodland Transition (3000–2500 cal B.P.) in the Mississippi River Basin." *American Antiquity* 71(2):195–231.

Kidder, Tristram R. 2011. "Transforming Hunter-Gatherer History at Poverty Point." In *Hunter-Gatherer Archaeology as Historical Process*, edited by Kenneth E. Sassaman and Donald H. Holly Jr., 95–119. University of Arizona Press, Tucson.

Kidder, Tristram R., Lee J. Arco, Anthony L. Ortmann, Timothy Schilling, Caroline Boeke, Rachel Bielitz, Tabitha Heet, and Katherine A. Adelsberger. 2009. "Poverty Point Mound A: Final Report of the 2005 and 2006 Field Seasons." Report on file, Louisiana Archaeological Survey and Antiquities Commission, Baton Rouge.

Kidder, Tristram R., Edward R. Henry, and Lee J. Arco. 2017. "Rapid Climate Change-Induced Collapse of Hunter-Gatherer Societies in the Lower Mississippi River Valley between 3300 and 2780 cal yr BP." *Science China Earth Sciences,* https://doi.org/10.1007/s11430-017-9128-8.

Kintigh, K. W., and S. E. Ingram. 2018. "Was the Drought Really Responsible? Assessing Statistical Relationships between Climate Extremes and Cultural Transitions." *Journal of Archaeological Science* 89:25–31.

Kirby, Anne V. T. 1973. *The Use of Land and Water Resources in the Past and Present Valley of Oaxaca, Mexico.* Memoirs of the Museum of Anthropology, University of Michigan, Ann Arbor.

Kirk, Athena. 2014. "The Semantics of Showcase in Herodotus's Histories." *Transactions of the American Philological Association* 144(1):19–40.

Klose, Heinrich. 1903. "Das Bassarivolk I." *Globus* 83(20):309–14.

Klose, Heinrich. [1899] 1964. *Klose's Journey to Northern Ghana, 1894.* Translated by Inge Killick, Institute of African Studies, University of Ghana at Legon. [Originally published as *Togo unter deutscher Flagge,* 285–544.]

Knapp, Bernard A., and Wendy Ashmore. 1999. "Archaeological Landscapes: Constructed, Conceptualized, Ideational." In *Archaeologies of Landscape: Contemporary Perspectives,* edited by Wendy Ashmore and Bernard A. Knapp, 1–30. Blackwell Publishers, Malden, MA.

Kohler, Timothy A., Scott G. Ortman, Katie E. Grundtisch, Carly Fitzpatrick, and Sarah M. Cole. 2014. "The Better Angels of Their Nature: Declining Conflict through Time among Prehispanic Farmers of the Pueblo Southwest." *American Antiquity* 79(3):444–64.

Kohler, Timothy A., and Lynne Sebastian. 1996. "Population Aggregation in the Prehistoric North American Southwest." *American Antiquity* 61(3):597–602.

Kopytoff, Igor. 1987. "The Internal African Frontier: The Making of African Political Culture." In *The African Frontier: The Reproduction of Traditional African Societies,* edited by Igor Kopytoff, 3–86. Indiana University Press, Bloomington.

Kowalewski, Stephen A. 2006. "Coalescent Societies." In *Light on the Path: The Anthropology and History of the Southeastern Indians,* edited by A. King, J. T. Milanich, E. E. Bowne, M. T. Smith, T. Purdue, S. C. Hahn, S. Kowalewski, J. E. Worth, S. Jones, W. M. Jurgelski, and M. Williams, 94–122. University of Alabama Press, Birmingham.

Kuckelman, Kristin A., Ricky R. Lightfoot, and Debra L. Martin. 2000. "Changing Patterns of Violence in the Northern San Juan Region." *Kiva* 66(1):147–66.

Kuckelman, Kristin A., Ricky R. Lightfoot, and Debra L. Martin. 2002. "The Bioarchaeology and Taphonomy of Violence at Castle Rock and Sand Canyon Pueblos, Southwestern Colorado." *American Antiquity* 67(3):486–513.

Kujit, Ian. 2008. "The Regeneration of Life: Neolithic Structures of Symbolic Remembering and Forgetting." *Current Anthropology* 49(2):171–97.

Kuzucuğlu, Catherine, and Catherine Marro. 2007. "Northern Syria and Upper Mesopotamia at the End of the Third Millennium BC: Did a Crisis Take Place?" In *Sociétés humaines et changement climatique à la fin du troisième millénaire: Une crise a-t-elle eu lieu en Haute Mésopotamie? Actes du Colloque de Lyon, 5–8 décembre 2005*, edited by Catherine Kuzucuğlu and Catherine Marro, 583–90. Varia Anatolica XIX. De Boccard Édition-Diffusion, Paris.

Lafitau, Pierre. 1977. *Customs of the American Indians Compared with the Customs of Primitive Times*. Translated by William N. Fenton and Elizabeth L. Moore. Champlain Society, Toronto.

Lamoureux-St-Hilaire, Maxime. 2011. "The Last Inhabitants of Minanha, Belize: Examining the Differential Abandonment of an Ancient Maya Community." MA thesis, Trent University, Peterborough, ON.

Lamoureux-St-Hilaire, Maxime. 2017. "La cuarta temporada de investigaciones en la sección norte del palacio real de La Corona." In *Proyecto Arqueológico La Corona: Informe Final, Temporada 2016*, edited by Marcello Canuto, Tomás Barrientos, and Eduardo Bustamante, 37–74. PRALC, Guatemala City.

Lamoureux-St-Hilaire, Maxime. 2018. *Palatial Politics: The Classic Maya Royal Court of La Corona, Guatemala*. PhD diss., Tulane University, New Orleans.

Lamoureux-St-Hilaire, Maxime. 2019. "El análisis de las tabletas y vasijas de cerámica del cuarto 13Q-4Pı." In *Proyecto Arqueológico La Corona: Informe Final, Temporada 2018*, edited by Marcello Canuto, Tomás Barrientos, and Marissa López. PRALC, Guatemala City.

Lamoureux-St-Hilaire, Maxime, and Eduardo Bustamante. 2016. "Investigaciones de desarrollo y funcionalidad en el palacio real de La Corona." In *XXIX Simposio de Investigaciones Arqueológicas en Guatemala*, edited by Bárbara Arroyo, Luis Méndez Salinas, and Gloria Ajú Álvarez, 311–28. Asociación Tikal, Guatemala City.

Lamoureux-St-Hilaire, Maxime, Marcello A. Canuto, E. Christian Wells, Clarissa Cagnato, and Tomás Q. Barrientos. 2019. "Ancillary Economic Activities in a Classic Maya Regal Palace: A Multi-Proxy Approach." *Geoarchaeology* 34(6):768–82.

Lamoureux-St-Hilaire, Maxime, Gyles Iannone, and Andrew Snetsinger. 2013. "Living amongst Ruins: The Use and Perception of Abandoned Architecture at Minanha, Belize." Paper presented at the 78th annual meeting of the SAA. Honolulu.

Lamoureux-St-Hilaire, Maxime, Scott Macrae, Carmen McCane, Evan Parker, and Gyles Iannone. 2015. "The Last Groups Standing: Living Abandonment at the Ancient Maya Center of Minanha, Belize." *Latin American Antiquity* 26(4):550–69.

Lamoureux-St-Hilaire, Maxime, and Rubén Morales-Forte. 2016. "La tercera temporada de investigación en la sección norte del palacio real de La Corona." In *Proyecto Arqueológico La Corona: Informe Final, Temporada 2015*, edited by Marcello Canuto, Tomás Barrientos, and Eduardo Bustamante, 53–96. PRALC, Guatemala City.

Lekson, Stephen H. 1999. *The Chaco Meridian: Centers of Political Power in the Ancient Southwest*. AltaMira, Walnut Creek, CA.

Lekson, Stephen H. 2008. *A History of the Ancient Southwest*. SAR Press, Santa Fe.

Lekson, S. H., C. P. Nepstad-Thornberry, B. E. Yunker, T. S. Laumbach, D. P. Cain, and K. W. Laumbach. 2002. "Migrations in the Southwest: Pinnacle Ruin, Southwestern New Mexico." *Kiva* 68(2):73–101.

Levtzion, Nehemiah. 1968. *Muslims and Chiefs in West Africa*. Clarendon Press, Oxford.

Levy, Jerrold E. 1992. *Orayvi Revisited, Social Stratification in an "Egalitarian" Society*. School of American Research Press, Santa Fe.

Lewis, David. 1994. *We, the Navigators: The Ancient Art of Landfinding in the Pacific*. University of Hawaii Press, Honolulu.

Liberski-Bagnoud, Danouta. 2002. *Les dieux du territoire. Penser autrement la généalogie*. Éditions de la Maison des Sciences de l'Homme / CNRS Éditions, Paris.

Lieberman, Victor B. 1987. "Reinterpreting Burmese History." *Comparative Studies in Society and History* 29(1):162–94.

Lieberman, Victor B. 2003. *Strange Parallels: Southeast Asia in Global Context, c. 800–1830*. Vol. 1: *Integration on the Mainland*. Cambridge University Press, New York.

Lieberman, Victor B. 2009. *Strange Parallels—Southeast Asia in Global Context, c. 800–1300*. Vol. 2: *Mainland Mirrors: Europe, Japan, China, South Asia, and the Island*. Cambridge University Press, New York.

Lieberman, Victor B. 2011. "Charter State Collapse in Southeast Asia, ca. 1250–1400, as a Problem in Regional and World History." *American Historical Review* 116(4):937–63.

Lieberman, Victor B., and Brendan Buckley. 2012. "The Impact of Climate on Southeast Asia, circa 950–1820: New Findings." *Modern Asian Studies* 46(5):1049–96.

Lipe, William D. 1995. "The Depopulation of the Northern San Juan: Conditions in the Turbulent 1200s." *Journal of Anthropological Archaeology* 14(2):143–69.

Lipe, William D. 2010. "Lost in Transition: The Central Mesa Verde Archaeological Complex." In *Leaving Mesa Verde: Peril and Change in the Thirteenth-Century Southwest*, edited by Timothy A. Kohler, Mark D. Varien, and Aaron M. Wright, 262–84. University of Arizona Press, Tucson.

Lipe, William D., and Scott G. Ortman. 2000. "Spatial Patterning in Northern San Juan Villages, AD 1050–1300." *Kiva* 66(1):91–122.

Lipe, William D., and Mark D. Varien. 1999. "Pueblo III (AD 1150–1300)." In *Colorado Prehistory: A Context for the Southern Colorado River Basin*, edited by W. D. Lipe, M. D. Varien, and R. H. Wilshusen, 290–352. Colorado Council of Professional Archaeologists and State Historical Fund, Colorado Historical Society, Denver.

Locke, John. [1689] 1993. *Two Treatises of Government*, edited by Mark Goldie. Everyman Library, London.

Longstaffe, Matthew S. 2010. *Ancient Maya Site Core Settlement at Minanha, Belize: Development, Integration, and Community Dynamics*. MA thesis, Trent University, Peterborough, ON.

Lowe, John W. G. 1985. *The Dynamics of Apocalypse: A Systems Simulation of the Late Classic Maya Collapse*. University of New Mexico Press, Albuquerque.

Lozny, Ludomir R. 2008. "Place, Historical Ecology and Cultural Landscape: New Directions for Culture Resource Management." In *Landscapes under Pressure: Theory and Practice of Cultural Heritage Research and Preservation*, edited by Ludomir R. Lozny, 15–25. Springer Science and Business Media, New York.

Luce, Gordon H. 1969. *Old Burma: Early Bagan*. Artibus Asiae and the Institute of Fine Arts, New York.

Lucien-Brun, Bernard. 1987. "Migration et colonisation des terres neuves." *Les migrations rurales des Kabiyè et des Losso (Togo)*, 5–216. Éditions de l'ORSTOM, maintenant l'IRD (l'Institut français de Recherche scientifique pour le Développement en coopération), Travaux et Documents de l'ORSTOM 202, edited by Lucien-B. et Pillet-Schwartz, A.-M., 5–221. Paris.

Macrae, Scott. 2010. *A Comparative Approach to the Socio-Political and Socio-Economic Organization of the Intensive Terrace Farming at the Ancient Maya Centre of Minanha, Belize*. MA thesis, Trent University, Peterborough, ON.

Macrae, Scott. 2017. *Terrace, Agricultural Strategies, and Resilience at the Ancient Maya Minor Center of Waybil*. PhD diss. University of Florida, Gainesville.

Macrae, Scott, and Pete Demarte. 2012. "The 2012 Waybil Settlement and Agricultural Terrace Study." In *Archaeological Investigations in the North Vaca Plateau, Belize: Progress Report of the Fourteenth (2012) Field Season*, edited by Gyles Iannone, Sonja A. Schwake, and Jaime J. Awe, 85–97. Social Archaeology Research Program, Trent University, Peterborough, ON.

Macrae, Scott, and Gyles Iannone. 2010. "Investigations of the Agricultural Terracing Surrounding the Ancient Maya Centre of Minanha, Belize." *Research Reports in Belizean Archaeology* 8:183–98.

Magee Labelle, Kathryn. 2014. *Le Pari de la dispersion: Une histoire des Ouendats au dix-septième siècle*. Presses de l'Université Laval, Levis.

Malterud, K. 2001. "Qualitative Research: Standards, Challenges, and Guidelines."
Lancet 358(9280):483–88.

Marcus, George E. 1995. "Ethnography in/of the World System: The Emergence of
Multi-Sited Ethnography." *Annual Review of Anthropology* 24:95–117.

Marin, Louis. 1984. *Utopics: Spatial Play*. Humanities Press, Atlantic Highlands, NJ.

Martin, Simon, and Nikolai Grube. 2008. *Chronicle of the Maya Kings and Queens:
Deciphering the Dynasties of the Ancient Maya*. Thames and Hudson, New York.

Martinelli, Bruno. 1982. *Métallurgistes Bassar: Technique et formation sociale*. Institut
national des Sciences de l'Education (INSE), Études et Documents des Sciences
humaines, Série A, No. 5. Lomé, Togo.

Martinelli, Bruno. 1984. "La Production des Outils agricoles en Pays Bassar (Nord-
Togo)." *Cahiers ORSTOM*, Série Sciences Humaines 20(3–4):484–504.

Massey, Douglas S., and Kristin E. Espinosa. 1997. "What's Driving Mexico-U.S.
Migration? A Theoretical, Empirical, and Policy Analysis." *American Journal of
Sociology* 102(4):939–99.

McAnany, Patricia A. 2010. *Ancestral Maya Economies in Archaeological Perspective*.
Cambridge University Press, Cambridge.

McAnany, Patricia A. 2013. *Living with the Ancestors: Kinship and Kingship in Ancient
Maya Society*. Rev. ed. Cambridge University Press, New York.

McAnany, Patricia A. 2019. "Soul Proprietors: Durable Ontologies of Maya Deep
Time." In *Sacred Matters. Animacy and Authority in Pre-Columbian America*, edited
by S. Kosiba, T. B. F. Cummins, and J. W. Janusek. Dumbarton Oaks Research
Library and Collections, Washington, DC. In press.

McAnany, Patricia A., and Linda A. Brown. 2016. "Perceptions of the Past within
Tz'utujil ontologies and Yucatec hybridities." *Antiquity* 90(350):487–503.

McAnany, Patricia A., and Maxime Lamoureux-St-Hilaire. 2013. "Detaching from
Place in Theory and Practice." Paper presented at the 78th Annual Meeting of the
Society for American Archaeology, Honolulu.

McAnany, Patricia A., and Sarah M. Rowe. 2015. "Re-visiting the Field: Collaborative Archaeology as Paradigm Shift." *Journal of Field Archaeology* 40(5):499–507.

McAnany, Patricia, Jeremy Sabloff, Maxime Lamoureux-St-Hilaire, and Gyles
Iannone. 2016. "Leaving Classic Maya Cities: Agent-based Modeling and the
Dynamics of Diaspora." In *Social Theory in Archaeology and Ancient History: The
Present and Future of Counternarratives*, edited by Geoffrey Emberling, 259–90.
Cambridge University Press, Cambridge.

McAnany, Patricia, Rebecca Storey, and Angela K. Lockard. 1999. "Mortuary Ritual
and Family Politics at Formative and Early Classic K'axob, Belize." *Ancient Mesoamerica* 10:129–46.

McAnany, Patricia A., and Norman Yoffee, eds. 2010. *Questioning Collapse: Human Resilience, Ecological Vulnerability, and the Aftermath of Empire*. Cambridge University Press, New York.

McCormick, Carmen. 2007 "What Was Going on Over Yonder? The Peripheral Investigations in Contreras, Minanha, Belize." In *Archaeological Investigations in the North Vaca Plateau, Belize: Progress Report of the Ninth (2007) Field Season*, edited by Gyles Iannone and Scott Macrae, 74–98. Department of Anthropology, Trent University, Peterborough, ON.

McCorriston, Joy. 1995. "Preliminary Archaeobotanical Analysis in the Middle Khabur Valley, Syria and Studies of Socioeconomic Change in the Early Third Millennium BC." *Canadian Society for Mesopotamian Studies Bulletin* 29:33–46.

McFadden, P. S. 2016. "Coastal Evolution and pre-Columbian Human Occupation in Horseshoe Cove on the Northern Gulf Coast of Florida." *Geoarchaeology* 31(5):355–75.

Middleton, Guy D. 2012. "Nothing Lasts Forever: Environmental Discourses on the Collapse of Past Societies." *Journal of Archaeological Research* 20(3):257–307.

Middleton, Guy D. 2017. *Understanding Collapse: Ancient History and Modern Myths*. Cambridge University Press, Cambridge.

Miller, Daniel, ed. 2005. *Materiality*. Duke University Press, Durham, NC.

Miller, Thomas E. 1996. "Geologic and Hydrologic Controls on Karst and Cave Development in Belize." *Journal of Cave and Karst Studies* 58(2):100–120.

Mills, Barbara J. 2011. "Themes and Models for Understanding Migration in the Southwest." In *Movement, Connectivity, and Landscape Change in the Ancient Southwest*, edited by Margaret C. Nelson and Colleen Strawhacker, 345–62. University Press of Colorado, Boulder.

Mock, Shirley Botelier, ed. 1998. *The Sowing and the Dawning: Termination, Dedication, and Transformation in the Archaeological Record of Mesoamerica*. University of New Mexico Press, Albuquerque.

Monaghan, John. 1995. *The Covenants with Earth and Rain: Exchange, Sacrifice, and Revelation in Mixtec Society*. University of Oklahoma Press, Norman.

Monaghan, John. 1998. "Dedication: Ritual or Production?" In *The Sowing and the Dawning: Termination, Dedication, and Transformation in the Archaeological and Ethnographic Record of Mesoamerica*, edited by S. B. Mock, 47–52. University of New Mexico Press, Albuquerque.

Moro Abadía, Oscar. 2017. "Bridging the Gap in Archaeological Theory: An Alternative Account of Scientific Progress in Archaeology." *World Archaeology* 49(2):271–80.

Moore, Elizabeth H. 2007. *Early Landscapes of Myanmar*. River Books, Bangkok.

Moore, Elizabeth, U San Win, and Pyiet Phyo Kyaw. 2016. "Water Management in the Urban Cultural Heritage of Myanmar." *Trans-Regional and -National Studies of Southeast Asia* 4(2):283–305.

Mrozoski, Stephen A. 2016. "Entangled Histories, Entangled Worlds: Reflections on Time, Space, and Place." In *Archaeology of Entanglement*, edited by Lindsay Der and Francesca Fernandini, 191–213. Left Coast Press, Walnut Grove.

Mt. Pleasant, Jane, and Robert F. Burt. 2010. "Estimating Productivity of Traditional Iroquoian Cropping Systems from Field Experiments and Historical Literature." *Journal of Ethnobiology* 30(1):52–79.

Murrell, Monica L., and Bradley J. Vierra, eds. 2014. "Bridging the Basin: Lands Use and Social history in the Southern Chuska Valley." Vol. 4: *Synthesis*. NMDOT, Santa Fe.

Naranjo, Tessie. 2008. "Life as Movement: A Tewa View of Community and Identity." In *The Social Construction of Communities: Agency, Structure, and Identity in the Prehispanic Southwest*, edited by Mark D. Varien and James M. Potter, 251–62. AltaMira, Lanham, MD.

Navarro-Farr, Olivia C., and Ana Lucía Arroyave-Prera. 2014. "A Palimpsest Effect: The Multi-Layered Meanings of Late-to-Terminal Classic Era, Above-Floor Deposits." In *Archaeology at El Perú-Waka': Ancient Maya Performances of Ritual, Memory, and Power*, edited by O. C. Navarro-Farr and M. Rich, 34–52. University of Arizona Press, Tucson.

Neiman, Fraser D. 1997. "Conspicuous Consumption as Wasteful Advertising: A Darwinian Perspective on Spatial Patterns in Classic Maya Terminal Monument Dates." *Archeological Papers of the American Anthropological Association* 7(1):267–90.

Nelson, Margaret C. 1999. *Mimbres during the Twelfth Century: Abandonment, Continuity, and Reorganization*. University of Arizona Press, Tucson.

Nelson, Margaret C., and Michelle Hegmon. 2001. "Abandonment Is Not as it Seems: An Approach to the Relationship between Site-Level and Regional Abandonment." *American Antiquity* 66(2):213–36.

Nelson, Margaret C., and Colleen A. Strawhacker. 2011. *Movement, Connectivity, and Landscape Change in the Ancient Southwest*. University Press of Colorado, Boulder.

Niemczycki, Mary Ann P. 1984. *The Origin and Development of the Seneca and Cayuga Tribes of New York State*. PhD diss., State University of New York at Buffalo, Buffalo.

Norris, E. G. 1984. "The Hausa Kola Trade through Togo, 1899–1912: Some Quantifications." *Paideuma* 30:161–84.

Norris, E. G. 1986. "Atakora Mountain Refuges: Systems of Exploitation in Northern Togo." *Anthropos* 81(1–3):103–36.

Nyunt Nyunt Shwe. 2011. "The Social Life of Bagan Period." *Dagon University Research Journal* 3:25–31.

O'Connor, Mary I. 2016. *Mixtec Evangelicals: Globalization, Migration, and Religious Change in a Oaxacan Indigenous Group*. University Press of Colorado.

Olsen, Bjørnar, Michael Shanks, Timothy Webmoor, and Christoper Withmore. 2012. *Archaeology: The Discipline of Things*. University of California Press, Berkeley.

O'Donoughue, Jason. 2017. *Water from Stone: Archaeology and Conservation at Florida's Springs*. University Press of Florida, Gainesville.

Oliveira, Gabrielle. 2017. "Caring for Your Children: How Mexican Immigrant Mothers Experience Care and the Ideals of Motherhood." In *Gender, Migration, and the Work of Care*, edited by Sonya Michel and Ito Peng, 91–112. Palgrave Macmillan, Cham, Switzerland.

Oppenheim, Max von. 1939. *Die Beduinen*. Vol. 1. Otto Harrassowitz, Leipzig.

Orthmann, Winfried. 1989. *Halawa 1980–1986*. Dr. Rudolf Habelt Verlag, Bonn, Germany.

Ortmann, Anthony L. 2010. "Placing the Poverty Point Mounds in Their Temporal Context." *American Antiquity* 75(3):657–78.

Ortmann, Anthony L., and Tristram R. Kidder. 2013. "Building Mound A at Poverty Point: Monumental Public Architecture, Ritual Practice, and Implications for Hunter-Gatherer Complexity." *Geoarchaeology* 28(1):66–86.

Ortman, Scott G. 2008. "Action, Place, and Space in the Castle Rock Community." In *The Social Construction of Communities: Agency, Structure, and Identity in the Prehispanic Southwest*, edited by Mark D. Varien and James M. Potter, 125–54. Rowman and Littlefield Publishers, Lanham, MD.

Ortman, Scott G. 2012. *Winds from the North: Tewa Origins and Historical Anthropology*. University of Utah Press, Salt Lake City.

Ortman, Scott G., and Catherine M. Cameron. 2011. "A Framework for Controlled Comparisons of Ancient Southwestern Movement." In *Movement, Connectivity, and Landscape Change in the Ancient Southwest*, edited by Margaret C. Nelson and Colleen Strawhacker, 233–52. University Press of Colorado, Boulder.

Ortman, Scott G., Varien, M. D., and T. L. Gripp. 2007. "Empirical Bayesian Methods for Archaeological Survey Data: An Application from the Mesa Verde region." *American Antiquity* 72(2):241–72.

Palka, Joel W. 2014. *Maya Pilgrimage to Ritual Landscapes: Insights from Archaeology, History, and Ethnography*. University Press of New Mexico, Albuquerque.

Parsons, Elsie Clews. 1939. *Pueblo Indian Religion*. Vols. 1 and 2. University of Chicago Press, Chicago.

Pauketat, Timothy. 2003. "Resettled Farmers and the Making of a Mississippian Polity." *American Antiquity* 68(1):39–66.

Pauketat, Timothy. 2007. *Chiefdoms and Other Archaeological Delusions*. AltaMira, Lanham, MD.

Pauketat, Timothy. 2011. "Getting Religion: Lessons from Ancestral Pueblo History." In *Religious Transformation in the Late Pre-Hispanic Pueblo World*, edited by D. M. Glowacki and Scott Van Keuren, 221–38. University of Arizona Press, Tucson.

Pauketat, Timothy. 2013. *An Archaeology of the Cosmos: Rethinking Agency and Religion in the Ancient American*. Routledge, London.

Pauketat, Timothy K., Susan M. Alt, and Jeffery D. Kruchten. 2017. "The Emerald Acropolis: Elevating the Moon and Water in the Rise of Cahokia." *Antiquity* 91(355):207–22.

Pearce, Robert. 1984. *Mapping Middleport: A Case Study in Societal Archaeology*. PhD diss., McGill University, Department of Anthropology, Montreal.

Peckham, Stewart. 1963. *Highway Salvage Archaeology*. Vol. 4. New Mexico Highway Department and Museum of New Mexico, Santa Fe.

Peltenburg, Edgar J. 1999. "Jerablus-Tahtani 1992–6: A Summary." In *Archaeology of the Upper Syrian Euphrates, The Tishrin Dam Area*, edited by Gregorio del Olmo Lete and Juan Luis Montero Fenollós, 97–105. Aula Orientalis-Supplementa 15. Editorial AUSA, Barcelona.

Peltenburg, Edgar J. 2007. "New Perspectives on the Carchemish Sector of the Middle Euphrates River Valley in the 3rd Millennium BC." In *Euphrates River Valley Settlement: The Carchemish Sector in the Third Millennium BC*, edited by Edgar J. Peltenburg, 1–27. OXbow Books, Oxford.

Peltenburg, Edgar J., Stuart Campbell, Paul Croft, Dorothy Lunt, Mary Ann Murray, and Marie E. Watt. 1995. "Jerablus-Tahtani, Syria, 1992–4: Preliminary Report." *Levant* 27(1):1–28.

Pe Maung Tin, and Gordon H. Luce, trans. 1923. *The Glass Palace Chronicle of the Kings of Burma*. Oxford University Press, London.

Perrin de Brichambaut, G., and Carl Christian Wallén. 1963. "A Study of Agroclimatology in the Near East." *World Meteorological Organization Technical Note* 56. World Meteorological Organization, Geneva.

Pétursdóttir, Þóra, and Bjørnar Olsen. 2018. "Theory Adrift: The Matter of Archaeological Theorizing." *Journal of Social Archaeology* 18(1):97–117.

Pfeiffer, Susan, Williamson, Ronald F., Judith C. Sealy, David G. Smith, and Meradeth H. Snow. 2014. "Stable Dietary Isotopes and mtDNA from Woodland Period Southern Ontario People: Results from a Tooth Sampling Protocol." *Journal of Archaeological Science* 42:334–45.

Pichard, Pierre. 1992–2003 *Inventory of Monuments at Pagan*. 8 vols. UNESCO, Paris.

Pinnock, Frances. 2009. "EB IVB—MBI in Northern Syria: Crisis and Change of a Mature Urban Civilisation." In *The Levant in Transition*, edited by Peter J. Parr, 69–79. Palestine Exploration Fund Annual 9. Maney, Leeds.

Polk, Jason. 2010. "Paleoenviromental Research a Minanha, Vaca Plateau, Belize: Summary of the 2010 Investigations." In *Archaeological Investigations in the North Vaca Plateau, Belize: Progress Report of the Twelfth (2010) Field Season*, edited by Gyles Iannone, Jaime J. Awe, Maxime Lamoureux St-Hilaire, and Matthew Longstaffe, 191–97. Social Archaeology Research Program, Trent University, Peterborough, ON.

Pollock, Adam J. 2007. *Investigating the Socio-Economic and Socio-Political Organization of Intensive Agricultural Production at the Ancient Maya Community of Minanha, Belize*. MA thesis, Trent University, Peterborough, ON.

Porter, Anne. 1995. "The Third Millennium Settlement Complex at Tell Banat: Tell Kebir." *Damaszener Mitteilungen* 8:1–50.

Premo, L. S. 2004. "Local Spatial Autocorrelation Statistics Quantify Multi-Scale Patterns in Distributional Data: An Example from the Maya Lowlands." *Journal of Archaeological Science* 31(7):855–66.

Raab, L. Mark, and Albert C. Goodyear. 1984. "Middle-Range Theory in Archaeology: A Critical Review of Origins and Applications." *American Antiquity* 49(2):255–68.

Ramsden, Peter G. 1990. "St. Lawrence Iroquoians in the Upper Trent Valley." *Man in the Northeast* 39:87–95.

Ramsden, Peter G. 2009. "Politics in a Huron Village." In *Painting the Past with a Broad Brush: Papers in Honor of James Valliere Wright*, edited by David L. Keenlyside and Jen-Luc Pilon, 299–318. Archaeological Survey of Canada, Mercury Series Paper No. 170. Canadian Museum of Civilization, Gatineau, QC.

Ramsden, Peter G. 2016a. "The Use of Style in Resistance, Politics and the Negotiation of Identity: St. Lawrence Iroquoians in a Huron-Wendat Community." *Canadian Journal of Archaeology* 40:1–22.

Ramsden, Peter G. 2016b. "Becoming Wendat: Negotiating a New Identity around Balsam Lake in the Late Sixteenth Century." *Ontario Archaeology* 96:121–32.

Randall, Asa R. 2015. *Constructing Histories: Archaic Freshwater Shell Mounds and Social Landscapes of the St. Johns River, Florida*. University Press of Florida, Gainesville.

Randall, Asa R., and Kenneth E. Sassaman. 2017. "Terraforming the Middle Ground in Ancient Florida." *Hunter-Gatherer Research* 3(1):9–29.

Rattray, Robert Sutherland. 1932. *The Tribes of the Ashanti Hinterland*. Clarendon Press, Oxford.

Reeder, Philip, Robert Brinkmann, and Edward Alt. 1996. "Karstification on the Northern Vaca Plateau, Belize." *Journal of Cave and Karst Studies* 58(2):121–30.

Reid, Anthony, and Jennifer Brewster. 1983. "Introduction: Slavery and Bondage in Southwest Asian History." In *Slavery, Bondage, and Dependency in Southeast Asia*, edited by Anthony Reid, 1–43. St. Martin's Press, New York.

Richard, Jean-François. 2016. "Territorial Precedence in Eighteenth- and Nineteenth-Century Huron-Wendat Oral Tradition." *Ontario Archaeology* 96:26–34.

Richards, Cara. 1967. "Huron and Iroquois Residence Patterns." In *Iroquois Culture, History and Prehistory: Proceedings of the 1965 Conference on Iroquois Research*, edited by Elizabeth Tooker, 51–56. University of the State of New York, State Education Department, and New York State Museum and Science Service, Albany.

Rice, Don S. 1976. "Middle Preclassic Maya Settlement in the Central Maya Lowlands." *Journal of Field Archaeology* 3(4):425–45.

Rice, Prudence M., Arthur Demarest, and Don S. Rice. 2004. "The Terminal Classic and the 'Classic Maya Collapse' in Perspective." In *The Terminal Classic in the Maya Lowlands*, edited by Arthur Demarest, Prudence D. Rice, and Don S. Rice, 1–11. University Press of Colorado, Boulder.

Ristvet, Lauren. 2012. "Resettling Apum: Tribalism and Tribal States in the Tell Leilan Region, Syria." *Looking North: The Socioeconomic Dynamics of Northern Mesopotamian and Anatolian Regions during the Late Third and Early Second Millennium* BC, edited by Nicola Laneri, Peter Pfälzner, and Stefano Valentini, 37–50. Studien zur Urbanisierung Nordmesopotamiens. Serie D Supplementa 2. Harrassowitz, Wiesbaden, Germany.

Robb, John, and Timothy R. Pauketat. 2013. "From Moments to Millennia: Theorizing Scale and Change in Human History." In *Big Histories, Human Lives: Tackling Problems of Scale in Archaeology*, edited by J. Robb and T. R. Pauketat, 3–33. School of American Research Press, Santa Fe.

Roberts, Norvell, Charles Satchfield, and Bob Lowry. 1968. "Steatite Bowls Found." *Mississippi Archaeological Association Newsletter* 4(1).

Rodning, Christopher B. 2009. "Mounds, Myths, and Cherokee Townhouses in Southwestern North Carolina." *American Antiquity* 74(4):627–63.

Rodning, Christopher B. 2013. "Community Aggregation through Public Architecture." In *From Prehistoric Villages to Cities: Settlement Aggregation and Community Transformation*, edited by Jennifer Birch, 179–200. Routledge, New York.

Romain, William F., and Norm L. Davis. 2013. "Astronomy and Geometry at Poverty Point." Louisiana Archaeological Society. Accessed October 21, 2013. http://www.laarchaeology.org/articles.html.

Romero Frizzi, Ma de los Angeles. 1996. *El sol y la cruz: Los pueblos indios de Oaxaca colonial*. INI, CIESAS, Tlalpan, Colonia Alpes, DF, Mexico.

Roney, John R. 1995. "Mesa Verdean Manifestations South of the San Juan River." *Journal of Anthropological Archaeology* 14(2):170–83.

Rose, Susan, and Robert Shaw. 2008. "The Gamble: Circular Mexican Migration and the Return on Remittances." *Mexican Studies/Estudios Mexicanos* 24(1):79–111.

Rozel, John R. 1979. "The Gunby Site and Late Pickering Interactions." MA thesis, McMaster University, Hamilton, ON.

Rumbaut Ruben, G. 1997. "Assimilation and Its Discontents: Between Rhetoric and Reality." *International Migration Review* 31(4):923–61.

Russell, Will G., Margaret C. Nelson, and Rebecca Harkness. 2013. "Exploring Ritual Dedication and Retirement: Ensouled Houses in the Mimbres Region." Paper presented to the 79th Annual Meeting of the Society for American Archaeology, Honolulu.

Ryan, Susan C. 2010. "Environmental Change, Population Movement, and the Post-Chaco Transition at Albert Porter Pueblo." *Kiva* 75:303–25.

Ryder, Michael L. 1993. "Sheep and Goat Husbandry with Particular Reference to Textile Fibre and Milk Production." *Bulletin on Sumerian Agriculture* 7(9):32.

Sassaman, Kenneth E. 2005. "Poverty Point as Structure, Event, Process." *Journal of Archaeological Method and Theory* 12(4):335–64.

Sassaman, Kenneth E. 2006. "Dating and Explaining Soapstone Vessels: A Comment on Truncer." *American Antiquity* 71(1):141–56.

Sassaman, Kenneth E. 2010. *The Eastern Archaic, Historicized.* AltaMira, Lanham, MD.

Sassaman, Kenneth E. 2016. "A Constellation of Practice in the Experience of Sea-Level Rise." In *Knowledge in Motion: Constellations of Learning across Time and Place*, edited by Andrew P. Roddick and Ann B. Stahl, 271–98. University of Arizona Press, Tucson.

Sassaman, Kenneth E., and Samuel O. Brookes. 2017. "Situating the Claiborne Vessel Cache in the History of Poverty Point." *American Antiquity* 82(4):791–87.

Sassaman, Kenneth E., John S. Krigbaum, Ginessa J. Mahar, and Andrea Palmiotto. 2015. *Archaeological Investigations at McClamory Key (8LV288), Levy County, Florida.* Technical Report 22. Laboratory of Southeastern Archaeology, Department of Anthropology, University of Florida, Gainesville.

Sassaman, Kenneth E., Neill J. Wallis, Paulette S. McFadden, Ginessa J. Mahar, Jessica A. Jenkins, Mark C. Donop, Micah P. Monés, Andrea Palmiotto, Anthony Boucher, Joshua M. Goodwin, and Cristina I. Oliveira. 2017. "Keeping Pace with Rising Sea: The First 6 Years of the Lower Suwannee Archaeological Survey." *Journal of Island and Coastal Archaeology* 12(2):173–99.

Sauvaget, Claude. 1981. *Boua, village de Koudé: Un terroir kabyè (Togo septentrional).* PhD diss., Université de Nanterre, Nanterre, France.

Schachner, Gregson. 2012. *Population Circulation and the Transformation of Ancient Zuni Communities.* University of Arizona Press, Tucson.

Schiffer, Michael B. 1972. "Archaeological Context and Systemic Context." *American Antiquity* 37(2):156–65.

Schiffer, Michael B. 1976. *Behavioral Archaeology*. Academic Press, New York.

Schiffer, Michael B. 1983. "Toward the Identification of Formation Processes." *American Antiquity* 48(4):675–706.

Schiffer, Michael B. 1985. "Is There a 'Pompeii Premise' in Archaeology?" *Journal of Anthropological Research* 41(1):18–41.

Schiffer, Michael B. 1987. *Formation Processes of the Archaeological Record*. University of New Mexico Press, Albuquerque.

Schillaci, M. A., and S. A. Lakatos. 2016. "Refiguring the Population History of the Tewa Basin." *Kiva* 82(4):364–86.

Schlegel, Alice. 1992. "African Political Models in the American Southwest: Hopi as an Internal Frontier Society." *American Anthropologist* 94(2):376–97.

Schneider, Tsim. 2015. "Placing Refuge and the Archaeology of Indigenous Hinterlands in Colonial California." *American Antiquity* 80(4):695–713.

Schwake, Sonja A., Natalie Baron, Megan Clarke, and Kevin Robitaille. 2012. "Minor Center Investigations in the Eastern Maya Lowlands: The 2012 Excavations in Group B at the Site of Waybil." In *Archaeological Investigations in the North Vaca Plateau, Belize: Progress Report of the Fourteenth (2012) Field Season*, edited by Gyles Iannone, Jaime J. Awe, Sonja A. Schwake, and Kendall Hills, 61–84. Social Archaeology Research Program, Trent University, Peterborough, ON.

Schwake, Sonja A., Kendall B. Hills, Gyles Iannone, Megan Clarke, Sarah Duignan, Spencer Kawell, Steve Lebrun, and Emma Schlegl. 2013. "Investigations in the Waybil Epicenter: Results from the 2013 Excavations in Group A." In *Archaeological Investigations in the North Vaca Plateau, Belize: Progress Report of the Fifteenth (2013) Field Season*, edited by Gyles Iannone, Jaime J. Awe, Sonja A. Schwake, and Kendall B. Hills, 127–44. Social Archaeology Research Program, Trent University, Peterborough, ON.

Schwake, Sonja A., and Gyles Iannone. 2016. "Destruction Events and Political Truncation at the Little Kingdom of Minanha, Belize." In *Ritual, Violence, and the Fall of the Classic Maya Kings*, edited by Gyles Iannone, Brett A. Houk and Sonja A. Schwake, 134–58. University of Florida Press, Gainesville.

Schwartz, Glenn M. 2017. "Western Syria and the Third- to Second-Millennium BC Transition." In *The Late Third Millennium in the Ancient Near East. Chronology, C14, and Climate Change*, edited by Felix Höflmayer, 87–128. Oriental Institute Seminars 11. Oriental Institute of the University of Chicago, Chicago.

Schwartz, Glenn M., Hans H. Curvers, Fokke A. Gerritsen, Jennifer A. MacCormack, Naomi F. Miller, and Jill A. Weber. 2000. "Excavation and Survey in the Jabbul Plain, Western Syria: The Umm el-Marra Project 1996–1997." *American Journal of Archaeology* 104(3):419–62.

Schwartz, Glenn M., and Naomi F. Miller. 2007. "The 'Crisis' of the Late Third Millennium BC: Ecofactual and Artifactual Evidence from Umm El-Marra and the Jabbul Plain." In *Sociétés humaines et changement climatique à la fin du troisième millénaire: Une crise a-t-elle eu lieu en Haute Mésopotamie? Actes du Colloque de Lyon, 5–8 décembre 2005*, edited by Catherine Kuzucuğlu and Catherine Marro, 179–203. Varia Anatolica XIX. De Boccard Édition-Diffusion, Paris.

Schwindt, D. M., R. K. Bocinsky, S. G. Ortman, D. M. Glowacki, T. A. Kohler, and M. D. Varien. 2016. "The Social Consequences of Climate Change in the Central Mesa Verde Region." *American Antiquity* 81(1):74–96.

Scoones, Ian. 1999. "New Ecology and the Social Sciences: What Prospects for a Fruitful Engagement?" *Annual Review of Anthropology* 28:479–507.

Sen, A. K. 1959. "The Choice of Agricultural Techniques in Underdeveloped Countries." *Economic Development and Cultural Change* 7(3):279–85.

Shackel, Paul A. 2001. "Public Memory and the Search for Power in American Historical Archaeology." *American Anthropologist* 103(3): 655–70.

Sirkeci, Ibrahim. 2009. "Transnational Mobility and Conflict." *Migration Letters* 6(1):3–14.

Smith, Robert C. 2003. "Diasporic Memberships in Historical Perspective: Comparative Insights from the Mexican, Italian and Polish Cases." *International Migration Review* 37(3):724–59.

Snead, James E. 2008. *Ancestral Landscapes of the Pueblo World*. University of Arizona Press, Tucson.

Snow, Dean R. 1994. *The Iroquois*. Blackwell, New York.

Snow, Dean R. 1995. *Mohawk Valley Archaeology: The Sites*. Occasional Papers in Anthropology No. 23, Matson Museum of Anthropology, Pennsylvania State University, University Park.

Snyder, Christina. 2010. *Slavery in Indian Country: The Changing Face of Captivity in Early America*. Harvard University Press, Cambridge.

Spate, O. H. K. 1945. "The Burmese Village." *Geographical Review* 35(4):523–43.

Spivey, Margaret S., Tristram R. Kidder, Anthony L. Ortmann, and Lee J. Arco. 2015. "Pilgrimage to Poverty Point?" In *The Archaeology of Events: Cultural Change and Continuity in the Pre-Columbian Southeast*, edited by Zachary I. Gilmore and Jason M. O'Donoughue, 141–59. University of Alabama Press, Tuscaloosa.

Stadtner, Donald M. 2011. *Sacred Sites of Burma: Myth and Folklore in an Evolving Spiritual Realm*. River Books, Bangkok.

Stadtner, Donald M. 2013. *Ancient Pagan: Buddhist Plain of Merit*. River Books, Bangkok.

Stanton, Travis W., and Aline Magnoni, eds. 2008. *Ruins of the Past: The Use and Perception of Abandoned Structures in the Maya Lowlands*. University Press of Colorado, Boulder.

Stark, Miriam T., Damian Evans, Chhay Rachna, Heng Piphal, and Alison Carter. 2015. "Residential Patterning at Angkor Wat." *Antiquity* 89(348):1439–55.

Staubwasser, Michael, and Harvey Weiss. 2006. "Holocene Climate and Cultural Evolution in Late Prehistoric–Early Historic West Asia." *Quaternary Research* 66(3):372–87.

Steckley, John. 2007. *Words of the Huron*. Wilfrid Laurier University Press, Waterloo, ON.

Steckley, John. 2016. "St. Lawrence Iroquoians among the Wendat: Linguistic Evidence." *Ontario Archaeology* 96:17–25.

Steinbeck, John. 1939. *The Grapes of Wrath*. Viking Press, New York.

Steinkeller, Piotr. 1991. "The Administrative and Economic Organization of the Ur III State: The Core and the Periphery." In *The Organization of Power*, edited by McGuire Gibson and Robert D. Biggs, 15–33. 2nd ed. Oriental Institute, Chicago.

Steinkeller, Piotr. 1995. "Sheep and Goat Terminology in Ur III Sources from Drehem." *Bulletin on Sumerian Agriculture* 8:49–70.

Stephen, Lynn. 2007. *Transborder Lines: Indigenous Oaxacans in Mexico, California, and Oregon*. Duke University Press, Durham, NC.

Stevenson, Marc G. 1982. "Toward an Understanding of Site Abandonment Behavior: Evidence from Historic Mining Camps in the Southwest Yukon." *Journal of Anthropological Archaeology* 1(3):237–65.

Stojanowski, Christopher M., and Glen H. Doran. 1998. "Osteology of the Late Archaic Bird Island Population." *Florida Anthropologist* 51:139–45.

Stone, Tammy. 2003. "Social Identity and Ethnic Interaction in the Western Pueblos of the American Southwest." *Journal of Archaeological Method and Theory* 10(1):31–67.

Storey, Rebecca. 2004. "Ancestors: Bioarchaeology of the Human Remains of K'axob." In *K'axob: Ritual, Work, and Family in an Ancient Maya Village*, edited by P. A. McAnany, 109–38. Monumenta Archaeologica 22, Cotsen Institute of Archaeology at UCLA, Los Angeles.

Strachan, Paul. 1989. *Imperial Pagan: Art and Architecture of Burma*. Kiscadale, Edinburgh.

Stuart, David. 2012. "Notes on a New Text from La Corona." In *Maya Decipherment: Ideas on Ancient Maya Writing and Iconography*. Online Blog. https://mayadecipherment.com/2012/06/30/notes-on-a-new-text-from-la-corona/.

Stuart, David. 2013. "New Drawing of the La Corona Panel." In *Maya Decipherment: Ideas on Ancient Maya Writing and Iconography*. Online Blog. https://mayadecipherment.com/2013/01/23/new-drawing-of-a-la-corona-panel/.

Stuart, David, Marcello A. Canuto, Tomás Barrientos, and Maxime Lamoureux-St-Hilaire. 2015. "Preliminary Notes on Two Recently Discovered Inscriptions from La Corona, Guatemala." In *Maya Decipherment: Ideas on Ancient Maya Writing and*

Iconography. Online Blog. https://mayadecipherment.com/2015/07/17/preliminary -notes-on-two-recently-discovered-inscriptions-from-la-corona-guatemala/.

Stuart, David, Peter Mathews, Marcello Canuto, Tomás Barrientos Q., Stanley Guenter, and Joanne Baron. 2014. "Un esquema de la historia y epigrafía de La Corona." In *XXIX Simposio de Investigaciones Arqueológicas en Guatemala*, edited by Bárbara Arroyo, Luis Méndez Salinas, and Andrea Rojas, 435–48. Asociación Tikal, Guatemala City.

Stuart, David E., and Rory P. Gauthier. 1981. *Prehistoric New Mexico: Background for Survey*. New Mexico Historic Preservation Bureau, Santa Fe.

Stuart-Fox, Martin, and Paul Reeve. 2011. "Symbolism in City Planning in Cambodia from Angkor to Phnom Penh." *Journal of the Siam Society* 99:105–38.

Sutton, Richard. 1996. "The Middle Iroquoian Colonization of Huronia." PhD diss., Department of Anthropology, McMaster University, Hamilton, ON.

Sutton, Richard. 1999. "The Barrie Site: A Pioneering Iroquoian Village Located in Simcoe County, Ontario." *Ontario Archaeology* 67:40–86.

Swentzell, Rina. 2000. *Younger-Older Ones*. Weaselsleeves Press, Santa Fe, NM.

Sykes, Clark M. 1980. "Swidden Horticulture and Iroquoian Settlement." *Archaeology of Eastern North America* 8(Fall 19):45–52.

Szwark, Marian, Father. 1981. *Proverbes et traditions des Bassar du Nord-Togo*. Collections Instituti Anthropos 22, edited by J. F. Thiel. Haus Volker und Kulturen, St. Augustin, Germany.

Tait, David. 1961. *The Konkomba of Northern Ghana*. Oxford University Press for the Institute of African Studies, Abingdon, Oxon.

Tamakloe, E. F. 1931. *A Brief History of the Dagomba People*. Accra, Ghana.

Tambiah, Stanley J. 1977. "The Galactic Polity: The Structure of Traditional Kingdoms in Southeast Asia." *Annals of the New York Academy of Sciences* 293(1):69–97.

Taylor, Christopher C. 2016. "Foreword." In *Ritual, Violence, and the Fall of the Classic Maya Kings*, edited by Gyles Iannone, Brett A. Houk, and Sonja A. Schwake, xiii–xv. University Press of Florida, Gainesville.

Taylor, William B. 1976. "Town and Country in the Valley of Oaxaca, 1750–1812." In *Provinces of Early Mexico: Variants of Spanish American Regional Evolution*, edited by Ida Altman and James Lockhart, 63–95. University of Pennsylvania Press, Philadelphia.

Tcham, Koffi Badjow. 2009. "Travail du fer et peuplement du centre du Togo: Les Koli du XIVe au XIXe Siècle." *Cahiers du* CERLESHS 24 (34):49–90.

Thieme, Mary Stevenson. 2009. "Continuity and Change in a Domestic Industry: Santa María Atzompa, a Pottery Making Town in Oaxaca, Mexico." *Fieldiana* (41):1–80.

Thomas, David Hurst, and Matthew C. Sanger, eds. 2010. *Trend, Tradition, and Turmoil: What Happened to the Southeastern Archaic?* Anthropological Papers of the American Museum of Natural History. Vol. 93. American Museum of Natural History, New York.

Thomas, Prentice M., Jr., and L. Janice Campbell. 1991. "The Elliott's Point Complex: New Date Regarding the Localized Poverty Point Expression on the Northwest Florida Gulf Coast, 2000 BC–500 BC." In *The Poverty Point Culture: Local Manifestations, Subsistence Practices, and Trade Networks*, edited by Kathleen M. Byrd, 7–25. *Geoscience and Man*, vol. 29. Louisiana State University, Baton Rouge.

Thomson, E. F., and F. Bahhady. 1995. "A Model-Farm Approach to Research on Crop-Livestock integration—I. Conceptual Framework and Methods." *Agricultural Systems* 49(1):1–16.

Thompson, Victor D., and Thomas J. Pluckhahn. 2012. "Monumentalization and Ritual Landscapes at Fort Center in the Lake Okeechobee Basin of South Florida." *Journal of Anthropological Archaeology* 31(1):49 65.

Thwaites, Reuben G. 1896–1901. *The Jesuit Relations and Allied Documents.* 73 vols. Burroughs Brothers, Cleveland.

Tilley, Christopher. 1994. *A Phenomenology of Landscape: Places, Paths, and Monuments.* Bournemouth, London.

Timmins, Peter G. 1997. *The Calvert Site: An Interpretive Framework for the Early Iroquoian Village.* Archaeological Survey of Canada Mercury Series Paper No. 156, Canadian Museum of Civilization, Gatineau.

Tomka, Steve A., and Marc G. Stevenson. 1993. "Understanding Abandonment Processes: Summary and Remaining Concerns." In *Abandonment of Settlements and Regions: Ethnoarchaeological and Archaeological Approaches*, edited by Catherine M. Cameron and Steve A. Tomka, 191–95. Cambridge University Press, Cambridge.

Tooker, Elizabeth. 1964. "An Ethnology of the Huron Indians, 1615–1649." Bulletin 190, Bureau of American Ethnology, Washington, DC.

Toselli, Stefania, and Emanuela Gualdi-Russo. 2008. "Psychosocial Indicators and Distress in Immigrants Living in Italian Reception Centres." *Stress and Health* 24(4):327–34.

Tremblay, Roland. 2006. *Les Iroquoiens du Saint-Laurent: Peuple du maïs.* Pointe-À-Callière Musée d'archéologie et d'histoire de Montréal, Montreal.

Trigger, Bruce G. 1969. *The Huron: Farmers of the North.* Holt, Rinehart and Winston, Toronto.

Trigger, Bruce G. 1976. *The Children of Aataensic: A History of the Huron People to 1660.* McGill-Queen's University Press, Montreal.

Trigger, Bruce G. 1978. "Iroquoian Matriliny." *Pennsylvania Archaeologist* 48(1 and 2):55–65.

Trigger, Bruce G. 1990. "Maintaining Economic Equality in Opposition to Complexity: An Iroquoian Case Study." In *The Evolution of Political Systems: Sociopolitics in Small-Scale Sedentary Societies*, edited by Steadman Upham, 119–45. Cambridge University Press, Cambridge.

Tripp, Grant. 1978. "The White Site: A Southern Division Huron Component." Manuscript on file at the London Museum of Archaeology, London, ON.

Tuck, James A. 1971. *Onondaga Iroquois Prehistory: A Study in Settlement Archaeology.* Syracuse University Press, Syracuse, NY.

Tyburski, Michael D. 2012. "The Resource Curse Reversed? Remittances and Corruption in Mexico." *International Studies Quarterly* 56(2):339–50.

Upham, S. 1984. "Adaptive Diversity and Southwestern Abandonment." *Journal of Anthropological Research* 40(2):235–56.

Urton, Gary. 1981. *At the Crossroads of the Earth and the Sky: An Andean Cosmology.* University of Texas Press, Austin.

Van Dyke, Ruth M. 2004. "Memory, Meaning, and Masonry: The Late Bonito Chacoan Landscape." *American Antiquity* 69(3): 413–43.

Van Loon, Maurits N., ed. 2001. *Selenkahiye: Final Report on the University of Chicago and University of Amsterdam Excavations in the Tabqa reservoir, Northern Syria, 1967–1975.* Uitgaven van het Nederlands Historisch-Archaeologisch Instituut te Istanbul 91. Nederlands Instituut voor het Nabije Oosten, Leiden.

Varien, Mark D. 1999. *Sedentism and Mobility in a Social Landscape: Mesa Verde and Beyond.* University of Arizona Press, Tucson.

Varien, Mark D. 2010. "Depopulation of the Northern San Juan Region: Historical Review and Archaeological Context." In *Leaving Mesa Verde: Peril and Change in the Thirteenth-Century Southwest*, edited by Timothy A. Kohler, Mark D. Varien, and Aaron M. Wright, 1–33. University of Arizona Press, Tucson.

Varien, Mark D., Scott G. Ortman, Timothy A. Kohler, Donna M. Glowacki, and C. David Johnson. 2007. "Historical Ecology in the Mesa Verde Region: Results from the Village Ecodynamics Project." *American Antiquity* 72(2):273–99.

Varien, Mark D., Carla R. Van West, and G. Stuart Patterson. 2000. "Competition, Cooperation, and Conflict: Agriculture and Community Catchments in the Central Northern San Juan Region." *Kiva* 66(1):45–66.

Verner, Dorte, ed. 2010. *Reducing Poverty, Protecting Livelihoods, and Building Assets in a Changing Climate: Social Implications of Climate Change in Latin America and the Caribbean.* World Bank, Washington, DC.

von Gernet, Alexander. 1994. "Saving the Souls: Reincarnation Beliefs of the Seventeenth-Century Huron." In *Amerindian Rebirth: Reincarnation Belief among North American Indians and Inuit*, edited by Antonia Mills and Richard Slobodin, 38–54. University of Toronto Press, Toronto.

von Zech, Le Comte, J. Graf. 1898. "Vermischte Notizen über Togo und das Togo Hinterlande." *Mitteilungen für Forschungsreisenden und Gelehrten aus den deutschen Schutzgebieten* 11:89–161.

Wallace, Eliza. 2014. "From Town to City: Urban Planning in the Early Bronze Age of Northern Mesopotamia at Tell es-Sweyhat, Syria." PhD diss., Department of Archaeology, Boston University, Boston.

Wallén, Carl C. 1968. "Agroclimatological Studies in the Levant." In *Agroclimatological Methods, Proceedings of the Reading Symposium*. Natural Resources Research 7:225–32.

Ware, John A. 2014. *A Pueblo Social History: Kinship, Sodality, and Community in the Northern Southwest*. SAR Press, Santa Fe, NM.

Warrick, Gary A. 1988. "Estimating Ontario Iroquoian Village Duration." *Man in the Northeast* 36:21–60.

Warrick, Gary A. 2008. *A Population History of the Huron-Petun*, AD *500–1650*. Cambridge University Press, Cambridge.

Warrick, Gary, and Louis Lesage. 2016. "The Huron-Wendat and the St. Lawrence Iroquoians: The Finding of a Close Relationship." *Ontario Archaeology* 96:133–43.

Watkins, Joe. 2006. Communicating Archaeology: Words to the Wise. *Journal of Social Archaeology* 6(1):100–18.

Watts, Christopher. 2013. *Relational Archaeologies: Humans, Animals, Things*. Routledge, New York.

Webb, Clarence H. 1944. "Stone Vessels from a Northeast Louisiana Site." *American Antiquity* 9(4):386–94.

Weber, Jill A. 1997. "Faunal Remains from Tell es-Sweyhat and Tell Hajji Ibrahim." In *Subsistence and Settlement in a Marginal Environment: Tell es-Sweyhat, 1989–1995 Preliminary Report*, edited by Richard L. Zettler, 133–67. MASCA Research Papers in Science and Archaeology 14. University of Pennsylvania Museum of Archaeology and Anthropology, Philadelphia.

Webster, James W. 2000. *Speleothem Evidence of Late Holocene Climate Variation in the Maya Lowlands of Belize Central American and Archaeological Implications*. PhD diss., University of Georgia. Athens.

Webster, James W., George A. Brook, L. B. Railsback, Hai Cheng, R. L. Edwards, Clark Alexander, and Philip P. Reeder. 2007. "Stalagmite Evidence from Belize Indicating Significant Droughts at the Time of Preclassic Abandonment, the Maya Hiatus, and the Classic Maya Collapse." *Palaeogeography, Palaeoclimatology, Palaeoecology* 250(1–4):1–17.

Weiss, Harvey. 2000. "Beyond the Younger Dryas: Collapse as Adaptation to Abrupt Climate Change in Ancient West Asia and the Eastern Mediterranean." In *Confronting Natural Disaster: Engaging the Past to Understand the Future*, edited by Garth Bawden and Richard Reycraft, 75–98. University of New Mexico Press, Albuquerque.

Weiss, Harvey. 2003. "Ninevite Periods and Processes." In *The Origins of Northern Mesopotamian Civilization*, ed. Elena Rova and Harvey Weiss, 593–624. Subartu IX. Brepols, Turnhout, Belgium.

Weiss, Harvey. 2015. "Megadrought, Collapse and Resilience in Late 3rd Millennium BC Mesopotamia." In *2200 BC: Ein Klimasturz als Ursache für den Zerfall den Alten Welt*, edited by Harald Meller, Helge Wolfgang Arz, Reinhard Jung, and Roberto Risch, 35–52. Tagungen des Landesmuseums für Vorgeschichte Halle 12. Landesamt für Denkmalpflege und Archäologie Sachsen-Anhalt, Landesmuseum für Vorgeschichte, Halle (Saale).

Weiss, Harvey. 2017. "Seventeen Kings Who Lived in Tents." In *The Late Third Millennium in the Ancient Near East. Chronology, C14, and Climate Change*, edited by Felix Höflmayer, 131–62. Oriental Institute Seminars 11. Oriental Institute of the University of Chicago, Chicago.

Weiss, Harvey, and Raymond S. Bradley. 2001. "What Drives Societal Collapse?" *Science* 291(5504):609–10.

Weiss, Harvey, Marie-Agnès Courty, Wilma Wetterstrom, Francois Guichard, Louise Senior, Richard H. Meadow, and Anne Curnow. 1993. "The Genesis and Collapse of Third Millennium North Mesopotamian Civilizations." *Science* 261(5124):995–1004.

Wheatley, Paul. 1971. *The Pivot of the Four Quarters*. Aldine, Chicago.

Whiteley, Peter M. 1988. *Deliberate Acts: Changing Hopi Culture through the Oraibi Split*. University of Arizona Press, Tucson.

Wilcox, Michael. 2010. "Marketing Conquest and the Vanishing Indian: An Indigenous Response to Jared Diamond's Archaeology of the American Southwest." In *Questioning Collapse: Human Resilience, Ecological Vulnerability, and the Aftermath of Empire*, edited by P. A. McAnany and N. Yoffee, 113–41. Cambridge University Press, New York.

Wilkinson, Tony J. 1997. "Environmental Fluctuations, Agricultural Production, and Collapse: A View from Bronze Age Upper Mesopotamia." In *Third Millennium BC Climate Change and Old World Collapse*, edited by Harvey Weiss, H. Nüzhet Dalfes, and George Kukla, 67–106. Springer, Berlin, Heidelberg.

Wilkinson, Tony J. 2004. *Excavations at Tell es-Sweyhat, Syria 1: On the margins of the Euphrates. Settlement and Land Use at Tell es-Sweyhat and in the Upper Lake Assad Area, Syria*. Oriental Institute Publication 124. Oriental Institute of the University of Chicago, Chicago.

Wilks, Ivor. 1975. *Asante in the Nineteenth Century*. Cambridge University Press, Cambridge.

Wilks, Ivor. 1995. *Forests of Gold: Essays on the Akan and the Kingdom of Asante.* Ohio University Press, Athens, Ohio.

Williamson, Meghan Burchell, William Fox, and Sarah Grant. 2016. "Looking Eastward: Fifteenth- and Early Sixteenth-Century Exchange System of the North Shore Ancestral Wendat." In *Contact in the 16th Century*, edited by Brad Loewen and Claude Chapdelaine, 235–55. Mercury Series Archaeology Paper 176, Canadian Museum of History and University of Ottawa Press.

Williamson, Ronald F. 1990. "The Early Iroquoian Period of Southern Ontario." In *The Archaeology of Southern Ontario to* AD *1650*, edited by Chris J. Ellis and Neal Ferris, 293–320. Occasional Publication of the London Chapter of the Ontario Archaeological Society. London, ON.

Williamson, Ronald F., ed. 1998. *The Meyers Road Site—Archaeology of the Early to Middle Iroquoian Transition.* Occasional Publication No. 7. Ontario Archaeological Society, London.

Williamson, Ronald F. 2007. "Ontinontsiskiaj ondaon' (The House of Cut-off Heads) The History and Archaeology of Northern Iroquoian Trophy Taking." In *The Taking and Displaying of Human Body Parts as Trophies*, edited by Richard J. Chacon and David H. Dye, 190–221. Springer Books, New York.

Williamson, Ronald F. 2010. "Planning for Ontario's Archaeological Past: Accomplishments and Continuing Challenges." *Revista de Arqueología Americana* 28:1–45.

Williamson, Ronald F. 2014. "The Archaeological History of the Wendat to AD 1651: An Overview." *Ontario Archaeology* 94:3–64.

Williamson, Ronald F. 2016. "East-West Interactions among Fifteenth-Century St. Lawrence Iroquoians and North Shore of lake Ontario Ancestral Wendat Communities." *Ontario Archaeology* 96:104–19.

Williamson, Ronald F., Shaun J. Austin, and Stephen Cox Thomas. 2003. *The Archaeology of the Grandview Site: A Fifteenth Century Community on the North Shore of Lake Ontario.* Arch Notes 8(5):5–49.

Williamson, Ronald F., and Susan Pfeiffer, eds. 2003. *Bones of the Ancestors: The Archaeology and Osteobiography of the Moatfield Ossuary.* Mercury Series Archaeology Paper 163. Canadian Museum of Civilization, Gatineau, QC.

Williamson, Ronald F., and David A. Robertson. 1994. "Peer Polities beyond the Periphery: Early and Middle Iroquoian Regional Interaction." *Ontario Archaeology* 58:27–40.

Williamson, Ronald F., and Debbie A. Steiss. 2003. "A History of Iroquoian Burial Practice." In *Bones of the Ancestors: The Archaeology and Osteobiography of the Moatfield Ossuary*, edited by Ronald F. Williamson and Susan Pfeiffer, 89–132. Mercury Series Archaeology Paper 163, Canadian Museum of Civilization, Gatineau, QC.

Wilson, Gregory D. 2010. "Community, Identity, and Social Memory at Moundville." *American Antiquity* 75(1):3–18.

Witschey, Walter R. T., and Clifford T. Brown. 2008. *The Electronic Atlas of Ancient Maya Sites*. http://MayaGIS.smv.org.

Wright, Aaron M. 2010. "The Climate of the Depopulation of the Northern Southwest." In *Leaving Mesa Verde: Peril and Change in the Thirteenth-Century Southwest*, edited by T. A. Kohler, M. D. Varien, and A. M. Wright, 75–101. University of Arizona Press, Tucson.

Wright, Eric E., Albert C. Hine, Steven L. Goodbred, Jr., and Stanley D. Locker. 2005. "The Effect of Sea-Level and Climate Change on the Development of a Mixed Siliciclastic-Carbonate, Deltaic Coastline: Suwannee River, Florida, US." *Journal of Sedimentary Research* 75(4):621–35.

Wright, Milton J. 1986. *The Uren Site (AfHd-3): An Analysis and Reappraisal of the Uren Substage Type Site*. Vol. 2 of Monographs in Ontario Archaeology. Ontario Archaeological Society, Toronto.

Wrong, George M. [1632] 1939. Sagard's Long Journey to the Country of the Hurons. Champlain Society, Toronto.

Wyatt, Andrew R. 2008. *Gardens on Hills: Ancient Maya Terracing and Agricultural Production at Chan, Belize*. PhD diss., University of Illinois at Chicago.

Xiang, B. 2013. "Multi-Scalar Ethnography: An Approach for Critical Engagement with Migration and Social Change." *Ethnography* 14(3):282–99.

Yaeger, Jason. 2010. "Shifting Political Dynamics as Seen from The Xunantunich Palace." In *Classic Maya Provincial Politics: Xunantunich and its Hinterlands*, edited by Lisa J. LeCount and Jason Yaeger, 145–60. University of Arizona Press, Tucson.

Yava, Albert, and Harold Courlander. 1978. *Big Falling Snow: A Tewa-Hopi Indian's Life and Times and the History and Traditions of His People*. University of New Mexico Press, Albuquerque.

Yoffee, Norman. 1988. "Orienting Collapse." In *The Collapse of Ancient States and Civilizations*, edited by Norman Yoffee and George L. Cowgill, 1–19. University of Arizona Press, Tucson.

Zettler, Richard L. 2003. "Reconstructing the World of Ancient Mesopotamia: Divided Beginnings and Holistic History." *Journal of the Economic and Social History of the Orient* 46(1):3–45.

Zettler, Richard L., James A. Armstrong, Andrew Bell, Matthew Braithwaite, Michael D. Danti, Naomi F. Miller, Peter N. Peregrine, and Jill A. Weber. 1997. *Subsistence and Settlement in a Marginal Environment: Tell es-Sweyhat, 1989–1995 Preliminary Report*, edited by Richard L. Zettler. MASCA Research Papers in Science and Archaeology 14. University of Pennsylvania Museum of Archaeology and Anthropology, Philadelphia.

Tomas Q. Barrientos is chair of the Archaeology Department and director of the Center for Archaeological and Anthropological Research at Universidad del Valle de Guatemala. He also is codirector of the La Corona Regional Archaeological Project. His research interests include Maya archaeology (Lowlands, Highlands, Pacific Coast), pre-Columbian Mesoamerican architecture, cultural heritage management, and identity studies.

Jennifer Birch is associate professor in the Department of Anthropology at the University of Georgia. She is the coauthor of "The Mantle Site: An archaeological history of an ancestral Wendat community" and coeditor of "The Archaeology of Villages in Eastern North America."

José Eduardo Bustamante is a *licenciatura* student in the Archaeology Department of the Universidad del Valle de Guatemala. He is currently working on his licenciatura thesis, which focuses on the early architecture at the regal palace of La Corona. His experience includes mapping and excavations in different sites in the Maya Lowlands, Highlands, and Pacific Coast

Catherine M. Cameron is professor at the University of Colorado, Boulder. She works in the American Southwest focusing on the Chaco regional system. She has worked in Chaco Canyon, northeast Arizona, and southeast Utah, including excavations at the Bluff Great House. Her research interests center on prehistoric demography and processes of cultural transmission, which have led to the study of captives in prehistory.

Marcello A. Canuto is professor of Anthropology and director of the Middle American Research Institute at Tulane University. His research interests include household and community dynamics, the development of sociopolitical complexity in ancient societies, the definition of identity through material culture, and the modern social contexts of archaeology in Mesoamerica. He now codirects a project at the Classic Maya site of La Corona in northwestern Guatemala, where he investigates the mechanisms by which complex sociopolitical organizations develop and were maintained.

Jeffrey H. Cohen is professor of anthropology at the Ohio State University. His research focuses on migration, economic development, and food in Mexico, Turkey, and China. His recent books include *The Cultures of Migration: The Global Nature of Contemporary Movement* (2011) and *Eating Soup without a Spoon: Anthropological Theory and Method in the Real World* (2015).

Michael D. Danti currently directs the Rowanduz Archaeological Program in Iraqi Kurdistan and serves as the program manager for the Mosul Heritage Stabilization Program at the University of Pennsylvania, working to preserve and protect cultural heritage impacted by recent terrorism and warfare in northern Iraq. Most recently, he designed and directed the American Schools of Oriental Research Cultural Heritage Initiatives (ASOR CHI) to assist local stakeholders in addressing the cultural heritage challenges caused by conflict and instability in Syria, Iraq, and Libya. His primary interests are safeguarding cultural heritage and the study of agropastoralism, conflict and warfare, Cultural Property, Art, and Antiquities crime, and the ancient and modern Middle East.

Philip de Barros is Professor Emeritus of Anthropology at Palomar College. His recent research focuses on the use of ethnoarchaeological data and oral traditions to interpret archaeological smithing sites in the Bassar region of northern Togo. A recent publication (de Barros and Lucidi 2017), entitled *Is This an Anvil? Iron Bloom Crushing Sites in Northern Togo*, concerns the multifunctionality of iron bloom crushing sites (in *African Archaeology without Frontiers*, edited by K. Sadr et al.) A major paper (de Barros et al.) reporting on a mid-to-late first millennium BC Bassar iron-smelting furnace and the metallurgical analysis of contemporaneous iron tools was also submitted in February 2019 for publication.

Pete Demarte is an MA candidate at Trent University. Over the past decade, Demarte has specialized in settlement and socioecological studies involving a variety of biologically and ecologically diverse cultural areas, including those of Central America, Ontario, Canada, and Southeast Asia.

Donna M. Glowacki is an associate professor of anthropology at the University of Notre Dame and a longtime research associate with Mesa Verde National Park and

Crow Canyon Archaeological Center. For over twenty-five years, she has been doing archaeological research in the Four Corners that focuses on understanding how societies change, particularly the social processes that lead to regional depopulation and migration, the formation of large, aggregated villages, and pottery production and exchange. Many of these issues were explored in her 2015 book, *Living and Leaving: A Social History of Regional Depopulation in Thirteenth-century Mesa Verde* (University of Arizona Press).

Gyles Iannone is a professor in the Anthropology Department at Trent University, and the director of both the Socio-ecological Entanglement in Tropical Societies (SETS) project, and the Integrated Socio-Ecological History of Residential Patterning, Agricultural Practices, and Water Management at the "Classical" Burmese (Bama) Capital of Bagan, Myanmar (eleventh to fourteenth century CE) Project (IRAW@ Bagan).

Maxime Lamoureux-St-Hilaire is a visiting assistant professor in the Anthropology Department at Davidson College and the publications director for American Foreign Academic Research. His archaeological work has led him to excavate in Belize, Guatemala, Mexico, Honduras, and Quebec. Before teaching at Davidson College, he was a George Stuart Residential Scholar at the Boundary End Archaeology Research Center (2018–19) and a Junior Fellow at the Dumbarton Oaks Research Library (2017–18). His research interests include ancient political resilience and collapse, Classic Maya architecture and ceramics, ancient foodways, geochemistry, and responsible scientific outreach practices.

Louis Lesage is a member of the Huron-Wendat Nation residing in Wendake, Quebec. He is the director of the Nionwentsio Office, Council of the Huron-Wendat Nation. He earned his MSc and PhD in Biology from Université Laval. Previously, he worked for the Canadian Wildlife Service (CWS) as aboriginal liaison biologist. He is also collaborating with various universities and scholars in archaeological projects related to Huron-Wendat sites, and he helps to complete interpretations of results from the Huron-Wendat perspective.

Scott Macrae is an adjunct graduate and research faculty in the Anthropology Department at Trent University and the codirector of the Integrated Socio-Ecological History of Residential Patterning, Agricultural Practices, and Water Management at the Classical Burmese (Bama) capital of Bagan, Myanmar (eleventh to fourteenth century CE) Project. His recent research and publications focus on the agricultural strategies and water management practices of both the ancient Maya and Classical Bagan.

Patricia A. McAnany is Kenan Eminent Professor and Chair of the Anthropology Department at the University of North Carolina, Chapel Hill. She is the codirector of

Proyecto Arqueológico Colaborativo del Oriente de Yucatán, a community-archaeology project located in Tahcabo, Yucatán, Mexico. She also cofounded and directs InHerit: Indigenous Heritage Passed to Present, a UNC program that generates collaborative research and education projects on topics of cultural heritage with communities in North Carolina and the Maya region.

Asa R. Randall is an associate professor of anthropology at the University of Oklahoma. His research examines histories of hunter-gatherer landscape use and terraforming in southeastern North America.

Kenneth E. Sassaman is Hyatt and Cici Brown Professor of Florida Archaeology at the University of Florida. His most recent work centers on the challenges of climate change on the gulf coast of Florida over the past 5,000 years. He is the author of over 100 articles and book chapters, and the author or editor of ten books.

Ancestor(s), 20, 46, 133–134, 140, 185; ancestralizing activity, 16; ancestral burials, 13, 136; ancestral cone, 136–138; ancestral heroes, 128; ancestral histories, 51; ancestral landscapes, *see* Landscape; ancestral places, 191; ancestral souls, 140; common, 129, 136; Huron-Wendat, 46, 49, 51, 55, 60–61; male, 139; protective, 142; sacralized, 4

Ancestral Pueblo people. *See* Pueblo

Ancillary, 110, 112, 113, 114, 118, 155

Animal bones, 142

Antrex site, 52

Archaeological site, 4, 197

Archaic, 6, 7, 72, 73, 74, 75, 187, 188, 192

Artisans, 197

Ascher, Robert, 4, 179

Ataronchronon, 59

Attawandaronon, 49

Attignawantan, 49, 58, 59

Attigneenongnahac, 49, 58

Attachment, 13, 152, 203; to home, 16; Hopi and Zuni, 61; to landscapes, 9, 51; to the past, 112; to place, 4, 46, 50, 56, 62, 127; sense of, 48; to settlement, 145

Bagan, 6, 8–9, 164–177, 188–192

Bandjeli, 121, 125–126, 129–135, 142

Bapuré, 126, 132

BAS (site name, Bassar region): BAS-3, 134; BAS-4, 132; BAS-295, 131; BAS-311, 134; BAS-319, 131, 137, 143; BAS-321, 143; BAS-323, 129, 130, 135, 136; BAS-366, 132; BAS-379, 129, 136

Basque, 50

Bassar, 19, 123, 125–128, 131, 140–143, 183, 185, 187, 192; Bassar culture, 127, 141; Bassar region, 6, 8, 120–124, 129–132, 137–138

Bathurst site, 57

Bear Nation, 54

Belemele Tapu A, 132; Belemele Tapu B, 132, 134

Belize, 8, 16, 20, 82, 85, 102

Bidjomambe, 129, 131, 137, 138, 142, 143

Bitakpambe, 126, 133, 134, 139, 140, 143; Tapu, 142

Bitampobe, 134

Bitchabe, 121, 125–131, 135–136, 140–143; Bitchabe Tapu, 129, 135, 141

Bitchobebe, 131, 137, 141–143

Blacksmiths, 123, 125, 129, 131, 140–141

Borrow pits, 143

British, 61

Buffer zone, 46

Burma: ancient kingdom of, 145; Upper, 170. *See also* Myanmar

Burmese: empire, 164; identity, 176; patronage 174; temples, 188

Buddhist, 9, 164, 165, 168, 169, 174, 175, 176

Cache(s), 66, 76–77, 117; caching, 77–78; dedicatory, 94, 97; foundational, 15; on-floor, 116. *See also* Soapstone

Calakmul. *See* Snake Kingdom

Calvert site, 51

Cameron, Catherine M., 5, 9–10, 30, 62, 65, 120

Canada, 18, 61, 102, 177

Capture/capturing: an area, 128; the earth, 128, 187; the land, 127, 135, 139; a locality, 141; rain/precipitation, 96

Cavalry, 124–125, 130, 134, 183

Cemeteries, 65–66, 72–75, 154

Ceremonial, 20; activities, 114; areas, 135; calendar, 54 center(s), 4, 9, 25, 94–95, 189, 191; civic-ceremonial 72, 88, 100; functions, 96, 98, 116; gatherings, 118; knowledge, 183; place, 142; royal ceremonialism, 114; sacrifices, 140; system, 39

Ceremony, 54–55, 115, 117–118, 135, 139–140, 142, 187; annual renewal, 136; vestiges of, 137

Chiefdoms, 122–127, 142; chief, 138–140, 142; chief installation, 136; council chief, 58; earth chief, 127; secular chief, 127; war chief, 58

Choctawhatchee Bay, 70–71

Claiborne site, 76

Clan: elder, 123, 135; exogamous clans, 122; group lines, 29; history, 28; identity, 127, 135, 141; lineage, 142; lower-status, 29; matrilineal, 56; subclans, 57, 183; territory, 128; transethnic, 140. *See also* Diwaal

Climate, 121, 207; change(s), 8, 12, 25, 27, 78, 81, 159, 172, 198; event(s), 145–147, 152, 155, 160–162; fluctuating, 99; global climate patterns, 144; Medieval Climate Anomaly, 172; model, 146; modern climate records, 157; paleoclimatic, 85, 96;

paleoclimatological methods, 146; paleo-climatology, 160; pleasant, 96; proxy, 87; regional climate trends, 86; worsening, 39. *See also* Environment

Cohen, Jeffrey H., 9–10, 18, 62

Collapse, 32, 192; of the Akkadian Empire, 148; of Bagan, 169–172; of buildings, 114–115; civilizational, 4, 104, 118; Classic Maya, 104–105, 189; complete, 24; discourse, 11, 16, 22; of Khabur, 160–162; political, 8; religio-political, 25; societal, 45, 146; sociopolitical, 170; trend of, 144; of Uruk, 146, 155

Colwell-Chanthaphonh, Chip, 17, 19, 61, 101

Community, 31, 47, 53, 55, 59, 79, 85, 102, 198, 200, 202, 209; abandonment of, 204; community-based activities, 99; contemporary, 179; detachment from, 203; entire, 13, 52; epicentral, 88, 90; formation, 7; growing, 95; home, 17; interdependent, 18; level, 98; members, 185; migrant, 201, 205; peripheral, 90; regional, 65; relocation, 46, 56; remaking of, 21; resources, 183; village, 54, 56; sending, 15; subcommunity, 57–58; surrounding, 96, 100; urban, 164

Confederacy, 46, 48–49, 51, 58–59

Consciousness, 64, 66, 80, 85

Conserved fodder, 152–153

Contreras Valley, 20, 82, 90–93, 96–102, 189–190

Cosmology, 7, 64–67, 69–71, 80–81, 185, 187

Cosmunity, 7, 65, 187

Cultivation, 121, 155, 161, 172

Cultural formation processes. *See* Site formation

Dagomba, 122, 125, 127; attacks, 126; emergence of, 123; slave raiding by, 19, 124, 131–132, 134, 138, 140; smiths, 130; State, 129

Depopulation: mass, 18; regional, 4, 23–25, 27, 31, 45, 180; and reorganization, 35; widespread, 26

Detachment/detaching (from), 144, 206; and abandonment, 194–200, 207–209; authority, 114; Bagan, 164, 173, 176–177; center, 189; community, 203; detachment-related behavior, 103, 118; institutional space, 113; landscapes, 4, 14, 22, 187; Late Classic royal courts, 12; place, 3, 6–9, 13, 15–21, 45–48, 50, 54, 56, 60, 62, 63–66, 79–81,

101, 103, 120, 129, 158, 178, 180–181, 185, 188, 191–193; population, 157, 159; power, 8, 104–105, 108, 117–118, 181, 188; rapid, 182; regions, 184, 186; seasonal, 155; settlements, 145, 148–149, 152, 162, 183; site, 77, 154; widespread, 147, 161

Disentanglement, 118; from Bagan, 177; from Classic Maya divine kingship, 111; landscape, 7, 13; people-place, 5; political, 105; social, 104; sociopolitical, 8

Displacement, 9, 47, 50, 52

Diwaal, 127–128, 134–143

Donzom, 125–126

Drought, 179, 181, 210; cycles, 12, 40; drought-related conservation practices, 34; drought-resistant, 150; impacts of, 25; major drought events, 99; major dry events (MDE), 86–87, 96, 99; megadrought, 36, 39, 144–149, 153, 157, 160; megadrought hypothesis, 8; periodic, 161; prolonged/long-term, 23, 33, 201; severe, 28, 32; and violence/warfare, 35, 36, 41, 186

Dzibanche. *See* Snake Kingdom

Earth Diver myth, 79

Ebla, 160

Ecology, 209; historical, 82–85, 101–102

Ecological: changes, 176; conditions, 64; knowledge, 14; perspectives, 8; processes, 195, 208–209; settings, 23; significance, 134; socioecological systems, 82; Socio-ecological Entanglement in Tropical Societies (SETS), 177; transformations, 202

Economic, 20, 30; activities, 110, 113–114; behavior, 181; center, 188; choice/decision, 186, 198; conditions, 48; contexts, 46; control, 165; crises, 201; devastation, 15; development, 172; economical feed sources 154; gain, 208; growth, 170; history, 85; independence, 169, 173; influence, 168; landscapes, 9; organization, 9; partner, 125; power, 104, 189; production, 117; region, 132; relationships, 23; resilience, 148; restructuring, 101; rights, 59; selective economic detachment, 159; stability, 19; standing, 171; success, 107; trauma, 14; units, 162; upheavals, 102; well-being, 18, 207. *See also* Socioeconomic

Elliott site, 51
Emigration. *See* Migration
Emplacement, 46–48, 52, 60, 66, 70–72, 75–77, 80–81, 184, 191
Enablers, 18, 27, 29, 36, 120, 131–132, 134, 140–141, 154, 208; primary, 130. *See also* Stressors
Entanglement(s), 27, 169, 171, 198–199; environmental, 18; human-place, 3–4; landscape, 7, 103, 178; with place, 12; social, 104; sociopolitical, 8; with things, 21. *See also* Disentanglement
Environment(s), 14, 83–85, 100, 155; built, 11, 13, 47, 53; changing, 144; of human insecurity, 18; of human security, 19; local, 86; man-made, 181; social, 180, 190. *See also* Climate
Environmental, 18, 121; abuse, 14, 16; attributes, 53; cause, 192; change, 7; conditions, 179; contexts, 4, 9; degradation, 159, 161–162; downturn, 181; features, 13; hazards, 15; insecurities, 208; interactions, 98; natural, 135; perspectives, 8; pressure, 96; problems, 189; research, 17; significance, 169; stressors, 102; understanding, 4; zone, 149
Erie, 49
Ethnic, ethnicity, 166; group(s), 19, 60; lines, 169; transethnic clan, 140
Ethnogenesis, 186, 191–192
Ethnography/ethnographic, 5, 24, 195–196; accounts, 183, 185; context, 15; data, 8, 182–183; framework, 9; history, 28; interviews, 187; multisited, 209; perspective, 7, 26, 28; Pueblo, 29–30; research, 202; short-focus, high-resolution, 200
Ethnohistory, 53–54, 56, 80, 182
Exit, 199
Experience: collective, 80; community, 204; contextual, 46, 48, 55; human, 12, 21, 29, 67; individual, 185, 192; lived, 24, 64, 85, 186, 200; long-term, 75; of movers, 202; and observations, 30; repeated, 66

Factionalism, 181, 184
Fairty ossuary, 54
Farming, 40, 123, 132, 201, 210; communities, 12, 17; dry, 145, 150, 152, 154, 162; intensive farming techniques, 122; populations, 96; and sedentism, 51

Feasting, 55
Feast of the Dead, 54
Ferguson, T. J., 17, 19, 61
Figurines, 116
First Nations, 61
Fission and fusion, 28–31, 36–38, 41, 183
Florida, 7, 66–70, 72, 74, 77, 80
Formation processes. *See* Site formation
Fragmentation, 199
French, 50, 65, 132
Futurescape, 73, 75, 187

Geomancy, 70
Georgian Bay, 50
Government(al), 8, 61, 111, 112, 118, 175; central, 173; Classic Maya, 104; funding, 201; Sak Nikte', 117. *See also* Administrative; Institution
Grandview site, 56
Greco-Persian wars, 198
Guatemala, 8, 85, 105
Gulf Coast (of Mexico), 7, 66–70, 72, 74, 76–80
Gunby site, 52

Hadidi, Tell, 160
Halawa, 160
Hajji Ibrahim, Tell, 152, 154
Hart, John, 57
Haudenosaunee (Iroquois), 48, 50, 59, 61
Herodotus, 198
Hodder, Ian, 5, 62
Holocene, 78; early, 72; Late, 150, 161, 163; Middle/mid, 74, 145, 150, 159, 161
Huron-Wendat: ancestral Huron-Wendat, 7, 46, 48, 50, 56–58, 60–62, 182, 186, 189; contemporary, 46, 49; emissaries, 50; historic heartland, 57; landscape, 55; Nation, 50–51, 60–62; region, 6
Hydrology, 86. *See also* Water management

Identity, 9; Burmese, 164, 176; clan, 127, 135, 139–141; community, 85; construction, 28; cultural, 3–4, 48; formation, 57; group, 47; Hopi, 28; Huron-Wendat, 60, 191; site, 96, 98; social, 43; St. Lawrence, 50
Immigration. *See* Migration
Incorporation (Iroquoian), 46, 50, 55, 60
Institution(al), 207; adaptation, 117;

landscape transformation, 9; mass, 147, 149; and mobility, 11–15, 209; Oaxacan, 200–201, 206–207; out-migration, 169; patterns, 24; planning, 17; population circulation, 55, 57–59, 182; resettlement, 5, 19, 46, 66, 149; seasonal, 159; serial, 29–31, 50, 182; small-scale, 127; and stressors, 132; studies, 178–179, 194; of the Sun, 75–76; transnational, 202; village relocation, 46, 51, 53–55, 58, 182, 185

Miller site, 54

Minanha, 20, 82–83, 85–86, 88–91, 93–96, 98–102, 188–192

Misrepresentation, 61, 197–198

Mississippian, 47, 48, 53

Mississippi River, 68–70, 75–77

Moatfield Ossuary, 54

Mobility, 11–12, 14, 196, 203–204; and abandonment, 202, 206–207; contemporary, 199–200; decisions, 184; human, 195, 198, 208–209; increasing, 161; research, 194; residential, 13, 56; as a response, 35; scale of, 18; as a strategy, 181

Mound(s), 65, 67, 72, 75, 77–78, 92, 149, 152, 191; building, 79; burial, 139; center, 53; complex, 76; earthen, 47, 63, 66

Moundville, 48

Myanmar, 6, 165, 173, 175–177, 189–190

Navajo, 191

Nelson, Margaret C., 17

New Mexico, 42–43

New York, 50, 58, 62

Nomadization, 144, 146–147

Non-Western, 13

North Atlantic Oscillation, 147

Northern Iroquoia, 46, 58

Northern Rio Grande, 42, 186

North Vaca Plateau, 7, 82, 85–90, 95–98, 102

Oaxaca, 197, 200–201, 203; Oaxaca City, 204; Oaxacan community, 201, 207; Oaxacan migration, 206; Oaxacans, 202–203; valley, 210

Oklahoma, 15, 50

On-floor: assemblage, 8, 114, 117; cache, 116; material, 115

Ontario, 50–51, 54, 57–58, 61–62, 186

Oral: history, 7, 25, 29–30, 45, 60; tradition, 5,

28–29, 42, 124, 126, 129, 131, 133, 141, 185

Ossuary (burial practice), 54

Palace(s), 156, 167; abandonment, 116; detachment from, 118; Classic Maya regal, 104, 188–189, 191–192; economy, 113; monumental, 107; regal palace of La Corona, 105–106, 108, 111, 114, 117, 119

Pastoralism, 8, 145, 153, 187; agropastoralism, 149, 155, 158–159, 162; sheep-goat, 152; transhumant, 154, 159

Periurban, 165, 167, 169, 171, 173

Pilgrimage, 20, 61; at Bagan, 164, 174, 176; Buddhist, 175; periodic, 142; pilgrim(s), 4; place of, 65, 79; at Poverty Point, 67, 78, 81

Place-making, 13, 22, 47, 52, 102, 180; complexities of, 6; deliberate, 15; Iroquoian, 51, 58; Preclassic Maya, 16; recursive, 11, 20–21

Place unmaking, 6, 13, 17, 20–22, 45, 51, 177–178

Population circulation. See Migration

Poverty Point, 7, 63, 66, 71, 78–81, 187; affiliation, 76; cache, 77; ceremonial center, 191; earthworks, 70; gatherings, 64–65; history, 67; and lithics, 68; and solstices, 75

Postmortem, 34, 40, 185

Pre-Colombian fakes, 197

Processual archaeology, 4, 179

Property rights, 13, 22

Pueblo(s), 182, 188, 190–192; ancestral Pueblo people, 7, 26, 180; artist, 29–30; ethnography, 29; how Pueblo people left, 41; masonry, 47; migrations, 7, 43; occupation, 27; people, 39; Pueblo III period, 185, 186; Southwest, 28; supposedly "sedentary," 181; understanding of abandonment, 44; villages, 40; World, 25, 32

Quebec City, 46, 50

Remaking, 13, 20–22, 177, 178

Ritual: closing, 76; deposits, 88; infrastructure, 79–80; interventions, 69; practice(s), 12, 17, 39, 67, 135; renewal, 65; site, 96; specialists, 29. See also Termination

Royal court. See Kingship

Ruler(s): at Bagan, 176; Classic Maya divine, 19; and collapse, 192; and inefficiencies, 90;